MANAGING ORGANIZATIONAL BEHAVIOR IN THE AFRICAN CONTEXT

Managing Organizational Behavior in the African Context discusses management and organization science theories as they apply within the social, cultural, and economic contexts in which organizations operate in Africa. The first organizational behavior book to cover the entire continent, it uses the findings of OB studies to establish a conceptual foundation, then explores how those topics apply in Africa's unique business environment. This integrative framework allows students and scholars to connect organizational phenomena in Africa with those in other parts of the globe. Illustrative examples, mini-cases, and self-assessment exercises all based on Africa-specific sectors, industries, and organizations round out this foundational guide to the OB field in Africa.

David B. Zoogah (Ph.D., Ohio State University) is Associate Professor of management at Morgan State University.

Constant D. Beugré (Ph.D. Rensselaer Polytechnic Institute) is a Professor of management at Delaware State University

MANAGING ORGANIZATIONAL BEHAVIOR IN THE AFRICAN CONTEXT

David B. Zoogah and Constant D. Beugré

Routledge
Taylor & Francis Group

NEW YORK AND LONDON

First published 2013
by Routledge
711 Third Avenue, New York, NY 10017

Simultaneously published in the UK
by Routledge
2 Park Square, Milton Park, Abingdon, Oxon OX14 4RN

Routledge is an imprint of the Taylor & Francis Group, an informa business

Library of Congress Cataloging in Publication Data
Zoogah, David B.
Managing Organizational Behavior in the African Context / David B. Zoogah
and Constant D. Beugré.
p. cm.
Includes bibliographical references and index.
1. Organizational behavior—Africa. 2. Organizational change—Africa.
3. Management—Africa. I. Beugré, Constant D. II. Title.
HD58.7.Z66 2012
658.0096–dc23
2012023860

ISBN: 978-0-415-53592-2 (hbk)
ISBN: 978-0-415-53593-9 (pbk)
ISBN: 978-0-203-10910-6 (ebk)

Typeset in Bembo and ITCStoneSans
by Book Now Ltd, London

Printed and bound in the United States of America
by Edwards Brothers, Inc.

DEDICATION

My *raison d'être*: Coniah Alahada Zoogah and Jalen Baniyelme Cloud Zoogah.
My caring wife Noelle and our lovely twins, Jane-Victoria and Constant Junior.

CONTENTS

TABLES

FIGURES

ACKNOWLEDGMENTS

Several people have contributed directly or indirectly in the completion of this first textbook on organizational behavior in the African context and deserve our thanks. We appreciate the help of Jonathan Imakando and Golshan Javadian in helping to find African studies on the different topics discussed in the book and Kittina Coursey, administrative secretary at Delaware State University, who provided secretarial assistance. We are particularly grateful to our respective spouses, Aleshia Zoogah and Noelle Beugré, who facilitated our tasks of revising and editing the chapters of this book by taking care of our lovely children. Other people also facilitated our arrival at this point: they supported and encouraged us. Dr David Zoogah owes a lot to his mentor and friend Peter Bycio, Robert and Margaret Cloud who were instrumental in his visit to the United States, Stephecca Sawyer who offered suggestions for facilitating student learning, Stephen Kolbil who provided moral support, and other acquaintances and friends who though not mentioned here are nevertheless significant and invaluable.

PREFACE

Although the field of organizational behavior is part of the mainstream curriculum in business education and several textbooks are published in this domain, few have focused on emerging economies in general and African economies in particular. The purpose of this *short* textbook is to fill this void by focusing on Africa to the extent that business education is flourishing in most African countries. Thus, the need for textbooks and educational materials geared toward business practices in the African context is of paramount importance. Western teaching materials are not always adapted to the African context. Our goal in writing this book is twofold. First, we want to write a textbook that includes examples and cases that African students can relate to. Second, we want to write a textbook that is affordable to African students due to the economic hardship faced by most of them. Thus, we kept the book relatively brief without sacrificing the quality of the content. For each topic, we discuss the general theories and techniques that define it. We then provide a section on African organizations. Where we do not provide a section focusing on the African context, we give examples specific to Africa. We also provide mini-cases at the end of several chapters. These mini-cases describe business situations faced by organizations operating in Africa. To enhance the educational value of the book, we provide examples and mini-cases focusing on Africa and self-assessment exercises at the end of each chapter. We believe that such an approach will help make the study of organizational behavior in African universities and business schools more relevant.

Managing people is important because, as Benjamin Schneider noted in a seminal article in 1987 in *Personnel Psychology*, the people make the place. Indeed, people can make or break organizations. In addition, organizations are populated by people. How these people are led and managed can help the organization prosper or falter. An African perspective of organizational behavior is important, as it could help instructors and students to tailor their teaching and learning to the African context. As a teaching tool, this book is intended to discuss the extant theories, techniques, and practices of organizational behavior in the African context. The ability of managers to understand, explain, and predict employee behavior enables them to manage effectively individual, group, and organizational activities. What drives employee behavior in African organizations? What types of behaviors maximize individual, group, and organizational performance in African organizations?

In this book we provide preliminary answers to these questions by analyzing decades of research in management and organizational behavior. For example, we discuss how organizational behavior theories and techniques developed in the West could be applied in the African context and help explain employee attitudes and behaviors, such as job satisfaction, commitment, productivity, performance, and turnover, to name but a few. The book is organized into three parts. In Part I, we provide an overview of organizational behavior as a field of study, discuss the external environment of African organizations, social perception and diversity, personality, affect, and stress, and motivational drivers in African organizations. In Part II, we focus on factors and dynamics of group-level behavior. Topics such as groups and teams, influence, power, leadership, decision-making, conflict, and communication are discussed. In Part III, we focus on organizational-level factors. Topics such as organizational structure and design, culture, strategy, and change and innovation are discussed.

Chapter 1. Introduction to Organizational Behavior

In this chapter, we discuss the types of organizations in Africa and provide a framework and definition of organizational behavior within the context of Africa. The framework serves as a guide for the rest of the book. The chapter also outlines the evolution of OB from its origins to extant trends as well as the challenges of doing research in organizational behavior in Africa. It concludes with the formula for behavior: interactive processes of traits and environment on behavior.

Chapter 2. The External Environment of African Organizations

In this chapter, we focus on the environmental component of the formula for behavior outlined in the previous chapter by discussing the types of environments (social, cultural, political, technological, and economic) present in Africa and their influences on organizational behavior. We conclude with a discussion of globalization and its influence on organizational behavior in Africa.

Chapter 3. Social Perception and Diversity in African Organizations

This chapter focuses on perceptual processes of employees. Because perception is critical to interactions, performance evaluation, and conflict, we discuss how it relates to organizational behavior. We also discuss impression management and attribution processes, and conclude with a discussion on perceptual errors.

Chapter 4. Personality, Affect, and Stress

This chapter discusses personality, affective processes and states, as well as stress. Frameworks of personality are presented along with their application to organizational behavior and the African context. Attitudes and values are included because of their importance to organizations. The two major types of affect – positive and negative – are discussed. In addition, we show how emotional intelligence has relevance to Africa. Stress is discussed because it seems a recent phenomenon associated with exposure of African organizations to globalization.

Chapter 5. Motivating the African Worker

First, we review the various theories of motivation before discussing those that have significance or relevance for Africa. Second, we discuss modern, particularly significant motivational mechanisms that seem applicable to Africa. All the major content and process theories of motivation are discussed with reference to Africa.

Chapter 6. Power, Influence, and Politics

We discuss power, influence, and politics as they relate to African organizations. We discuss the sources, bases, and applications of all three and point out the strengths and weakness of each in the context of Africa.

Chapter 7. Leadership in an African Context

We discuss the nature and types of leadership. We also distinguish leadership from followership. Further, we discuss the major theories of leadership including emergent theories. We also discuss how the major leadership theories apply in Africa. We emphasize leadership that is important to Africa.

Chapter 8. Groups and Teams

We focus on the congruence of teams and collectivism of African countries. Stages, types, and forms of teams as well as a team effectiveness model are discussed to show team antecedents, processes, consequences, and controls. We distinguish team processes from team states. Contingency factors are also considered.

Chapter 9. Decision Making

We discuss decision-making in organizations by focusing on the individual, team, and organizational levels. The nature, types, process, and models of decision making are emphasized. How decision making influences effectiveness of employees, teams, and organizations are also emphasized.

Chapter 10. Understanding Conflict in African Organizations

We discuss the nature, types, levels, and forms of workplace conflict. We also emphasize processes, determinants, and outcomes of conflict. Functional and dysfunctional forms of conflict are distinguished to show how managers can promote the former and avoid the latter.

Chapter 11. Communication in Organizations

Communication is a competency that impacts employee behavior. It is instrumental to interactions and work execution. We therefore discuss the nature, form, and process of communication as they relate to the African context. We also include barriers and skill-enhancing mechanisms for effective communication.

Chapter 12. Structure and Design of African Organizations

The context of employee behavior is the organization. How organizations are designed and structured facilitates workflow and employee behaviors. As a result, we discuss how jobs, functional units, and the entire organization are designed based on the prominent structure–conduct–performance (SCP) paradigm. The major forms of organizational structures are emphasized with specific examples from Africa.

Chapter 13. Culture and Strategy

Culture and strategy of organizations regulate behavior of employees. As a result, we discuss the organizational culture system (i.e., antecedents, process, and outcomes) as well as the nature of culture. We also discuss the forms of strategies organizations develop and how those strategies influence employee behavior motivation to accomplish strategic goals. The chapter concludes with the organizational strategy system.

Chapter 14. Change and Innovation in African Organizations

The chapter focuses on change in organizations. We discuss environmental dynamics and the adaptive processes with a focus on change as a response behavior. Various types and determinants of change are also discussed. The compliance and/or resistance behavior of employees are also discussed. We include information flow and the mechanisms that facilitate information distribution within African organizations.

In each chapter, a system's perspective is adopted. As a result, we discuss antecedents, processes, outcomes, and controls (feedback and feed-forward) of each topic. We also provide a summary, discussion questions, exercises, and mini-cases for each chapter. At the end, we provide a detailed case that integrates most of the topics. That case is intended to illustrated how the topics are interconnected. It supports higher forms of learning.

PART I

1

INTRODUCTION TO ORGANIZATIONAL BEHAVIOR

Overview

This chapter provides an introduction to organizational behavior (OB) by explaining the origins, levels, and behavioral systems in organizations. By the end of this chapter you should be able to:

- Define organizations
- Define organizational behavior
- Identify the levels of organizational behavior
- Discuss behavioral systems in organizations
- Identify contextual factors influencing behavior in organizations
- Understand the sources of OB knowledge

Introduction

The *Economist* (see Profile: "Africa Rising" at the end of the chapter) suggests that "after decades of slow growth, Africa has a real chance to follow in the footsteps of Asia." Since 2000, six of the world's ten fastest-growing economies are in Africa, and in eight of the past ten years, Africa has grown faster than East Asia, including Japan. Some major factors contributing to this growth potential include political stability, increased trade and aid, technological boom, and positive market outcomes in the form of commodity prices. First, African countries have recently become more stable, if only marginally more democratic. For example, Ghana has had free and fair democratic elections for over two decades now. Senegal and Mozambique are almost the same; they are considered more stable than other emerging economies such as Argentina, Ukraine, and the Philippines. This stability reduces overall country risk. A similar observation is made by the authors of "Cracking the Next Growth Market: Africa" (see Profile at the end of the chapter) on the growth potential of Africa. They discuss the challenges as well as opportunities for corporations, particularly foreign multinationals, interested in investing in Africa.

Second, public-private partnerships, which are based on collaboration between public sector and private actors, have opened up investment opportunities and facilitated cross-border trade within and across Africa. The collaborations enable risk sharing of governments with private firms, technology transfer from multinational corporations, and sustainability of investments. Third, the technological boom—telecommunication and Internet—has facilitated "leapfrogging" of African countries. African companies have also pioneered integrative technologies, such as mobile banking, where one in two mobile bankers globally is African (actually, Kenyan). Trade with non-traditional partners such as China and India has increased the demand for African resources. Some estimates show that increased commodities particularly with these partners have accounted for about a third of Africa's growth.[1]

Another factor contributing to growth is behavioral change. Africans are increasingly more competitive, wealth-driven, and peace-oriented than in the 50s when they were colonized; 60s when they struggled to gain independence; 70s when they strove to define their identities following independence; and 80s when hegemonic conflicts were rampant. They are ready to establish cooperative endeavors with individual and institutional partners if such deals will enable them to maximize their gains. This drive for increased wealth transfers to the workplace where increased salaries and bonuses push employees toward middle-income class status. The quest for the "good life" necessitates behaviors that facilitate achievement of that goal.

The "good life" depends partly on economic growth which is also a function of industrial activity. So, it can be said that the growth is based on the productivity or performance of African organizations. Behaviors of employees contribute to the performance of organizations. One challenge observed in the Profile "Africa Rising," is the lack of talent to sustain the growth in African economies. Talent refers to the skills and abilities of individuals; it includes behavioral and social skills. Individuals who develop behavioral and social skills are likely to achieve more or better individual outcomes such as promotion. It is therefore important to understand behaviors that optimize individual and organizational performance, contribute to economic productivity, and facilitate development of competence. Furthermore, it is important to know not only what we mean by OB but also how it evolved and what makes it unique as a discipline. We begin with an introduction of OB, its origin, components, and major frameworks.

Organizations

There are diverse definitions of organizations. Two definitions of significance focus on the legal and process characteristics. In the first, an organization refers to the registered, legally constituted enterprise that is endowed with rights and status similar to human beings. The second definition refers to the process of coordinating resources, personnel, materials, and finances to achieve specific goals. Modern African organizations encompass both meanings; they involve arrangements established by two or more individuals to pursue collective goals, control their own performance, and are separated from their environments. Organizations established by individuals for profit (private) differ from those established by governments for the welfare of their people (public) and those established either privately or by government to render important but neglected services (non-governmental agencies).

Characteristics of Organizations

Organizations have unique characteristics. Traditional characteristics focus on social, structure, management, process, resource dependence, and outcomes. They can also be categorized as public, semi-public, or private. Government ministries, agencies, and establishments fit within this category. Table 1.1 shows characteristics and examples of organizations in Africa.

TABLE 1.1 Characteristics and Types of Organizations

Characteristics	Types of Organizations	Examples
Outcome	Public	Government ministeries
	Semi-Public	Fee paying public universities; non-governmental organizations
	Private	Banks (e.g., Stanbic bank, South Africa)
Social	Co-Located	
	Virtual	
Structured	National	NEPA (Nigeria)
	International	Anglo-gold (South Africa)
	Global	DeBeers
Management	Internal	
	Contracted	
Process-Oriented	None	
	Partial	
	Complete	
Resource dependence	Deprived	Schools in the rural areas or villages
	Endowed	International schools in Accra, Lagos, Nairobi, Cairo, Tunis, Johannesburg

The majority of formal organizations are in the urban areas (e.g., Accra, Lagos, Nairobi, Cairo, Johannesburg, etc.) even though some can be found in the rural areas. Those in the latter tend to be informal.[1] Informal organizations are sometimes registered with the Trade Ministry and other times are not. A hairdresser in Nairobi requires a license to operate her kiosk. Her sister in the village of Kibera may not require that license. Informal organizations tend to have small operations that are characterized by a few local networks or customers. For example, a woman with an M-Pesa kiosk in a village has a small customer-base limited to her village or vicinity.[2] Even though they are registered with Safaricom Kenya, they are considered informal organizations.

Organizations are purpose-driven and have collective goals. They exist to achieve certain outcomes including profit, welfare, or service. These outcomes enable them to fulfill their purposes. Further, organizations have environments, settings that define their boundaries. Typically, the environments comprise internal and external components. Their operations, processes, and systems function in the internal environments.

Another characteristic is effectiveness of organizations. Effectiveness is a broad term that encompasses multiple outcomes including performance, productivity, profitability, customer satisfaction, product innovation, and stakeholder satisfaction. The effectiveness of African organizations thus includes financial outcomes, community development, employee welfare, customer satisfaction, and product or service innovation. Communities and employees are critical stakeholders that enable organizations to achieve their goals. Organizations, like individuals, have shared responsibility to support, promote, and develop the members of the community in which they are established.

Recently, organizations have been defined by the perception or admiration of individuals: the most admired companies.[3] Factors such as quality, stable strategy, managing talent, innovation, industry champions, investment value, social responsibility, trust (which encompasses credibility, respect, fairness, pride, and camaraderie), and culture (which encompasses history, incentives, hiring, inspiring, celebrating, and thanking) are used to determine effectiveness. The modern characteristics tend to focus on the climate of organizations and how they appeal to major stakeholders such as employees, customers, financiers, and supporters. FORTUNE, the company that generated these criteria in conjunction with the Hay Group, observes that the characteristics focus on business practices.[4] These criteria have been adopted in Africa. The Financial Technology of Africa has a list of the Most Admired Companies[5] and uses the following criteria: innovations; management quality; people management; financial soundness; long term investment; social responsibility; product/service quality; and global competitiveness.

Organizational Behavior

Organizations cannot exist without employees; expertise and behaviors of employees enable organizations to function, grow, and fulfill their missions. It is therefore important to understand what we mean by behavior and its various forms. Because we defined organizations as groups of people who work interdependently toward some purpose, we can define organizational behavior as *the accumulated knowledge of systematic research of multidisciplinary influences on behavior of individuals and groups in organizations*. We discuss the characteristics of this disciplinary definition next.

Systematic Research

First, it means we focus on what is already known (i.e., empirical evidence on factors influencing behavior in organizations). However, it can also refer to programmatic research activities that seek to add to the accumulated knowledge. Together, these factors focus on the research pillar of organizational behavior. The research pillar outlines how to conduct research that will yield significant results. By significant we mean the results that will be useful, acceptable, relevant, current, consistent, and valid. Rigorous systematic and programmatic research leads to these outcomes. Systematic research is based on adoption of scientific methods.

Multidisciplinary

This characteristic focuses on the repository of knowledge currently available. As discussed below (see section 1.6), our knowledge of OB is based on findings from diverse disciplines. Theories and practices from disciplines such as sociology, social psychology, and economics continue to be used today to improve OB. Scholars from other disciplines continue to enrich OB at various levels (see Figure 1.1). All the social sciences contribute to our understanding of individual, group, and organizational behavior. Even the physical sciences also contribute in one form or another. For example, our understanding of operations of systems derives from the physical sciences.

Dynamics

OB is dynamic. The accumulated knowledge can become obsolescent due to new knowledge or disconfirmation. Further, OB focuses on social entities whose attributes, psychology, and actions change from time to time. For example, an employee may exhibit identification and loyalty when he/she is new but show disloyalty and disidentification with increased tenure. The dynamics of OB are therefore natural or contrived. Natural dynamics are those that occur as a function of the natural life cycle of individuals. Contrived dynamics are those that emerge from the creations of groups and organizational systems. Both influence the behavior of employees.

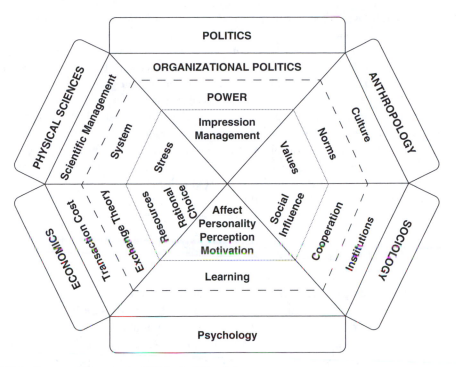

FIGURE 1.1   Sources of Organizational Behavior Knowledge
Note: Bottom = individual level; Middle = group level; top = organizational level.

Levels

There are three levels of study in OB: individual, group, and organizational (see Figures 1.1 and 1.3). What an individual does is different from what the group or organization does. For individuals, the group and organizational contexts affect their behaviors. As a result, we distinguish the lower level which focuses on behavioral systems (antecedents, processes, and outcomes) of individuals such as perception, personality, affect, and attitudes from the group level which focuses on interpersonal processes. The individual level is the foundation through which other higher level actions and behaviors emerge. For example, individual decisions differ from team decisions not only by *how* the team decides but also *what* decisions are taken. Further, some decisions are inherently group oriented (e.g., consensus) and therefore cannot be substitutes for individual actions, while others are aggregates of individual decisions. In the latter, representative criteria (e.g., the majority rule) can be established for the entire group, while action by all members is required in the former. Leadership, for example, involves one person (leader) influencing another (follower). Others include team dynamics and the change processes that occur within teams. The organizational level is the highest level and focuses on attributes of the entire organization. Topics here include structure of the organization which shows how all employees should relate to one another; culture or values, norms and beliefs shared by organizational members; change or restructuring of systems and processes throughout the entire organization; and strategy, the overall direction or plan of action for the future. They all affect individual and group behaviors.

Open Systems

Human beings are living organisms. As a result, they constantly interact with their environments. This interaction results in changes. The process of drawing inputs from the environment and transforming them through processes to specific outcomes is a systems approach. A system is any entity that is characterized by inputs, process, and output along with control relations.[6] Some systems may be closed in that they are self-contained and do not have to interact with the external environments (e.g., clocks); others are open and have to interact with the external environment to exist, develop, and mature. Social entities are characterized as open systems because they always interact with the environment. In that regard, African organizations have to interact with the local environments for resources (financial, human, and physical) to facilitate their productive activities; they influence and are influenced by those environments. For example, Shell in Nigeria which is based in Wari, depends on physical resources for oil but is affected by the persistent demands of the Ogoni tribe to engage in environmentally sustainable practices that will not harm the local communities. Behaviors of employees in its subsidiary, Shell (Nigeria), differ from those in the Netherlands or other parts of the world.

Epistemology of OB

By epistemology we mean the scope of OB knowledge obtained through valid and reliable (i.e., scientific) methods. Compared to other disciplines (e.g., physics), OB is fairly new; arguably it is about a century old. This nacency suggests that our knowledge of OB is limited; we are still discovering more about employee behaviors that are effective and those that are not. For example, cooperation is effective but stealing is destructive. However, there are other behaviors for which it is unclear whether they are effective or not. For example, politics can be effective and ineffective depending on the situation. In addition to the distinction between effective and ineffective behaviors, we can distinguish covert from overt behaviors.[7] Overt behaviors are readily observable and can be recognized when displayed. For example, when an employee helps a co-worker, the helping behavior can be observed. In some instances it can be electronically recorded on a computer. Such behaviors are neither sufficient nor the only kind; there are covert behaviors that complement overt behaviors. Covert behaviors are those that are not readily observable but which also enhance task and interpersonal relationships. An example is support from anonymous co-workers. In traditional Africa, children are socialized not to boast so as to avoid incurring the envy or jealousy of others.[8] Due to that socialization, they are likely to behave covertly out of cultural programming. However, when they are teens or adult workers, they may behave overtly due to social programming from urban and Western contexts where such behaviors are important for building social capital.

Why Study OB

As a student you may ask, why do I have to study OB? There are four major reasons why knowledge of OB is important for you. You are preparing for a career in organizations which means you will eventually become an employee, supervisor, manager, or executive in an organization. Each role requires knowledge of behaviors that improve performance, enable you to develop positive relationships with others which can advance your career, and help you to guide subordinates or run a department. In order to function effectively in each role, you will first need to understand the behavior of others. As you will discover in the following chapters, there are some behaviors that positively impact task execution, and others that negatively impact it; behaviors that develop relationships and those that destroy them. There are behaviors that enhance and others that inhibit interactions. As a supervisor, you will need to understand why your subordinate behaves the way he or she does.

The second reason for studying OB is prediction. As humans we are limited in our ability to know the future. But, to the extent that you, as a Stanbic Bank manager for example, can predict what is likely to happen in two years time, you can plan accordingly. Being able to predict when a supervisor will help a co-worker, show creativity, and even steal, is useful information that can facilitate effective supervision. Managers who are able to predict the behaviors of potential and actual employees can, for example, make effective hiring, retention, career advancement, and retirement decisions.

Third, you need to be able to explain the behaviors that you observe in organizations. Without knowing the system of behaviors (i.e., determinants, processes, and consequences), it is unlikely you will be able to explain them to others. For example, how can a supervisor explain the problem of 'herding behavior' when he/she has no clue as to what such behavior entails? The supervisor will not be able to model the appropriate behavior to others if he/she does not study it. For example, by studying cooperation behaviors, a manager can explain effective cooperation (e.g., sharing information with team members) and ineffective cooperation (e.g., social loafing) and thereby discourage the latter since it does not contribute to organizational effectiveness.

The fourth reason for studying OB is that it enables you to influence the behavior of others. Current thinking on interaction dynamics is that employees can influence one another. OB suggests that that influence is possible if each employee knows which behaviors to induce. Traditionally, it used to be thought that only leaders influenced followers; now we know that followers can also influence leaders. However, the influence of followers is limited to certain behaviors. Knowledge of such behaviors will help followers or subordinates influence leaders and supervisors.

In sum, there are benefits for studying OB. It enables you and other employees as co-workers or supervisors to participate more effectively in the organization. Upward influence (follower–leader inducement) as opposed to downward influence (leader–follower inducement) increases the participation of lower level employees in the organization and minimizes alienation. Other benefits include knowledge of behaviors that enhance career advancement, promotion, and compensation.

Origin of OB

In the case of Africa, the origins of OB stem from two sources: content and context. We discuss the latter as part of section 1.6, Sources of OB Knowledge. The content of OB can be traced back to classical management, the Hawthorne studies, human relations, contingency, and currently positive OB.

Classical Management

The classical origins begin arguably with F. W. Taylor[10] and scientific management, defined as the systematic study of relationships between people and tasks for the purpose of redesigning the work process to increase efficiency. Taylor argued that managers can reduce the amount of effort each employee expends to produce a unit of output by increasing specialization and the division of labor. He suggested that the principal object of management should be to secure the maximum prosperity of the employer, coupled with the maximum prosperity of each employee. He advocated studying the way employees perform their tasks, gathering job knowledge that employees possess, and experimenting with ways of improving task execution, codifying the new methods of performing tasks into written rules and standard operating procedures; methodically selecting employees with the requisite skills and abilities to match the needs of the task, and training them to perform the task according to the established rules and procedures; establishing acceptable levels of performance for tasks, and developing performance-based rewards systems above the acceptable level. In short, he proposed the integration of organizational design, employee relations, and human resource practices into organizational behaviour. Mary Parker Follett also proposed that managers consider the human side of the job. Specifically, she suggested involvement of employees in job analysis so that those with the requisite knowledge can be in control of the work process regardless of their positions. Follett viewed employees as individuals, and the organization, and environment as an interdependent system. As a result, she suggested not only consideration of the needs of employees as stakeholders of the organization but also cooperation between managers, employees, and communities. She also pioneered the understanding of lateral processes within hierarchical organizations (which influence the development of matrix structures of organizations), and the informal processes within organizations.[11]

Hawthorne Studies

Studies at the Hawthorne Works of the Western Electric Company (1924–32) which were initially an attempt to investigate how characteristics of the work setting affect employee fatigue and performance (e.g., lighting) led to information on the dynamics of groups and productivity. Our understanding of the effect of social or external influence (e.g., researchers' attention), managers' leadership approach, and work group norms on individuals and groups derive from the Hawthorne studies. The Hawthorne effect, a form of reaction whereby individuals improve or modify an aspect of their behavior simply in response to the fact that they know they are being studied, not in response to any particular experimental manipulation,[12] directly emerged from these studies. Since then managers and OB researchers have been careful to identify *real effects* from *Hawthorne effects*.

Human Relations Movement

The Human Relations Movement, which refers to researchers of organizational development who studied the behavior of people in groups (e.g., teams), examined the effects of social relations, motivation, and employee satisfaction on factory productivity. Consequently, our understanding of teams, motivation, and the achievement of individual goals within organizations directly arose from this movement. Unlike the above approaches that focused on employee, group, and organizational attributes, contingency researchers[13] proposed that the situations organizations face influence not only their structures but also the behavior of individuals and groups within them. Changes in technology might result in changes in structure to facilitate effective production. They introduced the contingency or situational perspective of OB.

   In addition to the above views, our understanding of the nature of individuals relative to work is enhanced by theory X, Y, and Z which make assumptions about individuals. Theory X assumes that the average employee is lazy, dislikes work, and will try to do as little as possible. As a result, managers are expected to supervise closely and control employees through reward and punishment. Theory Y, on the other hand, assumes that employees will do what is good for the organization when committed. Managers are therefore expected to create work settings that encourage commitment to organizational goals and provide opportunities for employees to exercise initiative. In contrast to Douglas McGregor, who proposed Theories X and Y, William Ouchi proposed Theory Z as a hybrid of the two extremes. He argued that employees are sometimes lazy and other times active. Similar to the contingency view, he proposed that the situations employees encounter may influence their behavior. Managers should therefore consider the situation and focus on increasing employee loyalty to the company by providing a job for life with a strong focus on the well-being of the employee, both on and off the job. Theory Z thus combines the assumptions of Theories X and Y by calling for workers to be involved in the work process and places more reliance on the attitude and responsibilities of the workers.

Positive OB

A recent source is positive OB. Positive OB is "the study and application of positively oriented human resource strengths and psychological capacities that can be measured, developed, and effectively managed for performance improvement in today's workplace."[14] It is the application of positive psychology to the workplace and focuses on human strengths, vitality, and on building the best in the workplace under the basic assumption that goodness and excellence can be analyzed and achieved. It developed from the Positive Psychology movement, initiated in 1998 by Martin Seligman and colleagues, and positive organizational scholarship proposed in 2003 by Cameron and colleagues. All aim to shift the focus in psychology and organizations from dysfunctional processes to functional ones by calling for an increased focus on the building of human strength.

Sources of OB Knowledge

Context

The current body of global OB knowledge derives from different disciplines and contexts. There are four major contextual sources: Western, Eastern, Southern, and African. Though it is difficult to determine the exact proportion, it is generally agreed that the bulk of OB knowledge is Western primarily because modern management began arguably around the time of the industrial revolution which started in the West. A slightly lower proportion is from the East, more specifically Japan and now China and India. The contribution of Africa and South America to management is significantly less than that of the other contexts.

Through colonialism, management science of which OB is a part was introduced to Africa. European management literature (books, journals, and magazines) was used. For Anglophone Africa, the literature was mainly British while Francophone countries used French literature. German colonies used German literature. The same pattern was observed for Portuguese and Spanish colonies. After independence, however, the pattern begun to change; African countries started developing and relying on their own literatures, paltry though they were. The change was accelerated with the dominance of America. Not only did the superior training and expertise of American management systems appeal to Africans but also the cooperative relationships between African governments and America facilitated the adoption of American literature in African countries. The American influence continues to this day.

Asia is the third source of contextual knowledge. The cold war was a mechanism by which the former Soviet Union spread socialist practices. Africans who were educated in the Soviet Union returned with expertise grounded in Russian ways of running organizations. Japan also introduced its management knowledge through its cooperative relationships with African governments. Now China and India seem to be doing the same. The Chinese and Indian multinationals are not only introducing the management practices of India and China but also their respective governments are distributing books, journals, and magazines based on their educational systems. They are also offering scholarships to Africans some of which are in Business. A number of Africans even pay their way to learn not only technology but also business training in China. As a result, there are Chinese business schools for Africa.[15] Thus, OB in Africa is predominantly foreign, a situation that should be changed by scholarship particularly in this era of increased industrial activity on the continent.[16]

Disciplines

The disciplinary sources range from psychology at the lower or individual level through sociology at the group level to anthropology at the organizational level, and philosophy at the societal level (see Figure 1.1).

Our understanding of the cognitive (mental and social) processes of individuals and small groups (i.e., teams) comes from cognitive and social psychology. Psychology is the science that seeks to measure, explain, and sometimes change the behavior of humans and other animals. Psychologists concern themselves with studying and attempting to understand individual behavior. Many of the theories dealing with personality, attitude, learning, motivation, and stress have been applied in organizational behavior to understand work-related phenomena such as job satisfaction, commitment, absenteeism, turnover, and worker well-being. Social psychology, an area within psychology that blends concepts from psychology and sociology, focuses on the influence of people on one another. One of the major areas receiving considerable investigation from social psychologists has been change—how to implement it and how to reduce barriers to its acceptance.

Sociologists, studying the structure and function of small groups within a society, have contributed greatly to a more complete understanding of behavior within organizations. Specifically, sociologists have made their greatest contribution to OB through their study of group behavior in organizations, particularly formal and complex organizations. Some of the areas within OB that received valuable input from sociologists include group dynamics, organizational technology, bureaucracy, communication, power, conflict, and intergroup behavior. Anthropology, the study of societies to learn about human beings and their activities, helps us understand differences in fundamental values and attitudes between people in different countries, and contributes knowledge on the dynamics and cultural processes of larger groups such as organizations. The economic motivations and behaviors of organizations derive from economics. It contributes knowledge on industrial dynamics and their effects on organizations. Specifically, economics has facilitated understanding of competition for scarce resources both within and between organizations and how this increases the commitment of organizations to efficiency and productivity. Political science, the study of people in a political environment and allocation of power among people to any single individual, also contributes knowledge on politics in organizations because human beings are inherently political through the quest for power and domination. Political scientists study individuals and groups within a political environment. Specific topics of concern here include structuring of conflict, allocation of power, and how people manipulate power for individual self-interest.

Organizations exist in societies. There is therefore an interdependent relationship between the two. Our knowledge of societal influences comes from philosophy which looks at how societies function. Other sources include medicine, biology, and physics; theories from these physical disciplines have been applied to OB. For example, our knowledge of stress derives from biology. Further, medicine, the applied science of healing or treating diseases, has enhanced our understanding of individuals' health and well-being. Medicine concerns itself with both physical and psychological health, as well as industrial mental health. Engineering, the applied science of energy and matter, has contributed knowledge on design of work. Frederick Taylor took basic engineering ideas and applied them to human behavior at work, influencing the early study of organizational behavior. With his engineering background, Taylor placed special emphasis on human productivity and efficiency in work behavior. His notions of performance standards and differential piece-rate systems still shape organizational goal-setting programs, particularly in the West. However, we have found that humans are unlike machines by their ability to circumvent mechanistic processes.

Interactive Processes of Behavior

Though simple, behavior is complex in terms of the factors that influence it. Behavior does not merely arise from a few factors that independently affect it; modern thinking is that the factors that influence behavior do so interdependently or interactively. Factors associated with the person (e.g., cognition, affect, and motivation) interact with the environment (e.g., culture, economics, technology, etc.) in influencing behavior. This idea is encapsulated in a formula for behavior: $B = f(P,E)$[17] where B = behavior; f = function, P = person, and E = environment. Others express it as $B = f(A,M, E)$[18] where B and f stand for behavior and function respectively while A, M, and E stand for ability, motivation, and environment respectively. This formula has been extended in extant research. It is suggested that individuals encode information from the environment or situational features, and integrate the encodings into the interactive dynamics of their cognitions, affect, and motivations to form decisions or intentions which then are transformed to actual behaviors through regulatory strategies, competencies, and resources.[19] The behavioral system depends as much on the particular situations, encodings, cognitions, affect, motivations, and regulation as on the dynamics.

The interactive process of behavior is heightened in Africa. Through cultural programming or socialization, individuals' behaviors depend on the interdependent influences of self-attributes and societal (e.g., kinship) influences. For example, managers' hiring behaviors are often based not only on the competence but also the origin or ethnic background of the applicants. Those related to the manager are more likely to be hired than those who are not. It is therefore important to know the interactive processes of behavior. Managers or supervisors who are concerned about the type and persistence of behavior, have to understand the specific "nature" and "nurture" variables and their dynamics. Through such understanding, they can establish mechanisms (skills, rewards, and climate) that facilitate behavior. When managers evaluate employees, they may look at the interactive determinants of behavior. For example, even though an employee may be low on skill or knowledge, he or she may be high on motivation and affect, which will significantly influence the person's behavior. Such information is useful for establishing fairness and a positive climate. Managers may also use the information in reward and promotion decisions. By considering the interdependence, managers can appropriately reward employees.

Benefits and Challenges of OB

In Africa, OB has unique benefits and challenges. OB is an opportunity to understand the behavior of employees in other parts of the world. Globalization has facilitated economic exchanges and career mobility across national borders. Ghanaian employees can learn from the behavior of Chinese employees in multinationals in Ghana. For example, a number of Africans from Ghana, Nigeria, Liberia, and so on work in Libya, Morocco, South Africa, and Botswana. Managers in the latter countries have to understand the needs, preferences, and attitudes of the former in order to better help, satisfy, and serve them. Second, as most African countries emerged from socialism and adopted capitalist or open market systems, companies seized the opportunity to establish operations in other parts of the continent and the world, which means they have had to deal with increased competition from other expanding companies and local ones. Quality, productivity, and good services are therefore essential. Unfortunately, these essential outcomes are wanting due to technological mechanisms that can improve quality, behaviors that maximize productivity, and skills that optimize service. Continuous improvement which facilitates these outcomes and is aided by technology therefore seems inadequate in most African companies.

A third challenge for organizations is empowerment. The cultural characteristic of most African countries—high power distance—centralizes authority in leaders. As a result, the concept of empowerment presents a challenge to managers who are used to clinging onto power. Modern managers therefore have to unlearn the traditional behaviors and empower subordinates. Empowerment increases the participation of employees and facilitates increased productivity. It also serves as a development mechanism as operatives learn to make effective decisions that are pushed down to them. The fourth challenge for managers in Africa is dealing with "permanency." It contrasts with managers in the West who have to deal with temporariness. Most employees either never quit their organizations (they work in one organization till retirement or death) or have never had to change jobs. The permanency becomes difficult for managers who may be prevented from hiring employees with "fresh" ideas. An additional challenge is the increasing trend of transparency or improved ethical behavior. Anecdotal evidence suggests that employees tend to seek "supplementary" income through graft, bribery, and other corrupt practices. The economic deprivation of employees, the drive to seek lifestyles commensurate in the West, and the cultural expectations all combine to heighten unethical behavior. Managers who are concerned about their subordinates are likely to understand such behavior even though they may disapprove of it. It therefore helps if managers define clearly the right and wrong conduct they accept; establish fair policies and appropriate systems; and increase confidence and trust in employees.

Lastly, managers have a challenge in creating positive work environments. There is so much negativity in the external and internal environments of organizations that it is not easy for them to harness the human strength and vitality of employees by assigning, preparing, and developing the right persons for the jobs to optimize the good of the organization. In this era of positive organizational scholarship, the extent to which managers exploit the positive capabilities of employees goes a long way to advance African organizations.

Behavioral Systems

Behavior as a system is defined by inputs, processes, and outputs at individual, group, and organizational levels. Figure 1.2 shows this system. Cognitions, affects, and motivations of individuals, groups, and organizations influence the decisions and intentions to enact some behaviors (and not

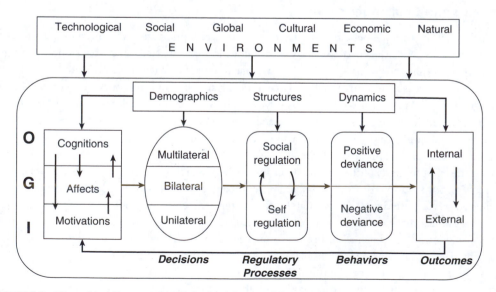

FIGURE 1.2   Hierarchical Framework of Behavioral System of Organizations

others). They do so independently and interactively. We show these processes by the up and down arrows.

The decisions may be unilateral, bilateral, or multilateral. They are transformed into behaviors through regulatory (self and social) processes. Individuals, groups, and organizations can regulate themselves but they can also be regulated by other social entities (e.g., friends, competitors, and government respectively). There are diverse individual, group, and organizational behaviors. Some scholars categorize them as task versus contextual behaviors.[20] They may also be negatively deviant (i.e., oriented toward problem solving) or positively deviant (i.e., oriented toward transcendence or demonstrating strength).[21] Business issues show either weakness or strengths. Negative and positive deviance behaviors address deficiencies and strengths respectively. In addition to these two forms that arrest a problem or advance a behavior, there are others (termed normalcy) that maintain a business issue; they focus on efficiencies. Behaviors of employees, teams, and organizations seek to prevent deterioration (negative deviance), maintain order (normalcy), or advance growth (positive deviance).

The outcomes of behaviors may be internal to the actor (e.g., employee) or external (e.g., supervisor of the employee). The same applies to groups whose actions may satisfy the members or fulfill the goals of the organization that assigned them to the task. The behavior of organizations may also yield outcomes for themselves (e.g., improved climate) or others (e.g., partners in collaborative relationships). We recognize that some behaviors are inherently internal (e.g., learning—actors learn for themselves but may share their knowledge with others) while others are external (e.g., cohesion—actors cohere with others, not themselves).

Within the behavioral system, cognitions, affects, motivations as well as decisions, regulations, behaviors, and outcomes are affected by demographics of the individuals, group, and organization, structural characteristics of the environment, and dynamics of the interaction processes of the social and economic exchanges they engage in. Age, composition, and size of employees, groups, and organizations respectively affect decision-making and self-regulation in influencing internal and external behaviors. For example, social networks which focus on structural characteristics of individuals, groups, and organizations show that the configuration of relationships and the roles actors occupy in that structure affects their behaviors.[22] When the actors do not achieve their goals, they reflect on *why*, *how*, and maybe *where* the outcomes were not achieved. The feedback is used in subsequent behaviors within the same domain or in another domain at a later time; it becomes an element of learning. Thus, behavior of individuals, groups, and organizations are affected by internal and external dynamics.

Behavioral systems of individuals, groups, and organizations can also be affected by the external environment. Technological advancement, and the social, global, cultural, economic, and natural environments affect behaviors within organizations. For example, the Internet changed the way tasks are executed at work; it facilitates telecommuting where employees can work from home. Social and global dynamics (e.g., globalization) which enable companies in China to permeate all regions of Africa not only affect interactions but the displacement of some labor. The tendency of Chinese firms in Africa to employ only Chinese implies that Kenyans or Angolans, or Guineans cannot find work. The values and norms of the culture also affect individual and collective behaviors because while some cultures facilitate cooperation or interdependence (i.e., African cultures) others (e.g., the United States) emphasize competition or independence. Obviously the decisions, regulations, and behaviors will be different in each culture. Further, economic conditions (e.g., booms and recessions) influence the behavior of employees, groups, and organizations. The same applies to concerns for the natural environment; organizations are increasingly changing their consumption patterns and orienting their employees to conserve resources or innovate to minimize destruction of the natural environment.

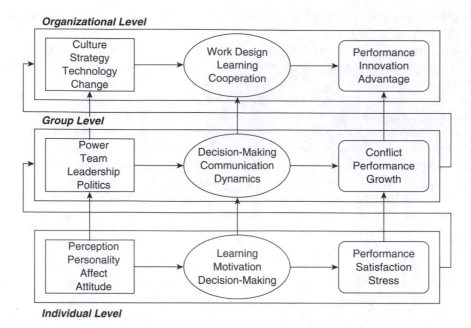

FIGURE 1.3 Framework for Book

Framework for Book

The framework for the rest of the book is summarized in Figure 1.3. We begin by examining inputs followed by processes and outcomes of the individual behavioral system. Then we move to the inputs, processes, and outcomes of the group or team behavioral system. We conclude with the inputs, processes, and outcomes of the organizational behavioral system.

We emphasize that this framework is a simplified version. For example, it does not include the moderators or contingencies that affect the relationships in each behavioral system. Nevertheless it serves as a useful guide for understanding the dynamics of OB in organizations. It is an emergent model in which behaviors and their determinants at the lower level emerge at the higher level through social or interaction processes within organizations.[23] We believe that structure facilitates learning and retention.

Summary

In this chapter we have discussed the background to organizational behavior by reviewing the origin and sources of knowledge as well as benefits, significance, and interdisciplinary influences on the field. A model of the factors that influence behavior is also presented. We conclude by presenting a system's framework to guide discussions in the rest of the chapters.

■ Individual Learning Questions

1. What is an organization? What types of organizations can you identify in Africa?
2. Where does the current knowledge of organizational behavior come from?
3. What is a behavioral system?

■ **Group Discussion Questions**

1. How does organizational behavior relate to organizational performance?
2. Discuss behavioral implications suggested by the article, "Africa Rising" (see below).
3. Discuss behavioral systems that can be inferred from the article, "Cracking The Next Growth Market" (see below).

Profile: "Africa Rising"

Business is booming across the continent from Sudan to South Africa, Guinea to Tanzania and Eritrea to Angola. The reasons for the boom include increased commodity prices, favorable demographic conditions (e.g., youthful populations), increased manufacturing and service activities.

These notwithstanding, there are still a number of problems that demand caution. They include environmental degradation (e.g., deforestation and desertification); corruption, and potential conflict from fraudulent elections.

These negative factors do not overcome the fast-growing middle class, soaring foreign investment, improved infrastructure from other developing countries (e.g., China, India, Malaysia), cross-border commerce, technological advancements, improved health systems, democratic governance, and better-educated young people of working age (demographic dividend).

To enhance these trends, there needs to be more trade than aid, regulatory mechanisms that facilitate starting of businesses, property rights and other institutional mechanisms that facilitate access to credit and business expansion, and avoidance of kleptocratic behaviors. In addition, Western governments have to provide support by opening up their markets to trade (e.g., America's African Growth and Opportunity Act), dealing transparently with African governments (e.g., sign the Extractive Industries Transparency Initiative), and negotiating favorable terms with foreign companies and governments. Such actions enable the development of good business climate that facilitates the thriving of African organizations.

In sum, Africa's continued rise will depend on the extent to which autocracy, corruption, and strife are minimized if not eliminated.

Source: "The Hopeful Continent: Africa Rising." *The Economist*, December 3, 2011.

Profile: "Cracking the Next Growth Market"

Is it the turn of Africa to rise up the rungs of the development ladder? Chironga, Leke, Lund, and van Wamelen, authors of "Cracking the Next Growth Market: Africa" certainly think so. They argue that Africa's moment has come because a number of favorable factors suggest that likelihood despite the political turmoil in North Africa, poor infrastructure, talent scarcity, poverty, famine, and disease. Real gross domestic product (real GDP) has been growing about 4.7% on average; Africans have spending power as indicated by the $860 billion they spent on goods and services in 2008 which is 35% more than Indians spent. Opportunities are also opening up in sectors such as retail, telecommunications, banking, infrastructure-related industries, resource-related business, and the agricultural value chain. Further, there is less competition, and pent-up consumer demand is strong because few foreign companies have a presence in Africa. Other companies (see Table 1) are exploiting that absence.

(Continued)

TABLE 1 Multinational Corporations and their Presence in Africa

Multinational*	Company	Presence†
Finland	Nokia	52
USA	Coca-Cola	52
UK/Netherlands	Unilever	20
Switzerland	Nestle	19
UK	Standard Chartered Bank	14
UK	Barclays	12
France	Societe Generale	15
Togo	Ecobank	30
South Africa	South African Breweries	30
South Africa	MTN	16
South Africa	Shoprite	16

*Country of Headquarters; †Number of countries company is in.

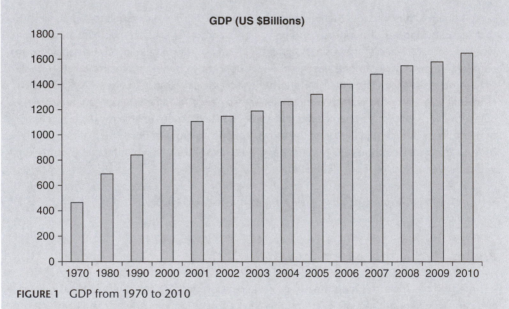

GDP (US $Billions)

FIGURE 1   GDP from 1970 to 2010

Africa's recent growth is due to increases in commodity prices (oil prices have increased from $20.00 a barrel in 1999 to $145.00 a barrel in 2008); natural resources exploitation which accounted for 24% of GDP growth from 2000 through 2008 (see Figure 1); halting of deadly hostilities that lead to political stability, healthier economies due to shrinkage in government budget deficits, trimmed foreign debt, and brought down inflation, adoption of market-friendly policies (privatization of state-owned enterprises, reduced trade barriers, cutting of corporate taxes, and strengthened regulatory and legal systems).

Given these factors, the trend will continue because of profit from rising global demand for oil, natural gas, minerals, food, and other natural resources, demographic (young, growing,

(*Continued*)

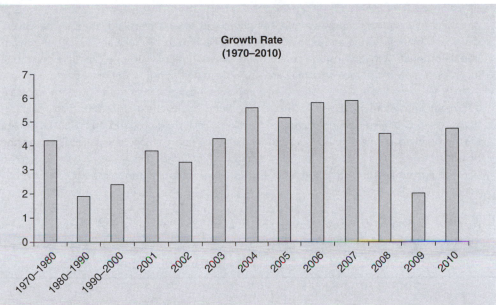

FIGURE 2   Growth Rates from 1970 to 2010

TABLE 2 Categories of African Economies

Diversified	Oil Exporters	Transition	Pre-transition	Unclassified
Botswana	Algeria	Cameroon	Djibouti	Benin
Congo (DRC)	Angola	Ghana	Ethiopia	Burkina Faso
Egypt	Chad	Kenya	Mali	Burundi
Libya	Congo	Madagascar	Sierra Leone	CAR
Mauritius	Equatorial Guinea	Mozambique		Côte d'Ivoire
Morocco	Gabon	Rwanda		Eritrea
Namibia	Nigeria	Senegal		Gambia
South Africa		Tanzania		Guinea
Tunisia		Uganda		Guinea-Bissau
		Zambia		Lesotho
				Liberia
				Malawi
				Mauritania
				Niger
				Swaziland
				Togo
				Zimbabwe
				Sudan

and migrating populations) and social (sizeable middle class on the continent with relatively high per capita income).

Given these conditions, African countries can be represented as opportunities sets. Table 2 categorizes the opportunities according to the level of diversification and exports as

(Continued)

diversified, oil exporters, transition, pre-transition, and other. Diversified countries have well-developed manufacturing and service industries. Oil exporters produce and export petroleum and its products. While transition countries are growing rapidly despite their low per capita incomes, the pre-transition economies are also expanding but not to the same degree.

In order to exploit these opportunities, companies must pick their right entry strategy, gain and maintain customers, fill the skills gap (i.e., bring midlevel expatriates to their organizations, set up extensive training programs, insist on global rotations, and buy talent), manage risk by building partnerships, wooing the influentials, and putting key stakeholders on the board. As the authors indicate "Just as investing in China embodies some poltical risk, so too does doing business in Africa. Companies must think carefully about the approaches they adopt, but it will be worthwhile."

From Mutsa Chironga, Acha Leke, Susan Lund, and Arend van Wamelen, "Cracking the Next Growth Market: Africa," *Harvard Business Review*, May, 2011.

2

THE EXTERNAL ENVIRONMENT OF AFRICAN ORGANIZATIONS

Overview

No organization functions in a vacuum. Thus, to explain employee behavior in African organizations, one must understand the external environment in which these organizations operate. In this chapter, we explore the external environment of African organizations. Factors discussed in this chapter include social-cultural, economic, political and legal, technological and international. By the end of this chapter you should be able to:

- Describe the importance of the external environment in understanding the behavior of African employees and managers
- Identify the different environmental factors that could influence human behavior in African organizations
- Describe the external environment in which organizations operate in Africa

The Social-Cultural Environment of African Organizations

Although Africa has about 54 countries with the addition of South Sudan as a new nation, it is still possible to talk about an African socio-cultural identity. The social and cultural environment includes the belief system of African employees and managers. We use Hofstede's[1] definition of culture as the mental programming of a given society to identify some of the values that could shape the behavior of African employees. Most African societies emphasize the role of traditions, wisdom as obtained through the aging process, the importance of maintaining harmonious relations with one's relatives and neighbors.

The African culture also encourages respect for authority. Hofstede[2] classifies cultures along five dimensions: collectivism/individualism, power distance, masculinity/femininity, uncertainty avoidance, and long-term orientation. Although these dimensions did not concern most African countries, a recent addition to the study includes data from East and West Africa.[3] Because these dimensions have been extensively discussed, we will only reference them here and explore their application to the African context.

Individualism/Collectivism

Collectivism refers to the degree to which a given culture emphasizes communal solidarity and the importance of the group. In most African countries, people expect each member to be loyal to the community and protect its interests. Failure to do so is often seen as a sign of not being sociable. The recent data of Hofstede's studies (see Table 2.1) show that African countries, represented in the table by East and West Africa, rank high on collectivism. This is understandable because in most African countries, the extended family still tends to be the norm. An employee or a manager should "help" relatives who are in need. Failure to do so would imply that one is failing to meet one's social obligations. Some authors have characterized this quasi-obligation to help relatives as the *solidarity tax*. In addition to helping his/her relatives, the African worker is also an agent of regional development. In most countries, African employees are required to participate in some forms of local economic development activities, including building schools, hospitals and other basic infrastructures in their native regions.

Power Distance

Power distance refers to the degree to which people defer to power and accept inequalities of power and wealth. It also refers to acceptance and obedience to those in power. Most African cultures value respect to authority and hierarchy. Again, African countries rank high on power distance. In most African cultures, people have a tendency to defer to authority. To some extent, people believe that gaining power is the will of God or some superior beings. Therefore, questioning those in power tends to be construed as a sign of disrespect.

Masculinity/Femininity

The construct of masculinity refers to the degree to which a given culture favors traditional gender roles. In such a culture, people view the role of men and women as different, with men having power and dominance over women. A high femininity culture, however, sees little difference between gender roles. In most African countries, there is a strong differentiation of gender roles although women tend to enjoy some privileges in the modern sectors of African economies.

Uncertainty Avoidance

This dimension refers to the extent to which people have an increased anxiety over novelty and change. Cultures high on uncertainty avoidance tend to emphasize maintaining traditions and the status quo compared to those low on this dimension. African countries again are ranked as high on uncertainty avoidance. This is understandable because traditions and customs still prevail in most African countries.

Long-term/Short-term Orientation

This dimension was later added to Hofstede's original four dimensions. It measures a society's devotion to traditional values. People in a culture with long-term orientation look to the future and value thrift, persistence, and tradition. In a short-term orientation, people value the here and now; they accept change more rapidly and don't see commitments as impediments to change.[4]

Ethics and Social Values

Concerns for ethical behavior are rising in most African organizations as well as in the public. Much has been written about corruption in Africa. However, few studies have investigated

TABLE 2.1 Hofstede's Cultural Values by Nation

Country	Power Distance		Individualism Collectivism		Masculinity Femininity		Uncertainty Avoidance		Long-term Short-term Orientation	
	Index	Rank	Index	Rank	Index	Rank	Index	Rank	Index	Rank
Argentina	59	35–36	46	22–23	56	20–21	86	10–15		
Australia	36	41	90	2	61	16	51	37	31	22–24
Austria	11	53	55	18	79	2	70	24–25	31	22–24
Belgium	65	20	75	8	54	22	94	5–6	38	18
Brazil	69	14	38	26–27	49	27	76	21–22	65	6
Canada	39	39	80	4–5	52	24	48	41–42	23	30
Chile	63	24–25	23	38	28	46	86	10–15		
Colombia	67	17	13	49	64	11–12	80	20		
Costa Rica	35	42–44	15	46	21	48–49	86	10–15		
Denmark	18	51	74	9	16	50	23	51	46	10
Ecuador	78	8–9	8	52	63	13–14	67	28		
El Salvador	66	18–19	19	42	40	40	94	5–6		
Finland	33	46	63	17	26	47	59	31–32	41	14
France	68	15–16	71	10–11	43	35–36	86	10–15	39	17
Germany	35	42–44	67	15	66	9–10	65	29	31	22–24
Great Britain	35	42–44	89	3	66	9–10	35	47–48	25	28–29
Greece	60	27–28	35	30	57	18–19	112	1		
Guatemala	95	2–3	6	53	37	43	101	3		
Hong Kong	68	15–16	25	37	57	18–19	29	49–50	96	2
India	77	10–11	48	21	56	20–21	40	45	61	7
Indonesia	78	8–9	14	47–48	46	30–31	48	41–42		
Iran	58	29–30	41	24	43	35–36	59	31–32		
Ireland	28	49	70	12	68	7–8	35	47–48	43	13
Israel	13	52	54	19	47	29	81	19		
Italy	50	34	76	7	70	4–5	75	23	34	19
Jamaica	45	37	39	25	68	7–8	13	52		
Japan	54	33	46	22–23	95	1	92	7	80	4
Korea (South)	60	27–28	18	43	39	41	85	16–17	75	5
Malaysia	104	1	26	36	50	25–26	36	46		
Mexico	81	5–6	30	32	69	6	82	18		
Netherlands	38	40	80	4–5	14	51	53	35	44	11–12
New Zealand	22	50	79	6	58	17	49	39–40	30	25–26
Norway	31	47–48	69	13	8	52	50	38	44	11–12
Pakistan	55	32	14	47–48	50	25–26	70	24–25	0	34
Panama	95	2–3	11	51	44	34	86	10–15		
Peru	64	21–23	16	45	42	37–38	87	9		
Philippines	94	4	32	31	64	11–12	44	44	19	31–32
Portugal	63	24–25	27	33–35	31	45	104	2	30	25–26
Singapore	74	13	20	39–41	48	28	8	53	48	9
South Africa	49	35–36	65	16	63	13–14	49	39–40		
Spain	57	31	51	20	42	37–38	86	10–15	19	31–32
Sweden	31	47–48	71	10–11	5	53	29	49–50	33	20
Switzerland	34	45	68	14	70	4–5	58	33	40	15–16
Taiwan	58	29–30	17	44	45	32–33	69	26	87	3

(*Continued*)

TABLE 2.1 (*Continued*)

Country	Power Distance		Individualism Collectivism		Masculinity Femininity		Uncertainty Avoidance		Long-term Short-term Orientation	
	Index	Rank	Index	Rank	Index	Rank	Index	Rank	Index	Rank
Thailand	64	21–23	20	39–41	34	44	64	30	56	8
Turkey	66	18–19	37	28	45	32–33	85	16–17		
United States	40	38	91	1	62	15	46	43	29	27
Uruguay	61	26	36	29	38	42	100	4		
Venezuela	81	5–6	12	50	73	3	76	21–22		
Yugoslavia	76	12	27	33–35	21	48–49	88	8		
Regions:										
Arab Countries	80	7	38	26–27	53	23	68	27		
East Africa	64	21–23	27	33–35	41	39	52	36	25	28–29
West Africa	77	10–11	20	39–41	46	30–31	54	34	16	33

Source: Hofstede & Peterson (2000).[3]
Scores range from 0 5 extremely low to 100 5 extremely high.
Note: 1 5 highest rank. LTO ranks: 1 5 China; 15–16 5 Bangladesh; 21 5 Poland; 34 5 lowest.

corruption and ethics in African organizations, especially those operating in the private sector. Although corruption is undeniable in Africa, one could argue that African employees and managers do not go to work with the desire to be corrupted or engage in corrupt practices. Rather, the environment in which they live and the operations of their organizations may induce corrupt tendencies. If obtaining a license to operate requires that one gives a "gift" to a government official or a civil servant, then a manager may act in this particular way. It may happen that certain actions could just be considered as the "normal" way of doing business. The concept of *guanxi* in Chinese business practices, which has been extensively studied in the literature in organizational behavior and management, is similar to what could be labeled *reciprocal favor* in Africa. Corruption should therefore be understood in this context. Historically, the subjects of the chief went to greet the chief with gifts, thus, today it is common to see a subordinate sending gifts to the supervisor. These practices are extensions of traditional gift giving practices to modern organizations.

One cannot talk about ethics in African organizations without exploring the concept of values. Values are basic convictions that a specific mode of conduct or end-state of existence is personally preferable to an opposite or converse mode of conduct or end-state of existence. To some extent, values contain an element of judgment to the extent that the individual views the context based on his or her ideas of what is right or wrong. Values are important because they lay the foundation for understanding a person's attitudes and behaviors. Thus, to understand the attitudes and behaviors of employees and managers in African organizations, we must know their values. Everyone has a set of values that he or she considers important. Such values constitute the person's value system.

The classical work of Milton Rokeach[5] on human values could be relevant to understanding the value systems of African employees. Rokeach divided human values into two sets of values: *terminal* values and *instrumental* values. Terminal values are desirable end-states, whereas instrumental values refer to means of achieving the end values. Table 2.2 provides examples of terminal values and instrumental values.

Understanding values can help explain corruption and ethical behaviors in African organizations. One way for African organizations to reduce the impact of corruption and unethical

TABLE 2.2 Terminal and Instrumental Values

Terminal Values	Instrumental Values
A comfortable life	Ambitious
An exciting life	Broad–Minded
A sense of accomplishment	Capable
A world at peace	Cheerful
Equality	Clean
Family security	Courageous
Freedom	Forgiving
Happiness	Helpful
Inner harmony	Honest
Mature love	Imaginative
National security	Independent
Pleasure	Intellectual
Salvation	Logical
Self-respect	Loving
Social recognition	Obedient
True friendship	Polite
Wisdom	Responsible
	Self-Controlled

practices is to develop codes of ethics. A code of ethics is a company booklet that describes what an organization stands for and the general rules of conduct it expects from its employees. However, developing a code of ethics is different from practicing what one preaches. Conducting ethics audits by senior managers or outside agencies could help to enhance the ethical practices of African organizations.

The Economic Environment

A recent *Harvard Business Review* article entitled "Cracking The Next Growth Market: Africa"[6] stresses the importance of the African market. This article was a follow up of a study conducted by the McKinsey Global Institute[7] that highlights the growth potential of the African continent. Despite several economic woes that have been depicted in the popular press and in policy-making circles, the African continent presents today undeniable business opportunities that have not been fully exploited. Several African countries, such as Angola, Ghana, Kenya, and South Africa, have seen their economies grow at faster rates than developed economies in the last decade. According to the *Harvard Business Review* article and the study of the McKinsey Global Institute, Africans spent $860 billion on goods and services in 2008, more than the $835 billion that Indians spent, and more than the $821 billion of consumer expenditures in Russia. If the continent maintains its growth trajectory, consumers will spend $1.4 trillion worth of goods and services in 2020, which will be a little less than India's projected $1.7 trillion but more than Russia's $960 billion (see Table 2.3).

African economies can be classified into four groups: diversified economies, oil exporting economies, economies in transition, and pre-transition economies (see Table 2.4). Diversified economies are characterized by a relative presence of several industrial and service sectors, while oil exporting countries mostly rely on oil revenues. Transition economies are setting the basis for

TABLE 2.3 Macroeconomic Data on the Present and Future of Africa

Africa Today	*Africa Tomorrow*
Collective GDP in 2008: $1.6 trillion	Collective GDP in 2020: $2.6 trillion
Combined consumer spending in 2008: $860 billion	Combined consumer spending in 2020: $1.4 trillion
Number of mobile phone subscribers since 2000: 316 million	Number of Africans of working age in 2040: 1.1 billion
Share of the world's total amount of uncultivated, arable land: 60%	Number of African households with discretionary income in 2020: 128 million
Number of cities with more than 1 million people: 52	Portion of Africans living in cities by 2030: 50%
Number of companies with revenues of at least $3 billion: 20	

TABLE 2.4 Groups of African Economies

Diversified Economies	*Oil Exporters*	*Transition Economies*	*Pre-Transition Economies*
Botswana	Algeria	Cameroon	DRC
Cote d'Ivoire	Angola	Ghana	Ethiopia
Egypt	Chad	Kenya	Mali
Lybia	Congo, Rep.	Madagascar	Sierra Leone
Mauritius	Equatorial	Mozambique	Sudan
Morocco	Guinea	Rwanda	
Namibia	Gabon	Senegal	
South Africa	Nigeria	Tanzania	
Tunisia		Uganda	
		Zambia	

Source: MGI (2010). The data included only countries whose 2008 GDP was approximately $10 billion or greater, or whose real GDP growth rate exceeded 7% over 2000–08 and excluded 22 countries that accounted for 3% of African GDP in 2008.

economic development and diversification and pre-transition economies are still finding their ways into the development process. They represent some of the poorest countries in Africa.

The current economic environments are shaped by past economic contexts such as economic reforms in the 1980s and 1990s. Most African countries restructured their economies by privatizing state-owned enterprises and instituting regulatory reforms that enabled locals and foreign companies to invest. Arguably, the economic reforms influenced the current economic environment.

The Technological Environment

The current century can be considered as the century of technological advancement and breakthroughs. From the Internet to the cellular phone and other information and communication technologies, each country and continent seems to be dramatically influenced by these technological advancements. African countries and organizations are not immune to such technologies although the pace of technological penetration may be less in African organizations than in those operating in developed countries, such as the United States. Nevertheless, technology permeates the African organization and influences the potential behavior of African employees and managers.

In describing the role of technology in organizations, we refer to technology as the physical and mental processes used to transform inputs into usable outputs. Technology also refers to the activities, equipment, and knowledge used to get things done. For instance, in explaining mass customization and mass production, we focus here on processes and how technology transforms such processes. Mass customization encompasses production processes that are flexible enough to create products and services that are tailored to individual customers; whereas mass production results in large quantities with little variation to control costs.

Technology influences work organization. An example is telecommuting. Telecommuting involves working away from the office, from a remote location (home or computer center). Some telecommuters work at home for at least two days a week on a computer linked to the office. There are three categories of jobs eligible for telecommuting: routine information-handling tasks, mobile activities, and professional and other knowledge-related tasks. Telecommuting is beneficial for both the company and the employee. For the company, it may help free up office space. For the employee, telecommuting may help balance work and family.

Technology also helps improve the performance monitoring process. For instance, computer performance monitoring is made possible by computer-based information technology. Computer performance monitoring refers to the use of computers to collect, store, analyze, and report information about work performance. Such monitoring may be continuous or intermittent. There is heated debate over computer performance monitoring. For the proponents of computer performance monitoring, it allows supervisors to gather more objective information about performance. However, for the opponents of computer performance monitoring, it constitutes an invasion of privacy, creates an atmosphere of distrust, and can be a source of work-related stress.

Technology affects the structure of an organization and helps create new forms of organizations. For instance, the use of information technology makes organizations more flexible and gives employees easy access to job-related information. Information technology has created a new breed of employees—knowledge workers.

E-organizations refer to applications of e-business concepts to all organizations. One must make a distinction between e-organizations, e-commerce, and e-business. E-Commerce refers to the sales side; whereas e-business is the full breadth of activities included in a successful Internet-based company. Using the Internet as a working tool can have both advantages and disadvantages. Information technology speeds the communication process, facilitates access to information, and reduces costs. It also helps employees develop highly marketable skills. However, at the individual level, using the Internet can lead to work distractions (cyber loafing). The Internet also creates new ways of interacting with colleagues. It reduces the emotions and warmth involved in face-to-face interpersonal relations. Thus, managers should develop new ways of leading employees in the Internet age.

Technology imposes different demands on people and organizations. Therefore, as technology changes or organizations use new technologies, they must design structures that fit these technologies. The goal of technology adoption in organizations is to improve efficiency. The extent to which such a goal is accomplished depends on how the technology is used. The technology should closely relate to the type of jobs performed in the organization.

Political and Legal Environment of African Organizations

One of the environmental factors that could affect organizations operating in Africa is the legal and political environment. Although tremendous progress has been made by Africa, there are still problems related to political instability, corruption, and issues related to the rule of law. Such factors could influence how employees and managers behave in the workplace. Hiring practices in some African organizations could be affected by political interference. In such cases, the manager could hire an employee because of his/her political connections rather than his/her expertise or work experience. The inability to enforce existing laws often leads to corruption and perceived injustices for both organizations and employees.

The political and legal environments of most African countries are shaped by the colonial and post-colonial traditions. The major colonial legacies—English, French, German, Portuguese, Spain, and Dutch—prevail in most countries in the form of language, judicial systems, and even multinational organizations. French multinational companies tend to dominate the francophone countries while English multinationals dominate Anglophone countries. The significance of the legacies is that they still influence business transactions in terms of the interactions (using English or French) for communication and the continued ties with the former colonial masters. The historical influences are not only in the political and legal environments; they also relate to the economic, cultural, and social environments because the educational, economic, and cultural activities are partly based on those historical legacies.

Globalization and African Organizations

Although we use the term African organizations, we must admit that some organizations operating in Africa are subsidiaries of multinational corporations and founded by non–Africans. In this regard, the term African organization is loosely used to describe any organization operating in an African country. Thus, organizations in Africa do not operate in a vacuum. They are influenced by the trends of globalization and internalization. For instance, some organizations in Africa function as suppliers of organizations located elsewhere in the world. Mercedes and BMW for example build cars in South Africa. The same is true for Nestlé, which operates several subsidiaries in Africa.

Statistics of these factors are summarized in Table 2.5.[8] They show how African political, legal, economic, social, and cultural environments are faring. Those with high and positive values suggest that the economies are doing well. For example, countries with high ratings of political environment suggest that there is peace in the country and therefore likelihood of order for conduct of enduring business.

The populations of most countries are high considering the economic welfare indicated by the gross domestic product per capita purchasing power parity (*GDP-pcppp*). This index is important for businesses that have to sell goods and services; the consumers can afford them. The economic environment indicators, gross domestic product (*GDP*), GDP per capita (*GDP-pc*), gross domestic product growth (*GDP-g*), and GDP-pcppp all seem to be high even though some countries have better indicators (e.g., South Africa, Egypt, Nigeria) than others (e.g., Sudan, Chad). The political environment indicator, *statd*, shows the status of the country. While some are authoritarian, others are democratic; still others are hybrid. The cultural index, *ed*, measures the diversity of ethnic or tribal groups in a country. Some countries are more diverse (e.g, Angola) than others (e.g., Libya).

As we briefly discussed in this chapter, the external environment could affect not only the behavior of employees and managers but also the behaviors and strategies of organizations. Understanding the external environment could help African organizations create internal environment where their employees could strive. For instance, subsidiaries of multinational corporations operating in Africa often employ expatriates from developed countries or third country nationals. Very often, those expatriates earn more than their local counterparts. Such compensation disparities create feelings of perceived distributive injustice. To remedy such feelings of inequity and injustice, organizations should clearly explain their compensation policies.

TABLE 2.5 Indices of Environmental Factors of Africa

Country	Population	GDP	GDP-pc	GDP-g	GDP-pcppp	rgn	HDI-rank	STATD
Algeria	33351137	117169320524.24	3508.91	2.00	7210.50	Northern	104	Authoritarian
Angola	17089111	45163239832.43	2655.04	18.56	4163.76	Southern	161	Authoritarian
Benin	8128208	4734839067.49	601.50	4.10	1315.22	Western	163	Full Democracy
Botswana	1858163	11255175568.25	5920.96	5.14	12296.24	Southern	132	Full Democracy
Burkina Faso	14358500	5771194544.67	394.69	5.50	1050.59	Western	176	Authoritarian
Burundi	7603492	918823350.84	122.93	5.12	347.02	Central	170	Hybrid
Cameroon	18174696	17956985510.83	1000.48	3.22	1979.67	Central	149	Authoritarian
CAR	4264806	1476870078.01	361.31	3.80	658.42	Central	172	Authoritarian
Chad	10468179	6099009022.99	604.82	0.20	1424.98	Central	174	Authoritarian
Congo	60643890	7731262789.50	2130.67	6.14	278.76	Central	168	Authoritarian
Congo (DR)	3486073	8543323220.41	144.59	5.08	3640.58	Central	142	Authoritarian
Côte d'Ivoire	19673411	17367306796.60	947.69	0.68	1536.51	Western	164	Authoritarian
Djibouti	818508	768873684.03	933.46	4.80	1892.05	Eastern	151	Authoritarian
Egypt	78602081	107484034648.25	1422.34	6.84	4529.64	Northern	119	Authoritarian
Eq. Guinea	625394	9603185319.30	15346.02	1.26	24416.68	Central	122	Authoritarian
Eritrea	4692115	1211186991.87	260.70	-0.96	601.96	Eastern	162	Authoritarian
Ethiopia	76627697	15164485977.36	199.55	10.83	683.38	Eastern	171	Hybrid
Gabon	1395613	9545984815.16	6832.26	1.18	12933.20	Central	124	Authoritarian
Gambia	1570883	508301859.90	323.58	6.55	1182.61	Western	156	Hybrid
Ghana	22393338	20388817031.72	919.61	6.40	1242.08	Western	139	Hybrid
Guinea	9411881	2821345794.39	306.60	2.50	1056.61	Western	157	Authoritarian
Guinea-Bissau	1506905	5785517470.21	414.56	2.14	503.01	Western	173	Authoritarian
Kenya	36553490	22502239913.45	615.81	6.32	1398.07	Eastern	155	Hybrid
Lesotho	1994888	1414900686.70	678.43	4.72	1358.63	Southern	149	Full Democracy
Liberia	3471020	611859674.74	184.64	7.80	334.31	Western		Hybrid
Libya	6038643	56484375000.00	9583.79	5.90	12949.14	Northern	58	Authoritarian
Madagascar	18105439	5515222624.39	299.30	5.02	901.25	Eastern	147	Hybrid
Malawi	13570713	3116942711.16	236.22	7.70	683.08	Southern	166	Hybrid

(*Continued*)

TABLE 2.5 (Continued)

Country	Population	GDP	GDP-pc	GDP-g	GDP-pcppp	regn	HDI-rank	STATD
Mali	11968376	5866095675.49	431.56	5.30	1025.47	Western	175	Full Democracy
Mauritania	3043639	2699180938.20	862.37	19.40	1831.67	Western	153	Authoritarian
Mauritius	1252987	6507112279.85	5193.28	3.95	10254.04	Eastern	65	Full Democracy
Morocco	30496553.37	65637107776.26	2106.20	7.76	3822.24	Northern	125	Authoritarian
Mozambique	20971449	7096128500.86	333.29	8.68	720.67	Southern	169	Hybrid
Namibia	2046555	7980502215.66	3766.78	7.07	5668.53	Southern	126	Full Democracy
Niger	13736722	3645126125.95	270.81	5.80	596.85	Western	178	Authoritarian
Nigeria	144719953	146867334823.52	1024.62	6.20	1795.26	Western	159	Authoritarian
Rwanda	9209997	3111203756.26	329.53	9.20	830.34	Central	160	Authoritarian
Senegal	11582863	9378279041.45	839.63	2.53	1609.60	Western	158	Hybrid
Sierra Leone	5270799	1422009797.58	266.93	7.28	665.55	Western	177	Authoritarian
South Africa	47391025	261007039378.85	5468.30	5.60	8861.93	Southern	121	Full Democracy
Swaziland	1136712	2669670497.79	2388.74	2.87	4410.89	Southern	148	Authoritarian
Tanzania	40117243	14331230928.99	367.64	6.74	1073.68	Eastern	165	Hybrid
Togo	6144899	2202809610.79	398.34	4.05	782.19	Western		Authoritarian
Tunisia	10128100	34377235161.53	3394.31	5.65	6743.00	Northern	89	Authoritarian
Uganda	29651734	9977209198.94	339.70	10.78	966.31	Eastern	145	Hybrid
Zambia	12019481	10702206685.72	910.82	6.23	1168.84	Southern	167	Hybrid
Zimbabwe	12459352	5203343319.97	415.28	-3.33		Southern	146	Authoritarian

TABLE 2.5 (Continued)

Country	Minfr0s	Mrusec10s	mwelf10s	meduc10r	mheal10s	ed	trade	mobcell	ecnstat
Algeria	36.48	55.69797217	68.4014	6	83.136869	0.0756	70.12	20997954.00	Oil Exporter
Angola	33.09	38.32036722	41.7436	51	55.080883	1.39718	109.89	3054620.00	Oil Exporter
Benin	27.83	65.5622253	51.3107	29	71.598807	1.79011	34.05	1055727.00	Unclassified
Botswana	63.12	61.77208932	76.5791	8	90.940159	0.74991	77.68	823070.00	Diversified
Burkina Faso	31.69	76.41031356	48.8958	47	59.269019	1.77854	38.34	1016605.00	Unclassified
Burundi	15.03	44.70208461	49.0953	48	51.910039	0.49989	57.71	200000.00	Unclassified
Cameroon	22.15	60.2729897	54.3221	27	57.48759	1.76164	43.96	3135946.00	Transition
CAR	17.74	36.06973914	33.4952	52	43.65096	1.68673	35.95	110000.00	Unclassified
Chad	16.84	36.54416195	29.8923	49	28.911331	1.99468	104.29	466088.00	Oil Exporter
Congo	27.18	43.31434127	45.2016	38	60.141671	1.34566	149.78	917499.00	Oil Exporter
Congo (DR)	0.84	44.39784098	32.535	41	43.195585	1.19711	75.03	4415470.00	Diversified
Côte d'Ivoire	28.56	35.97487536	35.5778	39	60.072691	1.51948	95.01	4065421.00	Unclassified
Djibouti	43.23	38.08838172	68.2959	36	64.449632	0.83763	97.22	44817.00	Pre-transition
Egypt	63.37	75.39578299	67.6588	7	81.434998	0.0458	61.52	18001106.00	Diversified
Eq. Guinea	27.94	41.5295904	31.8452	17	55.66544	0.64915	119.86	140000.00	Oil Exporter
Eritrea	23.13	49.91059754	37.9392	35	81.727207	1.21019	45.26	61996.00	Unclassified
Ethiopia	32.30	64.48008465	47.5038	28	55.783353	1.79952	50.47	866700.00	Pre-transition
Gabon	24.65	38.44763935	58.6225	12	68.970885	1.71391	93.74	897987.00	Oil Exporter
Gambia	35.49	62.92700531	65.4483	18	68.050144	1.56724	96.88	257.40	Unclassified
Ghana	27.86	60.1209211	69.0263	10	73.348781	1.64783	65.92	5207242.00	Transition
Guinea	1.89	43.70225462	41.0801	40	52.399497	1.27289	81.90		Unclassified
Guinea–Bissau	18.31	34.64928341	48.244	50	46.810449	1.67598		157330.00	Unclassified
Kenya	17.90	64.90999019	56.1334	20	68.148054	1.95361	62.73	7340317.00	Transition
Lesotho	49.84	47.92350774	58.0094	23	75.538111	0.04016	156.86	357913.00	Unclassified
Liberia	16.25	34.63797469	39.2194	21	46.865366	2.05613	111.86	280000.00	Unclassified
Libya	74.77	0.002	65.0794	4	97.806755	0.15393	96.77	3927562.00	Diversified
Madagascar	28.43	55.9348633	47.4569	34	60.270283	1.79165	75.51	1045888.00	Transition
Malawi	32.04	53.13715261	54.6885	43	71.168438	1.88385	69.73	620163.00	Unclassified

(*Continued*)

TABLE 2.5 (*Continued*)

Country	Minfr0s	Mrusec10s	mwelf10s	meduc10r	mheal10s	ed	trade	mobcell	ecnstat
Mali	15.62	61.87456709	52.4064	31	52.396384	1.46575	72.34	1512948.00	Pre-transition
Mauritania	38.15	60.90583403	46.4419	42	56.890039	1.08123	112.21	346.19	Unclassified
Mauritius	70.08	81.32195424	88.6826	3	87.217316	0.82258	134.52	616.44	Diversified
Morocco	47.08	66.54262861	63.6122	11	84.389531	0.0756	73.88	16004731.00	Diversified
Mozambique	29.16	60.18065202	49.5618	44	57.661247	1.21805	85.58	2339317.00	Transition
Namibia	64.28	57.52657303	65.875	15	87.845073	1.6321	81.41	608846.00	Diversified
Niger	6.01	59.4005088	39.6744	46	48.686208	1.29235		483000.00	Unclassified
Nigeria	10.07	51.69492503	46.2508	26	36.028643	1.77833	70.60	32322202.00	Oil Exporter
Rwanda	22.85	70.27019818	66.4879	37	78.938805	0.5013	36.34	314201.00	Transition
Senegal	23.18	67.06237177	57.1856	30	73.533694	1.50601	68.65	2982623.00	Transition
Sierra Leone	13.69	54.59933162	40.8363	45	38.217406	1.57117	57.48		Pre-transition
South Africa	44.53	64.23037013	80.2412	5	69.366848	0.74825	62.46	39662000.00	Diversified
Swaziland	39.79	45.47398776	56.6347	16	83.655391	0.75149	171.85	250000.00	Unclassified
Tanzania	32.15	74.09682455	56.7709	33	62.408437	1.73288	58.26	5766566.00	Transition
Togo	22.39	36.60192126	32.2128	32	67.104992	1.63161	104.84	708000.00	Unclassified
Tunisia	66.61	68.28245251	83.2128	2	94.746434	0.14083	93.94	7339047.00	Diversified
Uganda	28.77	64.75269831	64.9597	25	62.856048	2.07762	43.63	2008818.00	Transition
Zambia	33.66	51.35475776	54.3521	19	71.805694	1.82661	68.59	1663328.00	Transition
Zimbabwe	36.55	8.140014325	27.8674	24	55.863314	0.64685	86.65	68.15	Unclassified

Summary

We discussed macro factors influencing African organizations. These are important for understanding OB.

■ **Group Discussion Questions**

1. Describe the external environment of African organizations and indicate how such an environment could affect employee behavior.
2. What trends do you think will affect organizations operating in Africa in the next 10 years?
3. Do you think that the social and cultural environment confronting African workers is an impediment to their productivity? Yes? No? Justify your answer.

Exercise 2.1: The Stolen Drug[9]

In Europe, a woman was near death from a rare kind of cancer. There was one drug that the doctors thought might save her. It was a form of radium that a druggist in the same town had recently discovered. The drug was expensive to make, but the druggist was charging 10 times what the drug cost him. He paid $200 for the radium and charged $2,000 for a small dose of the drug. The sick woman's husband, Heinz, went to everyone he knew to borrow the money, but he could only get together about $1,000, which was half of what it cost. He told the druggist that his wife was dying and asked him to sell it cheaper, or let him pay later. But the druggist said, "No, I discovered the drug and I'm going to make money from it." Heinz became desperate and broke into the man's store to steal the drug for his wife.

Questions

1. Was Heinz right or wrong?
2. Use the levels and stages of moral development from the table below to explore Heinz's moral reasoning.

Heinz's Reasoning: Should I steal the drug?

Moral Stage	Argument for	Argument against
Stage 1. Orientation to punishment.		
Stage 2. Orientation to pleasure.		
Stage 3. Orientation to social approval.		
Stage 4. Orientation to social order.		
Stage 5. Orientation to social rights and responsibilities.		
Stage 6. Orientation to ethical principles.		

Duration: 10 minutes

Exercise 2.2: Writing a Value Statement

Identify five values that are important to you in life. Based on these values, write a value statement.

Duration: 10 minutes

Values:

1. _____
2. _____
3. _____
4. _____
5. _____

Write your value statement:

_____

_____

_____

_____

_____

_____

_____

_____

_____

_____

_____

_____

_____

_____

_____

_____

3

SOCIAL PERCEPTION AND DIVERSITY IN AFRICAN ORGANIZATIONS

Overview

This chapter focuses on perception and diversity and their influence on the behavior of employees. We discuss the determinants and consequences of social perception first, followed by diversity and its management. By the end of this chapter you should be able to:

- Explain social perception in organizations
- Explain attribution in organizations
- Discuss impression management
- Discuss diversity
- Distinguish various forms of diversity
- Explain tribal diversity

Perception

Perception is important because it affects both the decisions and behaviors of employees and managers. A decision taken by an individual is a complex process involving the intake of data, screening, processing, and interpreting and evaluating of data, based on the perception of the individual. Workplace interactions are also a function of how employees interpret and make sense of the world around them and each other. It is therefore important to understand perception and its dynamics.

Nature

As we all well know "perception is reality." How then does perception play out in African organizations? Even though perception is a complex cognitive process that differs from person to person—it occurs in every place, time, and space—it is a major fact of human interaction. Perception is defined as a process that involves receiving raw data from the senses and then filtering, modifying or transforming the data completely to give meaning to an individual's environment.

It therefore occurs during meetings, training, and travel. It involves five major subprocesses as discussed below.

Processes

Perception involves encounter or sensing, registration or selection, organizing, interpretation, and feedback processes. *Encounter* is when an individual confronts a perceptual stimulus, say another employee. It is followed by *registration or absorption*, and linking of the person to a co-worker with similar characteristics. *Organizing* occurs when the stimuli are grouped according to their relevance or basis. *Interpretation* refers to making sense or understanding the stimuli. It occurs through linkages with previous or current stimuli. *Feedback* occurs when a closer look confirms or disconfirms the interpretation. To illustrate these subprocesses consider the story of Okonle Koji who enters a meeting room, observes someone in a yellow shirt whose back or side is facing him, sits next to the person without a friendly gesture only to realize that that person is his best friend who happens to be in an unusual attire that day. The yellow color makes his best friend stand out. However, the others in the room have similar statures and Koji does not recognize his friend. Upon closer examination, Koji discerns that it is his friend, Kunle, who is absorbed in digesting a story in the Kenyan *Standard*. In this situation, Koji went through encounter (well-dressed individuals in a room), selection (bright yellow shirt), organizing (linking yellow shirts and his friend, Kunle), interpretation (the person wearing the yellow shirt must be Kunle), and feedback (confirmation that the yellow shirt person is his friend Kunle who is there to attend the meeting). Through these processes, Koji responds affirmatively toward Kunle.

Perception is important because workers form judgments based on it and their judgments are often translated into decisions. Accurate perceptions often lead to accurate judgments and right decisions. In addition, workers' behaviors result from their perceptions; if they perceive somebody as friendly, they are likely to reciprocate, resulting in healthy interactions. However, if their perceptions are wrong, they are likely to behave negatively. Workers are therefore likely to behave in a particular way based on their perception which may turn out to be inaccurate as a consequence. In short, accurate perceptions help workers make good decisions; motivate them to perform at a high level, to be fair and equitable, and to be ethical.

Selective Perception

One of the processes of perception is selection. People selectively interpret what they see on the basis of their interest, background, experience, and attitudes. According to the principle of perceptual selectivity, which explains how and why people select only a few stimuli out of the many stimuli they keep encountering at any given time, the features of some stimuli are attractive or salient. For example, at a meeting of managers, the person with a loud voice might be perceived more than another person with a normal voice.

There are a number of internal and external attention factors that can affect perceptual selectivity. Some of the internal factors include learning, motivation, and personality. When you learn something, the prior exposure makes you distinguish some social objects from others. Further, if an individual has a goal, for example, of becoming a manager, he/she is likely to focus on stimuli that relate to that goal. Moreover, some individuals have personality attributes associated with perception of environmental stimuli; they are self- and social-monitors. Consequently, their selective perception differs from those who do not have that attribute.

Some external factors that affect perceptual selectivity include intensity, size, contrast, repetition, motion, novelty and familiarity. Intensity raises the tempo above normal which draws attention. Repetition stands out because of the frequency of occurrence whilst contrast juxtaposes some attribute (e.g., red color) against another attribute (e.g., white color). Novel stimuli are salient because of their newness while big stimuli stand out because of their above normal size. Familiarity increases selective perception because of the congruence of encounter; the sense of *déjà vu* which the perceiver develops makes him/her home in on the familiar object rather than another object. Consequently, Kwesi, an Akan, is likely to select Ama during a job interview because of the familiarity of names.

Types of Perception

Humans cognitively process several stimuli that psychologists categorize as object and social perception. We are interested in social perception because of our desire to understand how employees perceive one another, and how that perception affects their judgments and decisions. Social perception is the process by which people interpret the input from their senses to give meaning and order to the social world around them. It focuses on sensing and interpreting social stimuli or attributes of people. Social perceptions occur in social interaction contexts such as meetings and contests.

Dimensions of Social Perception

Why do different individuals perceive the same thing differently? It could be the characteristics of the perceiver, situation, or target.[1] For example, the person's attitudes, motives, and expectations may influence which stimuli he/she cues in. The *perceiver's* knowledge base is organized into schemas, defined as abstract knowledge structures stored in memory that allow people to organize and interpret information about a given target of perception. In addition to the perceiver's schemas, the motivational state and mood also influence perception. Individuals in good motivational states and positive moods tend to have more positive perceptions than those in bad states and negative moods. The characteristics of *situations* or contexts (time, place, and ambience) also affect perception. In the morning for example, social stimuli draw greater attention because people still have vigor, alertness, and focus. That period of the day contrasts with the evening when people tend to be tired. The third factor is the *target* or what is perceived. Characteristics of the target influence perception. Ambiguous targets are subject to a lot of interpretation by the perceiver; the more ambiguous the target, the more likely perceivers are to differ in their perceptions of the social objective. The target's social status also affects how the target is perceived. The target's novelty, background, sounds, and size affect differences in perception. For example, an employee of a diminutive stature who perceives a very tall co-worker will differ from a very tall employee who perceives another very tall co-worker. In the latter situation, both are very tall and height difference is not salient unlike in the former situation where it was. These factors are summarized in Figure 3.1 below.

Perception Errors

There are several perception errors that prevent people from giving accurate meaning to the objects, events, and individuals they perceive. Such perception errors could make organizational life miserable for both the perceived and the target. In the following lines, we discuss some of these perception errors. The first perception error is the *halo effect*, a general impression about an individual which is based on a single positive characteristic. For example, an interviewer meeting a well-dressed applicant for the first time might conclude that the person will be a good

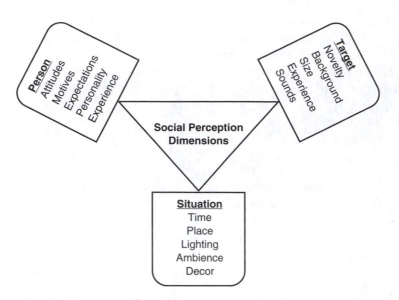

FIGURE 3.1   Dimensions of Social Perception

employee. That first and only encounter is insufficient for good judgment to be made about the candidate. The second is *contrast error*. It refers to evaluations of a person's characteristics that are affected by comparisons with other people recently encountered who rank higher or lower on the same characteristics. During the performance appraisal process, a supervisor may contrast the performance of an employee who performs moderately with one that performed excellently or poorly. The problem is that the attribution is relative rather than absolute, and may be magnified by the degree of contrast.

Another type of error is *projection*. It refers to the process of attributing one's own characteristics to other people. A supervisor who attributes his/her work style to subordinates commits the error of projection. Finally, *stereotyping* refers to judging someone on the basis of the group to which he/she belongs. It is a common dysfunctional schema. Stereotypes often lead perceivers to assume erroneously that targets have a whole range of characteristics simply because they possess one distinguishing characteristic (e.g., race, age, or gender). By associating the individual with a group, you "taint" the person with group characteristics. Stereotypes are not always negative; there are positive ones. However, most people complain about the negative stereotypes.

Impression Management

The errors and the desire of individuals to avoid the biases of perceivers sometimes cause some people to engage in impression management. Impression management is the process of editing, packaging, and communicating information to control one's own image as perceived by other people. Studies show that people use impression management to influence others, and that it eventually affects the overall quality of one's life. Even when people have no direct reason to influence others' behaviors, they are motivated to manage others' impressions of them in order to enhance their own self-esteem, to reduce negative emotions, and to construct and maintain their private identities. In the workplace, impression management occurs during job interviews, performance appraisal, or job promotion decisions. Figure 3.2 summarizes the impression management process.

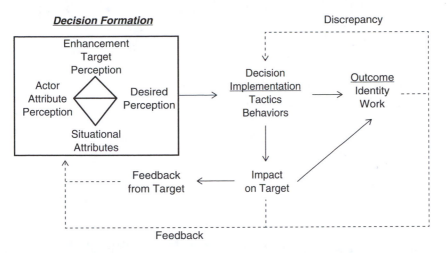

FIGURE 3.2 Impression Management Process

It begins with the actor forming a decision about how she/he will likely be perceived. That decision is a network of the actor's personal attributes, the target's attributes, the situation (e.g., job) to be encountered, and desired outcome (e.g., self-esteem). The implementation of the decision involves use of tactics and behaviors to impress which may impact the target and yield some outcomes. Feedback determines if the impression was good or not.

In Africa, impression management is important for at least two reasons. First, there is the global negative perception of Africa as backward and underdeveloped. Second, there are stereotypes about the attitudes and behaviors of Africans. For example, Nigerians are often perceived as criminal, typified by 419 scams that originate from Nigeria. Anecdotal evidence suggests that how Africans present themselves in job interviews in America and Europe often influences their hiring success.[2]

Applications of Perception in Organizations

Perception affects a number of organizational practices and processes that involve decision making. First, there is evidence that interviewers make perceptual judgments that are often inaccurate; different interviewers see different things in the same candidate and thus arrive at different conclusions about the applicant. Further, interviewers generally draw early impressions that become very quickly entrenched. Second, evidence indicates that people tend to validate their perceptions of reality, even when those perceptions are faulty. This occurs in the area of performance expectations. When one set of expectations is believed, responded to, and fulfilled, it becomes a self-fulfilling prophecy.[3]

As shown in Figure 3.3, when the expectations are positive, and lead to positive outcomes the result is a *galatea effect*.[4] However, when negative expectations lead to negative outcomes, the result is a *golem effect*.[5] To the degree that managers use subjective measures in appraising employees, what the evaluator perceives to be good or bad employee characteristics or behaviors will significantly influence the outcome of the appraisal.

Additional errors include *leniency*, the tendency to perceive the job performance of ratees as especially good; *harshness*, the tendency to perceive the job performance of ratees as especially ineffective; *central tendency*, the tendency to assign most ratees to middle-range job performance categories; and a *similar-to-me* error where a rater gives more favorable evaluations to people who

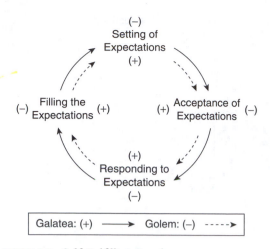

FIGURE 3.3 Self-Fulfilling Prophecy

are similar to the rater in terms of background or attitudes. All these (but particularly similar-to-me) errors can adversely affect women, minorities, and employees outside of the manager's tribe who are trying to climb the corporate ladder.

Attribution

Social perception induces individuals to attribute explanatory causes to behavior, attitudes, and events of others or themselves. This process is called causal attribution. Attribution is important because it occurs frequently in the workplace. Supervisors make attributions for high or low performance. If a supervisor attributes high performance to exceptional ability, challenging work is assigned, but if it is attributed to luck, no change in assignment will be made. Incorrect attributions could result in over-challenging or under-challenging assignments. Smooth day-to-day interactions often hinge on accurate attributions.

Assumptions of Attribution

Attribution theory has a number of assumptions.[6] First, it assumes that behavior is a function of the person and the environment. Second, individuals have a *locus of control*—defined as the extent to which people feel that they control their own destiny or that outside factors explain what happens to them. Individuals who have an internal locus of control, that is, believe they can change what happens to them, will likely take responsibility for events in their lives. Those who have external locus of control (i.e., they cannot change what happens to them) will likely not take responsibility for events in their lives, and believe that fate or luck or some other force controls their destiny. Third, individuals seek to understand the source of motivation, a quest that drives them to reflect on their outcomes. Finally, future behavior is influenced by belief systems. For example when Xhosa receives a poor grade that is attributed to a lack of ability, she will expect poor grades in the future, but when a poor grade is attributed to a lack of effort, the same result will not be expected in future situations.

Types of Attribution

There are two types of causal attributions: internal and external.[7] To understand the attribution process, consider the *observer* and the *actor*.[8] The observer is the person who witnesses the event and is trying to explain it. The actor is the person whose behavior is judged. Internal attribution occurs when the observer attributes the cause of the actor's behavior to the actor. The observer makes the attribution using dispositions such as personality traits, motivation or ability, and effort. An observer may thus attribute the cause of an employee's lack of promotion to laziness and incompetence and poor performance to lack of effort or ability.

External attribution occurs when the observer sees the cause of the actor's behavior as being situations over which the actor has no control. For example, if the employee's promotion was contingent on his performance on a fixed exam and on that day he fell ill and could not take the exam, the sickness would be the cause of his lack of promotion. The observer makes a situational attribution by attributing the behavior to external factors, such as a machine or car accident.

Components of Attribution

Given the assumptions discussed above, diverse sets of dimensions are often advanced to explain causal attributions. We focus on two sets of dimensions that have implications for organizational behavior in Africa.

Consistency, Consensus, and Distinctiveness

First, the behavior of individuals is often evaluated with reference to the actor or some situation (e.g., witchcraft). Thus, the *consistency*, *consensus*, and *distinctiveness* dimensions are of interest for behavioral evaluation (see Table 3.1). Consistency refers to the extent to which the person behaves the same way in other situations. Consensus refers to the extent to which others involved in the situation behave the same way as the individual whose behavior we are evaluating. Distinctiveness refers to the extent to which the behavior stands out; whether it is a singular occurrence or a repeated pattern.

As shown in Table 3.1, internal attributions are likely to be made when consistency, consensus, and distinctiveness are low. External attributions are likely to be made when consistency, consensus, and distinctiveness are high. When consistency is high and consensus and distinctiveness are low, external attributions are also likely to be made. Internal attributions are made when consistency is low, consensus high, and distinctiveness high. Other combinations are possible, as shown in Table 3.1. Though not explicit, these dimensions underlie external attributions of witches, ancestors, or fate for the cause of individual failure or mishap. When a director is removed from his post, albeit rarely in Africa, hardly ever is the cause attributed to incompetence; most often it is some "supernatural force."

TABLE 3.1 Dimensions and Types of Attribution

Attribution	Consistency	Consensus	Distinctiveness
Internal	Low	Low	Low
Internal	Low	Low	High
External	High	Low	High
External	High	High	Low
Internal	Low	High	High
Internal	Low	High	Low
External	High	High	Low
External	High	High	High

TABLE 3.2 Attribution of Achievement

Factors	Endowment	Stability	Controllability	Causality
Effort	High	Low	High	Internal
Ability	High	High	Low	Internal
Task Difficulty	High	Low	Low	External
Luck	High	Low	Low	External

Endowment, Stability, and Controllability

Another area of attributions common in organizations is achievement (see Table 3.2).[9] Achievements of individuals tend to also be evaluated based on internal and external attributions. The dimensions of endowment, stability, and controllability influence achievement attributions. Causality, for example, is either external or internal. In other words, you either believe that the cause of your particular achievement in an exam is due to your effort (internal) or is due to the fact that the test was too difficult (external).

When an individual can demonstrate effort and control over a task even though the effort seems unstable, the person is likely to make internal attributions. The same type of attribution is likely to be made when the person is highly endowed with ability. However, when the task is very difficult and the person cannot control what is going on, he/she is likely to make external attributions. The same applies to situations where the person is endowed with luck and greater uncontrollability. Employees who believe that they are endowed with resources and control over performance are likely to take responsibility for their achievement even if they are changing tasks or organizations.

In Ghana, it is not uncommon for external attributions to be made for a person's achievement particularly when there is perceived low effort, high task difficulty, and low ability. A supervisor who becomes a manager is more likely to be perceived as having been "helped" to that post.

Attribution Errors

Because attributions are based on perceptions, they also tend to be biased or error-prone. A bias occurs if the perceiver systematically distorts some otherwise correct procedure. Individuals are driven by needs or strategic reasons to make the biases. The information they have may also cause them to commit attribution errors. Four major attribution errors include the *fundamental attribution error*, *self-serving bias*, *actor–observer difference*, and *false consensus*. The fundamental attribution error refers to the tendency of individuals to underestimate the impact of situational factors and to overestimate the role of dispositional factors in controlling behavior.[10] The *self-serving bias* refers to the tendency to attribute one's success to internal causes, and failures to external causes. It is frequent and insidious among social actors. It manifests when employees attribute achievements to themselves and failures to supervisors or organizational systems. Self-serving bias has two forms: *self-enhancing bias* where individuals take credit for success, and *self-protecting bias* where they deny responsibility for failure. Another error is the *actor–observer difference*. Sometimes known as divergence bias it proposes that actors (self) are likely to attribute their actions to situational factors whereas the observers (others) are likely to attribute the same actions to stable personal dispositions. One reason for this tendency is that actors or self-raters have a greater amount of information about the behaviors (they know themselves more). In addition, they focus greater attention on the behavior which makes them understand it more. *False consensus* refers to the tendency for people to see their own behavior as typical and assume that others would do the same under similar circumstances. Why? There is some evidence that our own opinions are more salient to us, and tend to displace consideration of alternatives. It is possible that the tendency to subjectively justify the correctness of our opinions by grounding them in exaggerated consensus may enable stable perception of reality.

Context of Attribution

Are these errors or biases that distort attribution universal across different cultures? While there is no definitive answer there is some preliminary evidence that indicates cultural differences: Korean managers found that, contrary to the self-serving bias, they tended to accept responsibility for group failure. Attribution theory was developed largely based on experiments with Americans and Western Europeans. The Korean study suggests caution in making attribution theory predictions in non-Western societies, especially in countries with strong collectivist traditions. In Africa, it was also found in a study of Arab elites in the wake of the Gulf war that the attributions of Iraq's behavior by Egyptian elites, and attributions of the Coalition's behavior by Moroccan and Tunisian elites were not fully consistent with the fundamental attribution error predictions.[11]

Reducing Attribution Errors

How can you improve your attributions? First, admit that you cannot avoid them; no one can. Second, recognize the types of errors you make. Your awareness will help you minimize the biases overtime. Third, beware of the factors that elicit attributions—unexpected events, non-attainment of a goal, expectancy, locus of control, and emotions such as sadness and anger—and make the effort to avoid making attribution errors. Further, recognize relationships such as covariation—if a behavior or object is always present when another behavior or object is present, they covary; extremity—the more extreme the effect of a behavior, the more likely we are to make internal attributions; discounting—the more you know about environmental conditions surrounding a behavior, the less likely you are to make internal attributions; and augmentation—the strength of a facilitative force will be perceived as greater if an event occurs in the presence of an inhibitory force.

Diversity

Organizations comprise different and multiple individuals and groups that have distinct attributes or characteristics. For example, there are men and women as well as managers and subordinates. The diverse attributes can be harnessed to improve organizations. That is why diversity has become important in organizations.

Definition

Diversity has numerous definitions. The generally accepted definition is one that combines all aspects of human attributes in organizations. It refers to the set of multiple and different human attributes, including but not limited to: race, religion, color, gender, national origin, disability, sexual orientation, age, education, geographic origin, and skill of individuals and groups in organizations. It endows organizations with unique strength, resilience, and richness.

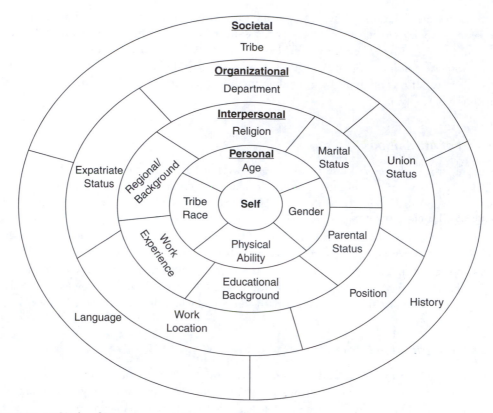

FIGURE 3.4   Circle of Heterogeneous Demographic Factors

Dimensions

The diverse attributes of employees in the workplace can be grouped into several categories. Some scholars propose core, internal, external, and organizational dimensions of workplace diversity (see Figure 3.4).[12] At the core is personality. It is the most diverse form; there are as many personalities in organizations as there are individuals. The internal dimension focuses on attributes that center on the individual such as age, gender, or race. The external dimension focuses on the groups the individual belongs to such as educational background, geographic location, recreational habits, marital status, and so on. The organizational dimension focuses on organizational attributes such as managerial level, union status, or work content domain. What is important is that diversity moves from the most heterogeneous (core) to the less heterogeneous (organizational); there are fewer people in the latter categories than the former ones.

Diversity in Africa

Africa is often considered the most diverse continent. Not only are there diverse ethnic groups but also the historical, cultural, political, economic, and geographic diversity of the continent is so profuse that the underdevelopment of the various countries is sometimes attributed to that heterogeneity. Diversity also permeates African organizations. The organizations can be grouped according to the degree to which their structures and resources are exploitated. Organizations with open or closed structures either embrace or avoid diversity. Further, some organizations focus on exploiting homogeneous or heterogeneous resources. The combination of the two

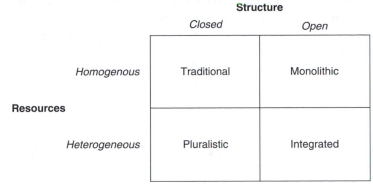

FIGURE 3.5 Typology of Diversity Organizations

dimensions results in four types of organizations: traditional, monolithic, pluralistic, and integrated (see Figure 3.5).[13]

Traditional organizations have closed structures and focus on exploiting homogeneous resources. In that regard, they employ individuals and groups that have homogeneous attributes (e.g., women only, Ibos, Afrikaans, etc). Such organizations differ from monolithic organizations that are defined by open structures but homogeneous resource exploitation. The amount of structural integration (the presence of persons from different cultural groups in a single organization) is minimal. These types of organization have other diverse attributes but one major attribute (e.g., tribal group) dominates the organization with regard to leadership or power. Pluralistic organizations have more heterogeneous membership than monolithic organizations. They also take steps to be more inclusive of other diverse attributes. Opportunities are provided and limited empowering structures are established but only available to a few. Their structures are not open to all levels. The integrated organizations have open structures and seek to exploit resources from heterogeneous sources. Diversity is across the board. All systems are integrated to exploit diversity potentials and to minimize challenges or eliminate constraints. At the moment, there are very few of such organizations in Africa.

Value of Diversity

The value of diversity is reflected in what it does for individuals, organizations, and society. For each African society, diversity enables the countries to achieve the long-term goal of having a workforce that generally reflects the population of the countries in all its dimensions. For example, when one group dominates, as was the case in South Africa, the outcome is marginalization of other groups. The marginalization can serve as a basis for conflict or excess deprivation, as reflected in apartheid.

For organizations, diversity enables them to create environments that respect and include differences, recognizes the unique contributions that individuals with many types of differences can make, and maximizes the potential of all employees. Such environments facilitate learning about dignity and respect for all from others who are not the same. They also enhance decision making and improved problem solving, greater creativity and innovation, all of which lead to enhanced product development, and more successful marketing to different types of customers. Diversity provides organizations with the ability to compete in regional and global markets. For example, a Nigerian in Ghana Commercial can help the organization in Nigeria either through customer increase or harnessing of the talent of Nigerians.

For the individuals, diversity helps them to learn about themselves. Through learning about others, they learn about themselves, their limited perceptions, and the possibilities presented to them. Inclusiveness helps them build trust by promoting understanding and breaking down prejudice. It also allows employees with talents to feel needed and to have a sense of belonging, which in turn increases their commitment to the company and enables each of them to contribute in a unique way.

Challenges

Even though diversity is good for organizations and society, there are challenges to optimizing its potential. First, it is not easy to change the mindsets of individuals, particularly the dominant groups that have privileges. The majority generally seek to maintain their hegemonic structures within the organization and society. Indeed, most of the past and current conflicts are due to the majority or dominant groups refusing to allow opportunities to the minority or less influential groups. Second, it is not easy to assimilate members of the minority group. It has been observed that "those who assimilate are denied the ability to express their genuine selves in the workplace; they are forced to repress significant parts of their lives within a social context that frames a large part of their daily encounters with other people."[14] Assimilation can therefore create a situation in which people who are different are likely to fail, and for the organization to experience decreased productivity.

Another challenge is management of a diverse population. Managing diversity is more than simply acknowledging differences in people; it requires ability to motivate, which is not easy. Miscommunication may also occur because the competencies—self-monitoring, empathy, and strategic decision making—associated with diversity communication are lacking. Self-monitoring refers to a communicator's awareness of how his/her behavior affects another person along with his/her willingness to modify this behavior based on knowledge of its impact. Empathy enables the receiver to go beyond the literal meaning of a message and consider the communicator's feelings, values, assumptions, and needs. Strategic decision making implies that the communication sources and channels used to reach organization members, as well as the substance of the messages conveyed, are mindfully selected.[15]

Finally, maintaining a culture which supports the idea of employee voice especially for marginalized group members is not easy. When the environment is not supportive of dissenting viewpoints, employees may remain silent for fear of repercussions, or may seek alternative safe avenues to express their concerns and frustrations. This situation is compounded by the high power distant culture of African countries. Cultivating participative voice is not easy when traditionally subordinates are limited in what they can say. Overcoming the cultural humdrums is not easy.

Managing Diversity in African Organizations

As we discussed above, diversity has different layers and facets. Can and should managers worry about all of the facets? Not only will it be too stressful and probably counterproductive for managers to do that but also some facets are less problematic. For example, the hierarchical differences are embedded within the structure of organizations for motivational, legitimacy, and accountability purposes. It is therefore unlikely that those differences will be problematic for managers. However, there are other facets that may create problems for the organization; each of the facets may negatively affect the climate and interactions or demotivate and reduce productivity of employees. One such facet is tribal differences. Tribal affiliations are so strong in Africa that they have been the cause of major national conflicts in Rwanda, Liberia, Sierra Leone, Kenya, Nigeria,

Sudan, Morocco, Congo, and Zimbabwe. How managers handle tribal diversity is therefore critical.

Steps to Managing Diversity

How should managers approach tribal diversity? First, they should ensure fairness in dealing with employees. Second, they should organize socialization programs to integrate the various groups. Such programs neutralize the salience of tribal identities. Third, they should serve as role models. Employees are likely to learn vicariously the modeling behavior of managers. Finally, they should ensure fair representation across the organizational hierarchy of leaders from the diverse tribal units in the company. Such representation fosters participation and engagement. It also enables organizations to harness the acumen of specific tribal members.

Another diversity facet that managers should pay attention to is gender. Africa is traditionally hierarchical and biases against women are frequent; females have always occupied subordinate roles in the society even though they are the linchpins of families and societies. By facilitating gender representation managers enable the capabilities of women to be transferred to their organizations. Women also have unique capabilities for harnessing the efforts or capabilities of others. To the extent that organizations can utilize those capabilities, they are likely to enhance their human capital.

Summary

In this chapter we have discussed social perception, attribution and diversity by highlighting the antecedents, processes, and consequences of each of them. We have also discussed how to manage each of them to achieve effective individual, departmental, and organizational outcomes.

■ Individual Learning Questions

1.   What is social perception?
2.   What is attribution?
3.   What perceptual errors tend to be made by people?
4.   Why is diversity important in Africa?

■ Group Discussion Questions

1.   Discuss the dimensions of attribution.
2.   What challenges do African organizations face in managing diversity?
3.   What is the relationship between attribution, stereotypes, and prejudice?
4.   How should diversity be managed in African organizations?

Exercise 3.1: Case Study

Mr Apem, an HR manager of a gold mining company in Ghana, was meticulous in his tasks. He met required deadlines, treated his subordinates respectfully and fairly, and supported peers who needed his help. He went out of his way to assist even subordinates who did not need his help. It was no surprise that he was promoted to manage the small but influential human capital department. He did not know that Mr Manu, the previous manager, had left him a problem. Mr Manu contrasted sharply with him on personality, attitude, behavior, and tribal origin. Mr Manu was neither agreeable nor helpful; he was also not dedicated to his work. He neither cared very much about his subordinates nor interacted with his fellow managers. He was also from the tribe that is generally recognized in Ghana as boastful, condescending, and disrespectful of other tribes.

Mr Manu had completed annual performance appraisals of his staff but could not distribute them before leaving. Most (three employees) received relatively strong evaluations except Kolbil who was appraised lower than the other employees even though everyone in the department regarded him as the hardest and most productive worker. It was rumored that the rating of Kolbil was discriminatory and based on his tribal origin; Mr Kolbil was a Frafra. Mr Apem now had the responsibility of distributing the annual raises based, in large part, on the appraisals of Mr Manu.

Of the five employees Mr Apem now manages, all received fairly strong appraisals mostly in the "above average" range although no one received the highest rating of "excellent." Given the constraint of no budget growth for the next three years, and a consequent inability to give salary increases, Mr Apem was further handicapped by the lack of excellent performers which would have given him the opportunity to apply for extra merit pay funding. Mr Apem is trying to decide how to reveal the disappointing news to all his staff. As for Mr Kolbil he plans to meet with him separately. He is weighing a number of options including the following:

1. Explain to the staff that they deserve higher raises but, based on the long-term departmental budget, this is the best he can do for them.
2. Explain to the staff that he could have gotten them higher raises if their performance levels had been higher.
3. Explain to the staff that they deserve higher raises and that he, as their boss, failed them by not doing more for them.
4. Explain to the staff that these raises are fair, given their performance levels.
5. Explain that he inherited the constraint even though he would have liked to do more for them.

Questions

1. What attribution is being communicated in each option? Is it internal or external?
2. Which of the five options do you think would not satisfy the staff?
3. What should Mr Apem tell Mr Kolbil?

Exercise 3.2: Individual Exercise

Listed below are phrases or inscriptions on vehicles in an African country that have work, perceptual, attribution, and diversity applications. For each phrase write its application in the second column.

A friend in need	_____	Never rush in your life	_____
What else should I have done?	_____	No wonder	_____
When you hear, ask (it may not be true)	_____	Patience & Confidence	_____
Be bold	_____	People will talk of you	_____
Unless you work very hard	_____	You do well	_____
Remember how I toiled	_____	Good friend	_____
Remember what I have done (for you)	_____	Good luck	_____
Not all people are like that	_____	Good name	_____
People should be careful	_____	Good never lost	_____
No cross no crown	_____	Good partner	_____
No money no friends (sticker)	_____	Comfort	_____
No victory without struggle	_____	Consider	_____
No condition is permanent	_____	Determination	_____
Keep smiling	_____	No hurry in life	_____
Keep what you get	_____	No problem	_____
Love and respect	_____	Remember	_____
Mind your own	_____	Respect	_____

Exercise 3.3: Identifying Occupational Stereotypes

What we expect of people and the way we treat them is likely to be affected by stereotypes about their professions. This exercise helps you to understand this phenomenon better.

Directions

Using the following scale, rate each of the occupational groups listed here according to how much of each characteristic the people in these groups tend to show:

Not at all	A slight amount	A moderate amount	A great amount	An extreme amount
1	2	3	4	5

Accountants
__ Interesting
__ Generous
__ Intelligent
__ Conservative
__ Shy
__ Ambitious

College Professors
__ Interesting
__ Generous
__ Intelligent
__ Conservative
__ Shy
__ Ambitious

Lawyers
__ Interesting
__ Generous
__ Intelligent
__ Conservative
__ Shy
__ Ambitious

Clergy
__ Interesting
__ Generous
__ Intelligent
__ Conservative
__ Shy
__ Ambitious

Physicians
__ Interesting
__ Generous
__ Intelligent
__ Conservative
__ Shy
__ Ambitious

Plumbers
__ Interesting
__ Generous
__ Intelligent
__ Conservative
__ Shy
__ Ambitious

Nigerians
__ Interesting
__ Generous
__ Intelligent
__ Conservative
__ Shy
__ Ambitious

Egyptians
__ Interesting
__ Generous
__ Intelligent
__ Conservative
__ Shy
__ Ambitious

Liberians
__ Interesting
__ Generous
__ Intelligent
__ Conservative
__ Shy
__ Ambitious

Questions for Discussion

1. Did your ratings of the various groups differ? If so, which groups were perceived most positively and which were perceived most negatively?
2. On what characteristics, if any, did you find no differences among the various groups? What do you think this means?
3. To what extent did your ratings agree with those of others? Was there general agreement about the stereotypical nature of people in various occupational groups?
4. To what extent were your responses based on specific people you know? How did specific knowledge—or lack of knowledge—regarding members of the various occupational groups influence your ratings?
5. By becoming aware of these stereotypes, do you believe that you will perpetuate them in the future or that you will refrain from behaving in accord with them? Explain.

Exercise 3.4: Group Exercise

(A) Perception and Attribution

A certain man used to work as a driver for the Director of a company. One day he decided that he did not want to continue that job because he was not making enough money. Ironically, the very day that he ended his employment, thieves stole the vehicle from the garage. Naturally he became a suspect and was arrested by the police and detained for one week. He felt humiliated and so peeved that he decided to seek spiritual intervention to settle scores for an offence he did not commit.

A few weeks after the incident, someone from the Director's family died in mysterious circumstances. Before the funeral retinue returned from the cemetery, another family member of the Director died and a third followed. After these mysterious deaths, the family of the Director also decided to find out from the spiritual world what was going on. They were told that those deaths were happening to them because someone in the family had wrongfully offended another person. Upon further inquiries, the offended person turned out to be the former driver. To overturn the curse, they were asked to compensate the man. When the driver was approached to indicate what he would want for compensation, he asked for a job as supervisor of the company's drivers. The Director agreed to offer him the job. To celebrate his exoneration and redeemed image, the driver inscribed 'The Truth' on the front of the taxi he bought shortly after his promotion and 'Shall set you free' on the back to tell the world his story.

Questions

1. In this story, what internal attributions are made?
2. What external attributions are made?
3. What errors of attributions can you identify?
4. What perceptual errors can you identify

(B) How Much of a Diversity Change Agent are You?

Directions: Respond to the following statements by checking the appropriate column.

	Usually	Sometimes	Rarely
1. I challenge stereotypic comments and assumptions.			
2. I engage colleagues in discussions about diversity.			
3. I spend time (e.g., lunch, breaks) with people who are different from me.			
4. I bring diversity concerns to the attention of my manager.			
5. I let people know that ethnic, gender, racial, religious, etc., jokes are off limits.			
6. I suggest diversity issues and topics for the agenda at regular management or work team meetings.			
7. I challenge us vs. them comments and complaints about other groups.			
8. I listen to others' concerns with an open mind and questioning attitude.			
9. I suggest resolution strategies when there are diversity-related conflicts.			
10. I explain the business advantages of effectively dealing with diversity.			
11. I ask for suggestions about ways to make the work environment more inclusive.			
12. I speak enthusiastically about the organization's diversity plans and initiatives.			
13. I speak up and educate when I hear a derogatory comment, slur, or joke.			
14. I seek out people to talk with whose views are different from mine.			
15. I challenge my own assumptions and stereotypic thoughts.			

Source: Adapted from Lee Gardenswartz and Anita Rowe, "How Much of A Diversity Change Agent Are You," © http://www.gardenswartzrowe.com/activity.html

Suggestions for Using "How Much of a Diversity Change Agent Are You?"

Objectives:

- To raise awareness of behaviors necessary for creating diversity change in organizations
- To assess oneself as a change agent
- To stimulate development of change agency within the organization

Intended Audience

- Diversity Council/Task Force members
- Diversity trainers
- Leaders and managers in diverse organizations

Time: 45 Minutes

Materials

- Copies of "How Much of a Diversity Change Agent Are You?" worksheet for all participants
- pens/pencils
- easel/chart (optional)
- felt tip markers (optional)

Processing the Activity

- Participants are asked to share (in pairs, small groups, or with the entire group) the behavior they do which most helps the diversity process in their organization.
- Facilitator elicits responses and charts responses on chart pad (optional).
- Facilitator explains that while organizational change around diversity happens at three levels, organizational, managerial, and individual, participants can have a significant influence on that change process through their own behavior. The activity they are about to experience will give them a chance to examine these behaviors, assess themselves against them, and set goals for their own growth.
- Facilitator distributes worksheets and asks participants to respond, following directions.
- Participants then pair up and discuss their responses focusing on greatest strengths and most important areas for growth.
- Each participant commits to working on behavior for development and shares in pairs or with entire group. Facilitator may chart commitments (optional).

Questions for Discussion

- Which behaviors do you often do?
- Which are most difficult for you?
- What blocks you from doing these?
- What other behaviors would you add to the list?
- Which behaviors are most important to develop in order to be more effective in moving the diversity process forward?
- Where/how can you begin developing your ability to do this behavior?
- What would help you in this process?

Caveats, Considerations, and Variations

- You may tailor this list to specific activities and processes in your organization (e.g., mentoring, training, brown bag forums, hiring panels, etc.).
- Participants can make contracts with specific individuals to check back with one another at predetermined intervals regarding their development commitments.
- This activity is best used with those who see their role as change agents regarding diversity and is most effective when combined with information about long-term change processes and the role as facilitators in making change happen.

4

PERSONALITY, AFFECT, AND STRESS

Overview

In this chapter we examine personality, affect, and stress. Under personality, we present the major frameworks and functions of personality identified through decades of research in psychology (cognitive, social, industrial/organizational). We also discuss the affect and stress systems and how they relate to employee behavior. By the end of this chapter you should be able to:

- Discuss the personality system and its functions
- Discuss the affect system and its functions
- Discuss the stress system and its effects

Personality

Nature of Personality

Ask a friend what his/her personality is and you are likely to get the response, "what do you mean?" It is not that your friend does not have a personality; rather it is more likely he/she has not reflected on, analyzed, or studied it. The lack of studies of personality of Africans is the major problem why your friend will not be able to describe to you his/her personality. Assuming he/she grew up in the city, he/she is more likely to use terms that are identical to those used by peers in the West in describing his/her personality. This is the Western influence. Had he/she grown up in the rural or traditional setting with little exposure to the West, he/she is more likely to describe his/her personality by linking it to traditional symbols, kins, or totems. This is the traditional way by which individuals' personalities were identified.

In modern organizations, however, personality is often described from the Western perspective. It turns out that the difficulty your friend would have also applies in the West. That is because personality is often difficult to describe; it does not refer to one thing. Sometimes it refers to the thoughts or thinking style of individuals. Other times, it refers to their behaviors. Still others view it from their experiential tendencies. Lastly, some describe it from the traits or characteristics associated with individuals. Consequently, most scholars define personality as the characteristic patterns of thoughts, feelings, and behaviors that make a person unique, and which arise from within the individual, and remain fairly consistent throughout life. This definition combines the various perspectives of personality.

Importance of Personality

Why is it important to study personality? There is overwhelming evidence across decades of research which shows that behavior of individuals partly depends on their personality. As we discussed in Chapter 1, behavior is a function of the environment and characteristic features that define a person. These features constitute personality. The work behaviors of employees therefore partly depend on the work environment and the formative features of employees in the workplace. Such knowledge, first, helps managers understand why employees are either helpful toward others or Johnny-come-latelies at work. Second, personality influences how individuals interact with peers, subordinates, and superiors. For example, an employee who does not speak during meetings may be doing so because he/she is introverted. Third, knowledge of personality is important for attributing causes to behavior of employees. As we discussed in Chapter 3 on perception and attribution, studying personality enables managers to make accurate attributions about the behavior of subordinates. In other words, they are less likely to err in attributing factors for why an employee comes in late versus another that comes in early. Further, the decision-making process of individuals can be understood from their personalities because cognitive style or individuals' way of thinking defines their personality.[1] In sum, personality influences the attitudes, interactions, and orientations of individuals toward work, projects, and activities. That knowledge is useful for effective management.

Perspectives of Personality

There are four major perspectives of personality. Table 4.1 summarizes these perspectives. Examples are also provided and prominent scholars identified with each perspective. We elaborate on each below.

Knowledge Structures

The first is knowledge structures. Scholars here view personality in terms of the way individuals define themselves. They try to evaluate a response to the question, "Who am I?" Typically, individuals who answer this question focus on their self-knowledge. Self-knowledge comprises esteem, image, and identity. Self-esteem is based on an individual's appraisal or estimation of his/her importance or value. No one is in a better position to determine the worth of a person than the individual him/herself. Self-esteem is divided between low self-esteem (LSE) and high self-esteem (HSE). It affects how people behave and tends to influence attitudes related to success. Low self-esteem individuals are susceptible to external influences, whereas people with high self-esteem are less susceptible to external influences. Another trait related to self-esteem but different from it, is self-efficacy. Self-efficacy refers to the feelings individuals have that they can successfully perform certain tasks. People may have "generalized" self-efficacy or "specific" self-efficacy. In generalized self-efficacy, the individual believes that he/she has the ability to be successful in most tasks. In specific self-efficacy, the individual believes that he/she can successfully perform

TABLE 4.1 Perspectives of Personality

	Perspective	Dimension	Factors	Exemplary Scholars
1	Knowledge structures	Self-concept	Working self Self-esteem Self-complexity Self-image	Markus (1977)
2	Behavioral regularities	Big Five Factors	Conscientiousness Agreeableness Extraversion Openness to experience Emotional stability	Costa & McCrae (1992)
3	Cognitive style	Thinking style	Preference Cognitive complexity Cognitive ability	Briggs & Myers (1962) Streufert & Streufert (1978) Kirton (1976)
4	Subjective experience	Flow	Autotelia Vocational Preference	Czikszentmihalyi (1992) Holland (1997)

particular tasks. Self-efficacy is important because people with a high level of self-efficacy tend to set high goals and perform better than people with a low level of self-efficacy.

Self-image refers to how the individual represents him/herself to others. There is often an image that a person desires and it is this image he/she tries to portray to others. No one knows this image more than the individual him/herself. Self-identity refers to the sense of self that characterizes an individual over a period of time. It affects the extent to which individuals want to belong to a group. Some individuals may want to be assimilated within the group but that means their identity is not unique. Others may want to be totally different from the group. Of course, differentiation would mean loss of legitimacy that a group may provide. An option is to optimally balance the needs for differentiation and assimilation.[2]

Self-monitoring refers to the degree to which individuals can modify their behavior to fit particular situations. Individuals high on self-monitoring can change their behavior to fit specific situations. This implies that people can have different attitudes and behaviors depending on the contingencies. By being able to adjust to the situation, they can hide their true feelings. Such individuals are called "social chameleons." Self-monitoring can be both good and bad. High self-monitoring individuals can be flexible and adjust to several situations and changes within organizations. However, they may face trouble building lasting and trustful relations with colleagues who may see them as playing organizational politics or games.

Collectively, these terms are often referred to as the self-concept, an individual's perception of his/her abilities, weaknesses, status, and worth in the past, present, or future. Sometimes the self-concept is defined normatively (i.e., what he/she would like to be) or proscriptively (what he/she should be). The self-concept is mercurial; it changes as a function of time, place, and situation. Given that dynamic, some scholars define the self-concept as a system of affective-cognitive structures about the self that lends coherence and structure to the individual's self-relevant experiences.[3] Self-relevant experiences refer to experiences that affect the self.

Studies of the self-concept of Africans are not as voluminous as in the West. Nevertheless, the few studies that have examined it have found that the definitions of Africans about themselves vary wildly. One study found that Africans defined their self-concepts as collectivistic and

TABLE 4.2 Descriptions of Big Five Personality Factors and Exemplary Traits

	Factor	Definition	Some Traits
1	Conscientiousness v. Undirectedness	Describes socially prescribed impulse control that facilitates task and goal-directed behavior, such as thinking before acting, delaying gratification, following norms and rules, and planning, organizing, and prioritizing tasks	Responsible, orderly, and dependable
2	Agreeableness v. Antagonism	Contrasts a pro-social and communal orientation toward others with antagonism and includes traits such as altruism, tender-mindedness, trust, and modesty	Good natured, co-operative and trusting
3	Extraversion v. Introversion	Implies an energetic approach to the social and material world and includes traits such as sociability, activity, assertiveness, and positive emotionality	Talkative, social, and assertive
4	Openness to experience v. Closed to experience	Describes the breadth, depth, originality, and complexity of an individual's mental and experiential life	Imaginative, independent minded
5	Emotional stability v. Neuroticism	Contrasts emotional stability and even-temperedness with negative emotionality, such as feeling anxious, nervous, sad, and tense	Anxious, prone to depression, and worries a lot

moralistic.[4] Another study found that Africans who currently sojourned in Europe and America tended to define themselves differently from when they lived in Africa (before the sojourn) and after they returned to Africa. It seems that those who were studied have complex selves.[5]

Behavioral Regularities

The second perspective of personality is behavioral regularities. Personality here is viewed by the way individuals regulate themselves. Often described in terms of attributes, such as conscientiousness or agreeableness, individuals have traits that show how they conduct themselves. Scholars have organized the traits that define behavioral regularities of individuals into what is called the Big Five Factors—conscientiousness, agreeableness, extraversion, openness to experience, and emotional stability. Table 4.2 shows the definitions of each factor and some specific traits that fall within each factor.

The Big Five Factors focus on the individual's sense of self with regard to psychological, task, social, and economic exchanges. Because organizational activities and processes involve all these exchanges, personality is often considered an important factor by managers when they are selecting applicants. They want individuals who will focus on organizational tasks diligently, interact with other employees, particularly new ones, meaningfully, and have a sense of calm in times of crisis.

Another attribute in this perspective is locus of control. Locus of control refers to the degree to which a person believes that he/she can control his/her own destiny. Two dimensions of locus of control are usually identified, *internal locus of control* and *external locus of control*. People with an internal locus of control believe that they can control their destiny and can influence events. However, those with an external locus of control believe that they cannot control events and that what happens to them is beyond their control. The implication of this personality trait is that employees who have an internal locus of control tend to perform better than those who have an external locus of control. Locus of control also affects the level of engagement people have in dealing with some problems at work or in life. People with an internal locus of control would be involved in trying to solve their problems since they believe that they can influence the course of events.

The relationship of locus of control to culture suggests that some people may view their personality as changeable since they can control events and subjugate their environment. An example is Americans, who tend to have high internal locus of control. Others may view their personality as immutable; they were endowed with it by God. Individuals from the Middle East tend to believe this because external locus of control is high among them.

Cognitive Style

The third perspective of personality is the *cognitive style*. Studies here focus on an individual's way of thinking. A "thinking style" describes the way individuals think, perceive, and remember information. Cognitive style encompasses thinking preferences, information integration of what is called cognitive complexity, and cognitive ability (or level). The Myers–Briggs Type Indicator (MBTI) seems to be the most popular instrument used to determine the cognitive preferences of individuals. It is a 100-question personality test that asks people how they usually feel or act in particular situations. The answers provided help classify individuals into the following four categories: Extrovert or Introvert (E, I); Sensing or Intuitive (S, N); Thinking or Feeling (T, F); Perceiving or Judging (P, J). These classifications are then combined into 16 personality types. For instance, INTJs are considered as visionaries, ESTJs as organizers, and ENTPs are conceptualizers. Intuitive thinkers are rare and some authors speculate that only 10 percent of American people can be considered as intuitive thinkers. This typology helps predict employee behavior at work or understand why some people in organizations may be considered as visionaries. Several organizations such as AT&T and General Electric (USA) use the MBTI in their recruitment and selection process.

Holland also developed a theory of personality the intent of which is to match personality traits to particular occupations. The theory argues that people with a certain personality trait would prefer certain types of jobs. According to the theory employees are likely to remain in the organization when their personality fits the work environment. The theory uses a hexagonal figure to depict the six personality traits: Realistic, Artistic, Investigative, Social, Enterprising, and Conventional (RAISEC). Two traits that are close to each other in the figure are similar and those that are diagonally opposite are highly dissimilar. According to the theory, congruence between personality and occupation leads to a high level of satisfaction and a low level of turnover. This view is supported by research which indicates that "personalities seek out and flourish in career environments they fit and that jobs and career environments are classifiable by the personalities that flourish in them."[6] Implicit in these studies is the notion that individuals seek happiness and make career choices that would yield outcomes that are consistent with their self-definitions.

Subjective Experience

Subjective experience, the fourth perspective, focuses on the experiences of individuals. There are some individuals who do certain things, participate in some events, and engage in certain situations, all because they enjoy them. For example, hikers, mountain climbers, and musicians immerse themselves completely in their activities repetitively and incessantly because they enjoy

TABLE 4.3 Theories and Major Proponents of Personality Development

Personality Development Theory	Focus	Perspective	Major Proponent
Motor and cognitive development	Cognitive ability	Cognitive style	Jean Piaget (1896–1980)
Psychosocial development	Social interactions	Behavioral regularities	Erik Erikson (1902–1994)
Structural model of self development	Self-awareness	Knowledge structures	Sigmund Freud (1856–1939)
Moral development	Morality	Subjective experience	Lawrence Kohlberg (1973)

those activities. Studies show that such individuals are in a state of flow.[7] They are described as having autotelic personalities. Autotelic personality refers to characteristics that define individuals who behave in a certain way automatically (i.e., without external inducement) because they enjoy it. There is limited knowledge of autotelic personality of Africans. Nevertheless, there are drummers in my village, Sheagah, who behave similarly to those observed in subjective experience. Dancers in Kumasi also seem to have identical characteristics. What is unique about these individuals is that they define their selves by the experiences they enjoy. Further, there are students who incessantly read books because they enjoy learning. Otherwise called "book worms," such individuals constantly study because of the fun or joy in learning old, current, and new things. In the work context autotelic employees are likely to accept challenging tasks because the tasks present opportunities for learning. Further, they are likely to perceive the tasks as new avenues of learning.

Development and Dynamics of Personality

How does personality form? There is no consensus on an accurate answer to that question partly because different scholars have different views consistent with each of the perspectives discussed earlier (see Table 4.3). Four major theories of personality development, focus, representative perspective, and major proponent are shown in Table 4.3. The motor and cognitive development theory which focuses on dynamics of cognitive ability represents the cognitive style perspective as proposed by Jean Piaget. The psychosocial development theory focuses on social interactions and represents the behavioral regularities perspective. A major proponent of that theory is Erik Erikson. The structural model of self-development focuses on self-awareness and represents knowledge structures. It was originally proposed by Sigmund Freud. The moral development theory focuses on morality and represents the subjective experience perspective. Lawrence Kohlberg is the major proponent.

Nevertheless, all the major perspectives seem to agree on the following: first, personality is expansive. It not only grows but its potential is optimized overtime. So, an individual may start out with lack of self-confidence or with self-doubt but through repeated successes develops confidence that enables him/her to actualize him/herself. The perspectives discussed above also view the development of personality in diverse ways. For example, in the knowledge structures perspective, individuals, particularly those who are high self-monitors, shed some characteristics and adopt others overtime. As a result, they may have past selves, present selves, and future selves.

Second, the environment influences personality development. As discussed in Chapter 2, the social and cultural environments significantly affect the self-perception, thinking, regulation, and experiences of individuals through cultural programming. The belief in witches and the supernatural world affects the extent to which individuals are creative; risky behavior that contributes to learning and growth is often not permitted. The extent to which one describes him or herself is also limited. While the Akans would want to show off what they can do, the Talensis socialize individuals against that orientation.

The above discussion shows the independent effects of nature and nurture in the development of personality. However, there is now consensus among scholars that nature and nurture interact in influencing the development of personality. That interaction accounts for differential growth patterns of, say identical twins.[8] Good environments (those that enhance positive development) foster positive behaviors of individuals with good personality attributes while bad environments do not foster such behaviors or at least to the same degree.

Effects of Personality on Behavior

We are interested in personality because of its effect on the behavior of individuals. Each of the perspectives discussed above shows that personality influences the behavior of individuals. Their thought processes, self-evaluations, and experiences alter how they conduct themselves. For example, individuals with conscientious attributes have been overwhelmingly shown to perform well at tasks or jobs. Self-monitors also interact well in social settings. Subjective experience is also associated with creative behaviors.

Given the fact that personality is expansive, organizational environments are therefore contexts that can foster the development of employees' personalities. Positive organizational environments are likely to foster personality attributes that are desirable to the organization. To the extent that organizations create such environments they are likely to achieve positive behaviors that enhance performance, creativity, and good interactions.

Affect

Nature of Affect

In addition to personality, affect influences the behavior of employees. Affect generally refers to the positive and negative orientations and reactions of individuals toward situations, events, co-workers, supervisors, and subordinates. It includes emotions, moods, and attitudes. The activation of affect is measured by the positive affect and negative affect schedule (PANAS).[9]

Emotions

Emotions are intense and relatively enduring negative or positive feelings that are directed at someone or something. Thus there are negative and positive emotions. While negative emotions occur in disapproving contexts, positive emotions manifest when employees approve a situation or person. Because a person's emotions affect him/her as well as the environment and person at whom they are directed, it is important for that person to regulate his/her emotions. Emotional regulation, the process by which a person influences which emotions are shown, when they are displayed, and how they are expressed, is part of emotional intelligence (EI). Emotional intelligence generally refers to a person's ability to identify, assess, and control his/her emotions as well as those of others. Emotionally intelligent individuals display their emotions in ways that minimize emotional labor, the social requirement of expressing desired emotions during interpersonal exchanges. Emotional labor is a form of emotional regulation; employees who are able to regulate

TABLE 4.4 Dimensions and Illustrations of Emotions Likely to be Observed in African Organizations

Dimension	Type	Situations/Job	Typical Person
Variety	Positive	Parties	Leader
	Negative	Funerals	Representative
Intensity	High	Contest	Director
	Low	Conversations	Coworker
Activation	Task-Related	Theft	Supervisor
	Self-Related	Deprivation	Peer
Frequency	Often	Meeting	Receptionist
	Rarely	Conflict	Negotiator
Regulation	Controlled	Crisis	HR Manager
	Uncontrolled	Injustice	Production Manager

their emotions make interpersonal exchanges less burdensome while those who are unable to regulate create undesirable exchanges. For example, the emotions Gatobu has to display when transacting with Omolowu, the supervisor, differ from those that may be required when Gatobu is interacting with Kolbil, a peer and a friend. Similarly, the emotional labor required of Nyathi during a meeting is different from that expected during a festival when he is representing the organization. The different situations and their emotional requirements sometimes create what is referred to as emotional dissonance, a situation in which Kenyata, for example, must project cheerfulness toward others (e.g., customers) when he is experiencing sadness associated with his imminent firing. Emotional dissonance suggests that Kenyata's actual emotions, that is, felt emotions, are different from his displayed emotions, those required by the organization and which are deemed appropriate for a particular job.

Table 4.4 summarizes the dimensions, types, situational context, and exemplars of emotions likely to be observed in African employees or organizations. Emotions range in variety, intensity, activation, frequency, and regulation. Work-related situations and contexts in which they are likely to be observed are also shown. The exemplars suggest the emotions individuals are likely to display in the specific contexts.

Attitudes

The behavior of individuals and groups is often preceded by their attitudes. An attitude is defined as the orientation of an individual toward an event, person, object, or situation. Attitudes can therefore be positive or negative. General attitudes include satisfaction, commitment, intention, involvement, engagement, and identity. In the workplace, the focus tends to be on job satisfaction, commitment, involvement or engagement, and identity.

Job Satisfaction

Job satisfaction has been defined as a positive emotion that results from appraisal of the job or job experiences. Two major theories explain job satisfaction. Variance theory suggests that if a person desires something (x) from work then the person is satisfied to the extent that the job provides that x. As you know individuals either have difficulty defining what they want from work or have innumerable expectations of work. The Job Characteristics model suggests that job satisfaction depends on the characteristics of the job such as autonomy, skill variety, task identity, task significance, and feedback. As discussed in Chapter 5, the core job characteristics lead to critical psychological states such as experienced meaningfulness, experienced responsibility for outcomes, and knowledge of the actual results which in turn influence work outcomes such as job satisfaction, absenteeism, work motivation, and so on.

Commitment

Similar to satisfaction, commitment has different facets. It focuses on the extent to which the individual is loyal and dedicated to the job (job commitment), team (team commitment), and organization (organizational commitment). Commitment can be affective (when the individual is dedicated to the job, team, or organization out of desire or admiration), normative (when the dedication is based on norms), or obligation (when there is no other recourse). Otherwise termed engagement, commitment yields positive outcomes to individuals, teams, and organizations. Commitment derives from personal and situational characteristics including those of the organization.

Involvement

Individuals can be involved in their jobs, teams, and organizations. Consequently, involvement is a psychological statement that shows the extent to which an individual is immersed in a job, team, and organization. Involvement may be strategic. Like commitment, it has been linked to absenteeism, turnover or intent to leave, and job satisfaction.

Identification

Identification often focuses on the organization even though it can apply to the job and team. Identification generally refers to the extent to which a person perceives a sense of connection with a job, group, or organization. It is based on a sense of worth from the job, group, or organization. Individuals that identify with a group or organization seek to be associated with it probably because of what the group or organization has to offer to them. It emerges from social identity theory which focuses on perceived membership in a relevant social group.[10] It derives from self-identity which focuses on the self-worth of the individual. The identification may be based on the individual's liking of the organization (i.e., affective identification) or the norms prevailing within the organization (i.e., normative identification). It could also be because the individual has no other alternative but to be in the organization (i.e., continuance identification).

Attitudes in African Organizations

Attitudes of employees in African organizations seem to be identical to those observed in the West. They are as concerned about job satisfaction as their peers in other parts of the world. How they express that satisfaction, however, may be different because of the cultural difference. Instead of talking about it, they may be silent which could increase their stress level. Job, team, and organizational commitment among African employees also tends to be high. However, comparisons with employees in other parts of the world are lacking. Nevertheless, we know that organizational commitment affects service behavior of employees in South Africa.[11] Organizational identities also drive the goals of individuals and tactics of employees in organizations.[12] Third, the job, team, and organizational involvement of employees also tend to be high, albeit not in relative terms.

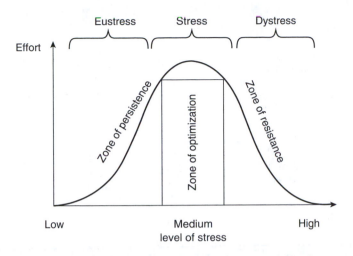

FIGURE 4.1   The Stress–Effort Relationship and Zones of Performance

Stress

Nature of Stress

One significant trend in Africa is increased reports of stress, and psychosomatic and physical ailments among employees. A friend who is a director at a government agency remarked to the first author that "the level of stress in this country has reached the pyramid level" during the funeral of a colleague who had passed away due to stroke and excessive stress of work demands. Arguably, the increasing competition and drive to live by Western standards without the means (e.g., effective health care systems) to manage the attendant consequences suggests that workers will continue to be stressed as organizations strive for competitive advantage. This necessitates understanding of the stress system.

Stress generally refers to a feeling of tension when a person perceives that a given situation is exceeding his/her ability to cope and consequently could affect the person's welfare. In such situations, the person is likely to ask, "Can I handle this situation?" If the person can handle it the stress is beneficial or what is often called eustress. The person's ability to handle the stress increases to an optimum point beyond which he/she can no longer perform the task. Dystress or negative stress begins from that point to when the person completely withdraws from the situation. Figure 4.1 shows the relationship between stress and effort.

When stress is low, there is increasing drive to achieve more or to persist in one's effort. That is the *zone of persistence*. The persistence continues till the *zone of optimization*, that region where the individual optimizes his/her effort; it is the peak of a person's endurance or capability. Thereafter, there is an urge to resist continued effort; every attempt is increasingly resisted. That is the *zone of resistance*.

The Stress System

What are the sources and consequence of stress? Currently, the stress system is viewed as originating from, and affecting, not only the individual but also the organization and society in which the person lives. In other words, the stress has multilevel characteristics, as shown in Figure 4.2.

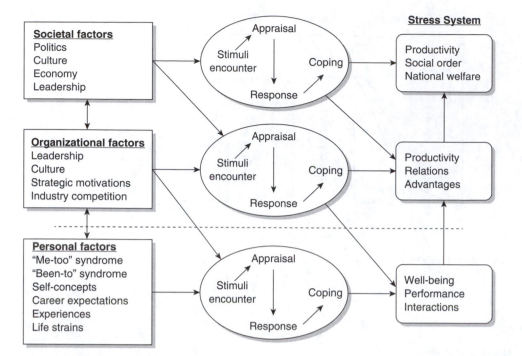

FIGURE 4.2 Multilevel Model of Stress System

Stress Process

Stress begins with the encounter of a stimulus. The nature of that stimulus is appraised to form a judgment of the threat posed. A stimulus that can be manipulated will be endured until it is perceived as exceeding the capability of the individual. Appraisal of the strength of the stress stimulus determines the response of the individual—approach or avoidance is based on the judgment from the stimulus appraisal. The individual then copes with the stress situation. As a behavior, the coping may be acceptable (i.e., easy) or unacceptable (i.e., difficult). The coping will persist up to the optimal level of effort beyond which resistance begins. Coping therefore encompasses persistence, endurance, and resistance.

Antecedents of Stress

Multiple factors ranging from the national or societal level through the organizational to the individual level cause stress.

Individual factors. At the individual level life strains associated with family responsibility, experiences from failed endeavors, career expectations, and self-concepts (expected versus actual self-representations) cause stress. In Africa two additional causes are significant. First, the "Me-too" syndrome where individuals strive to be like others (e.g., the poor striving to be like the rich) seems pervasive in African countries. It also occurs in organizations where operatives strive to be like managers even though they lack the requisite capabilities and resources to function in that capacity. Second, the "been-to" syndrome can also cause individual stress. A "been-to" is an individual who has sojourned abroad particularly in the Western hemisphere (i.e., Europe and America) and returned home. Because been-tos are often perceived as superior, others strive to also be like them (i.e., go abroad).[13]

Organizational factors that contribute to stress are leadership, culture, strategic motivation, and industry competition. Stress at the organizational level is a collective state. It occurs when the organization as a whole is undergoing some crisis or transformation. The collective stress has the same process but differs from, and affects, the individual stress. In addition, the leadership or supervisory systems an organization has can cause stress. Dystress occurs if supervision is bad. The leadership of the organization can also cause stress; it occurs when executives are malicious. The culture of the organization can also cause stress, particularly if its values are incongruent with those of the individual. For example, if the culture does not support tribal diversity, an employee from a minority tribe is likely to feel dystress. The strategic direction of the company causes stress when the executives challenge employees to achieve the strategic objectives of the organization. For example, an organization that adopts an innovation strategy is likely to have an environment that is stressful because of pressure to meet quality and new product expectations. Lastly, the nature of competition in the industry can affect the stress level of employees. In Ghana for example, the level of competition in the Banking sector is so high that some employees change jobs to less competitive industries just to escape from the high stress level in that industry.

National factors. Similar to that at the organizational level, stress at the national level is collective but influences organizations and individuals. The nature of politics in the country increases the stress level of individuals by heightening fear of conflict. Most civil conflicts (e.g. Kenya in 2009) arise from political conflicts. Related to politics is the leadership of the country. Because of the dictatorial tendencies and lack of participation in military leadership, the stress level of employees tends to increase during such regimes. The values and beliefs of the nation can also create stress levels that either impede or enhance employee behaviors. For example, during the apartheid era, the values and beliefs heightened stress particularly among the black employees. Lastly, the economy can also be a source of stress. The well-being of individuals depends on economic performance. When the economy is in recession, job opportunities, wages, and welfare systems tend to be limited, which increases the stress level of employees.

Consequence of Stress

Individual. Stress has positive and negative consequences. As shown in Figure 4.1, stress can influence individual performance (see zone of persistence and zone of optimizing). So long as the stress level is low to medium, it will have positive effects. However, when stress is high, it has deleterious effects on well-being, performance, and interactions. Dystress limits the ability of individuals to interact with co-workers, perform effectively, and achieve outcomes that improve their welfare. For example, attendance of dystressed employees reduces and alienation increases which means task and contextual (e.g., organizational citizenship) behaviors will be low.

Organizational. Similar to the individual employee the organization can experience negative and positive outcomes from collective stress. When change pressures, for example, induce employees to increase productivity, the outcome enhances the growth of the company. However, when the pressures are so high they can negatively affect the performance, employee relations (i.e., climate), and advantages the company can gain. Through the insidiousness of stress, the performance of employees can be transferred across co-workers and result in collective underperformance. Further, competitive and market leader advantages emerge from the behaviors of employees. To the extent that dystress limits their behaviors, workers cannot contribute meaningfully to enhance competitive advantages. In addition, collective stress affects individual employees' performance, interactions, and well-being.

Societal. Stress at the national level affects industries, organizations, and individuals. A civil war, for example, constrains not only industrial activity but also organizational performance by limiting access to raw materials and markets. National stress therefore limits economic productivity. In addition, it affects social order and national welfare. Rwanda, Sierra Leone, and Liberia, for example, are still recording negative low productivity, tremors of conflict, and poor national welfares from the wars they experienced. Industrial activities are low and employees are psychologically traumatized. Interpersonal mistrust is high as a consequence which affects workplace interactions.[14]

Summary

The behavior of individuals in organizations depends on their personalities, affect, and stress. These factors are dynamic and derive from diverse sources resulting in multiple perspectives, types, and effects.

■ Individual Learning Questions

1. Define personality.
2. List the major perspectives of personality.
3. List the major types of attitudes in organizations.
4. Identify the major elements of the stress system.

■ Group Discussion Questions

1. Discuss personality and its dynamics.
2. What are the various types of work attitudes?
3. How applicable is the stress model in Africa?
4. What is the relationship between stress and work attributes?

Exercise 4.1: Case Study

Agbonu was delighted to leave his village for the city, Dar es Saalem. Unlike his village, Dar es Saalem had opportunities for him to train, go to a vocational school and develop a career. He had heard that it is a place where he could make money, particularly from the foreigners who visited Dar es Saalem from Europe and the United States. Determined to improve himself including wealth, Agbonu enrolled in a video recording and filming school. Soon he had the opportunity to demonstrate his skills when some visitors from the Middle East asked him to film their visit to Dar es Saalem. He did an excellent job to the point that the footage was reported in Al Jazeera, the world-renowned TV station in the Emirates. That gave him greater confidence. As a result, he had three job referrals. He was careful not to charge the guests. However, he needed money to fit the city lifestyle he had developed.

A month after his resolution, he was recommended by a manager to American professors who were organizing a workshop and wanted to film the event. Even though the negotiations during the referral process concluded with him working pro bono, Agbonu thought he could seize the opportunity to make money. He was unaware that one of the professors organizing the workshop, Prof. David, was from Tanzania. That professor was familiar with the negotiations and the cultural context. Asked by the principal director of the workshop, Prof. Jim, how much he would charge for the film, Agbonu quoted $2700.00. Prof. Jim was dumbfounded but only told him to wait a few hours for a consent response. The director was neither able nor willing to pay that amount.

When Agbonu did not hear a response several hours later and no return call, he called Prof. David who admonished him for his behavior and attitude. Prof. David added that he was blocking future opportunities including tangible and fair rewards. Upon reflection, Agbonu agreed to film the event without charge. Prof. Jim could not believe when Prof. David told him that Agbonu would film the event without charge.

Discussion Questions

1. Describe the attitude of Agbonu toward the workshop.
2. Discuss the types of attitude in the case.
3. How would you describe the personality of Agbonu?

Exercise 4.2: Individual Exercise—Assessing Your Self-Efficacy

Objective

The purpose of this exercise is to help you understand the concept of self-efficacy and to estimate your general self-efficacy.

Definition

Self-efficacy refers to a person's belief that he or she has the ability, motivation, and situational contingencies to complete a task successfully. Self-efficacy is usually conceptualized as a situation-specific belief. You may believe that you can perform a certain task in one situation, but are less confident with the task in another. However, there is also evidence that people develop a more general self-efficacy that influences their beliefs in specific situations. This exercise helps you to estimate your general self-efficacy.

Instructions

Read each of the statements below and circle the response that best fits your personal belief. Then use the scoring key to calculate your results.

General Self-Efficacy Scale

To what extent does each statement describe you? Indicate the level of agreement by circling the appropriate response on the right. Use the following categories: Strongly Agree (SA), Agree (A), Neutral (N), Disagree (DA), and Strongly Disagree (SD).

1.	When I make plans, I am certain I can make them work.	SA	A	N	DA	SD
2.	One of my problems is that I cannot get down to work when I should	SA	A	N	DA	SD
3.	If I can't do a job the first time, I keep trying until I can.	SA	A	N	DA	SD
4.	When I set important goals for myself, I rarely achieve them.	SA	A	N	DA	SD
5.	I give up on things before completing them.	SA	A	N	DA	SD
6.	I avoid facing difficulties.	SA	A	N	DA	SD
7.	If something looks too complicated, I will not even bother to try it.	SA	A	N	DA	SD
8.	When I have something unpleasant to do, I stick to it until I finish it.	SA	A	N	DA	SD
9.	When I decide to do something, I go right to work on it.	SA	A	N	DA	SD
10.	When trying to learn something new, I soon give up if I am not initially successful.	SA	A	N	DA	SD
11.	When unexpected problems occur, I don't handle them well.	SA	A	N	DA	SD
12.	I avoid trying to learn new things when they look too difficult for me.	SD	SA	A	N	DA
13.	Failure just makes me tried harder.	SA	A	N	DA	SD
14.	I feel insecure about my ability to do things.	SA	A	N	DA	SD
15.	I am a self-reliant person.	SA	A	N	DA	SD
16.	I give up easily.	SA	A	N	DA	SD
17.	I do not seem capable of dealing with most problems that come up in life.	SA	A	N	DA	SD

Scoring Key

To calculate your score, assign the appropriate number to each question from the scoring key below. Then add up the numbers. The higher the score, the higher your self-efficacy is.

For items 1, 3, 8, 9, 13, and 15, Strongly agree = 5; Agree = 4; Neutral = 3, Disagree = 2, and Strongly Disagree = 1. For items 2, 4, 5, 6, 7, 10, 11, 12, 14, 16, and 17, Strongly agree = 1; Agree = 2; Neutral = 3, Disagree = 4, and Strongly Disagree = 5.

Exercise 4.3: Group Exercise—Self-Concept Exercise

The following exercise is meant to help you discover yourself. It has three parts.

Part I

List 10 adjectives that tell your *family members* who:

1. You are NOW
2. You would want to be in the FUTURE
3. You should have been in the PAST

Part II

List 10 adjectives that tell your *co-workers* who:

1. You are NOW
2. You would want to be in the FUTURE
3. You should have been in the PAST

Part III

Reconcile differences by writing why you are seen as different to friends and family.

5

MOTIVATING THE AFRICAN WORKER

Overview

By the end of this chapter you should be able to:

- Explain the nature of motivation
- Explain the need theories of motivation
- Explain the process theories of motivation
- Apply motivation theories in organizations
- Explain the job characteristics model
- Explain Herzberg's two-factor theory

Nature of Motivation

Motivation is often considered as the energy that drives someone to engage in a particular course of action. Motivation refers to the forces within a person that affect the *direction*, *intensity*, and *persistence* of a voluntary behavior.[1] In defining motivation, one should consider the three factors of direction, intensity, and persistence. Motivation cannot be observed; it can only be inferred from a person's actual behavior. To illustrate this point, let's take an example of a student who wants to get an A. The desire to get an A represents the goal (the direction). The student will have several choices. Work hard, ask the instructor for leniency (which is unlikely), or display another type of behavior. Let's assume that the student makes a choice among these three alternatives. If he or she decides to work hard, the decision to work hard to earn a grade of A would be the direction of his or her motivation. The degree to which the student will work hard to obtain the grade will be considered the intensity of the motivation. If the student continues to work hard, particularly after performing poorly in the first exam, this will represent the persistence of his or her behavior.

The motivation of individuals derives from diverse sources including incentives, drives, arousal, and needs. These factors are explained by several theories that have been organized into content and process theories of motivation. Unlike process theories which focus on *how* an individual is aroused and sustained in his/her motivation, content theories focus on *what* motivates individuals.

Need Theories of Motivation

Three major need theories of motivation are often emphasized in OB: Maslow's hierarchy of needs, Alderfer's ERG theory, and McClelland's need theory. The common thread of need theories is that what motivates a person is a desire to satisfy a particular need. But what is a need? A need is a deficiency, something we lack and for which we are determined to take action. The reasoning is this. A need creates a tension and the person is motivated to reduce the tension by fulfilling the need.

Maslow's Hierarchy of Needs

Maslow's theory is the most popular need theory. Maslow identified five types of needs, including physiological needs, safety needs, social needs, esteem needs, and self-actualization needs.[2] According to Maslow, these needs form a hierarchy. When a need is not satisfied, the person experiences a tension and acts to fulfill this need. Once the need is satisfied, it no longer motivates the person. Since Maslow considers his needs as forming a hierarchy, people must satisfy lower level needs before satisfying higher level needs. For example, a person will first satisfy physiological needs before satisfying safety needs. As the person satisfies a lower level need, the next higher need in the hierarchy becomes the primary motivator. This principle is known as the *satisfaction-progression hypothesis*.[3] The exception to the satisfaction-progression process is self-actualization. As people experience self-actualization, they desire more rather than less of this need primarily because it is the highest need.

There is evidence that Africans seem to focus more on security needs.[4] This is probably due to the development stage of Africa economies; Africans are more concerned about survival needs.[5] In a study of national quality of life across time, it was found that participants from 21 African countries seemed to follow Maslow's hierarchy of needs.[6] The satisfaction-progression hypothesis seems to have been confirmed in this study. The authors observed that participants followed the sequence described by Maslow. Given the clear socio-economic bifurcation of the economies into rural and urban, it is likely that those in the rural areas will be more on the lower levels of need of the hierarchy while those in the urban areas will be at the upper levels (social and esteem needs) with very few reaching self-actualization.

Alderfer's Existence, Relatedness, and Growth Need Theory

Alderfer developed a three-factor need theory.[7] Contrary to Maslow, he identified three needs: *existence needs*, *relatedness needs*, and *growth needs*. Relatedness needs correspond to social needs, and growth needs correspond to esteem and self-actualization needs. What is the difference between Maslow's hierarchy of needs and Alderfer's ERG Theory? ERG theory states that a person can be motivated by several needs at the same time. For instance, an employee may try to satisfy his/her growth need without having completely satisfied his/her relatedness need. ERG theory includes a *frustration-regression hypothesis* unlike Maslow's theory. According to this hypothesis, when an individual is unable to satisfy a higher level need, he/she becomes frustrated and regresses back to the next lower level need. For instance, if existence and relatedness needs have been satisfied but growth need has not been satisfied, the individual will become frustrated and relatedness needs will again emerge as the dominant source of motivation.

Studies of ERG in African organizations are few, if any. However, the developmental status of most economies suggests that the majority of employees will be motivated by existence needs, particularly those in the rural areas. The collectivistic characteristics of the countries also suggest relatedness needs will likely be a source of motivation. Growth needs are likely to be strong among employees in the middle to top levels of the hierarchy.

McClelland's Need Theory

McClelland also identified three types of need—the *need for achievement*, the *need for affiliation*, and the *need for power*—that drive people.[8] According to McClelland, these needs are learned through childhood learning, parental influences, and social norms.

Need for Achievement

The need for achievement refers to the need to accomplish challenging goals. High need achievement people prefer challenging assignments, competition, and prefer to receive feedback on their actions. Entrepreneurs tend to have high need for achievement. They are mostly motivated by the expectations of satisfying their need for achievement. However, money tends to motivate individuals who have low need for achievement.

Need for Affiliation

The need for affiliation refers to the desire to seek approval and acceptance from others. People with a strong need for affiliation want to have positive relationships with others. The need for affiliation is similar to Maslow's social needs and Alderfer's relatedness needs.

Need for Power

The need for power refers to the willingness to control one's environment. People with a high need for power will seek positions of power, and would prefer to stay in control of things. McClelland identified two types of power: *personalized power* and *socialized power*. People with personalized power use power to advance their own interests, whereas people with socialized power use power to advance the interests of the group or the organization.

Employees at the lower level of the hierarchy are likely to be driven by the need for achievement more than those at the top partly because the latter have already achieved some career progression; those at the lower level are driven to rise to the level of those at the top.[9] Employees in rural areas are also likely to be driven by need for achievement rather than other needs (e.g., need for power).[10]

Practical Implications of Need Theories

How would managers help employees meet the various needs described above? By focusing on lower level needs and using extrinsic mechanisms such as adequate compensation and cost-of-living adjustment, managers could help lower level employees satisfy their physiological needs. The compensation will help employees meet basic needs, such as food and shelter. Managers could also help employees meet safety needs by providing job security, insurance benefits, and safer working conditions. Events that foster teamwork and social needs in the workplace can help employees satisfy their social needs. Recognizing employees' accomplishments through formal employee recognition programs could help satisfy their esteem needs. Providing challenging assignments and opportunities for continuous learning could help employees satisfy their self-actualization needs.

Process Theories of Motivation

Process theories of motivation contend that behavior is a function of beliefs, expectations, and values. Behavior is viewed as a result of rational and conscious choices. These theories include: goal setting theory, equity theory, and valence/expectancy theory.

Goal Setting Theory

A goal is what an individual is trying to accomplish; it is the object or aim of an action. Edwin Locke is an organizational behavior scholar who has written extensively on goal setting theory.[11] In goal setting theory, the driver of a person's motivation is the desire to accomplish a goal. According to Locke, goal setting has four motivational mechanisms:

1.   Goals direct attention; they focus a person's attention on what is relevant.
2.   Goals regulate effort; they motivate a person to act.
3.   Goals increase persistence. Persistence represents the effort expended on a task over an extended period of time. For example, it takes effort to run 100 meters but it takes persistence to run a 26-mile marathon. Persistent individuals tend to view obstacles as challenges to be overcome rather than reasons to fail.
4.   Goals foster strategies and action plans. Having a goal allows a person to develop concrete actions to reach that goal.

Conditions that enhance the motivational power of a goal include difficulty of the goal, specificity of the goal, opportunities for feedback, goal acceptance, and goal commitment.

Managers could use goal setting theory as a motivational technique. To this end, they should set specific, measurable, attainable, results-oriented, and timely (SMART) goals. Managers should also provide feedback and ensure that employees accept the goals. Research and experience have shown that employees tend to perform well when they have participated in setting the goals.

The importance of goal setting is evidenced by the millennium development goals (MDG) in Africa; the MDGs are SMART. Goal difficulty and specificity have, for example, influenced the behavior of entrepreneurs in Zimbabwean microenterprises.[12]

Equity Theory

J. S. Adams developed equity theory based on social comparison.[13] The theory postulates that the individual compares him or herself to another individual. In so doing, the individual compares his/her input/output ratio to that of another person called the comparison other or the referent. Three elements, input, output, and referent, are important in equity theory. Input is what the individual brings to the exchange relationship. Examples of input include effort, education, and experience. Output is what the person gets from the exchange relationship. Examples of output include compensation, bonus, and promotion. The referent is the comparison other—the individual with whom the person compares him or herself.

The person experiences feelings of equity when the two ratios are equal. However, when the person's ratio is greater than that of the comparison other, he/she experiences feelings of inequity. This is a situation of positive inequity. If the person's ratio is less than that of the comparison other, he/she experiences feelings of inequity. This is a situation of negative inequity. Negative inequity is less tolerable than positive inequity. Inequity can be reduced in a variety of ways: reduce one's inputs, increase one's inputs, increase one's output, psychologically distort inputs and outputs of the comparison other, quit the exchange relationship, or change the comparison other. Managers can implement equity theory by creating conditions of equity. The driver of a person's behavior in equity theory is the feeling of equity he/she experiences.

The concern of Africans for equity is tempered by the hierarchical structure of the cultural systems. Most African countries are characterized by wide gaps between chiefs and subordinates. Further, traditional practices dictate that seniors more than juniors have the right of say. Consequently the distribution of rewards and process of interactions tend to be skewed particularly against those at the bottom. The same cultural practices are likely to be transferred to the workplace. Even though an employee may not be paid well (output), he/she might still be expected to work harder and more frequently (input) because that is what the supervisor wants.

Expectancy Theory

Expectancy theory contends that we are motivated to behave in ways that produce desired combinations of expected outcomes. There are three components of expectancy theory: *expectancy*, *instrumentality*, and *valence*.[14] Expectancy refers to the relationship between effort and performance. An employee may clearly see that performing a given task will lead to a certain level of performance. Instrumentality refers to the relationship between performance and rewards. Valence refers to the value of the reward. Managers can implement expectancy theory by clearly explaining the link between effort and performance, performance and reward, and making rewards attractive to employees.

Because of differences in expectancies, employees are likely to differ in motivation. White managers in South Africa tend to show different expectancies than their black colleagues.[15] In Botswana, expectancies alone seemed insufficient in motivating employees; they had to be supplemented with goals and extrinsic mechanisms such as pay and promotion.[16]

The Job as a Motivator

This section focuses on the job itself as a motivator.

Job Characteristics Model

The job characteristics model includes five components: skill variety, task identity, task significance, feedback, and autonomy.[17] Skill variety refers to the extent to which a job requires workers to use different skills and talents. Task identity refers to the extent to which an entire piece of work is completed from beginning to end. Task significance refers to the impact of the job on others. Feedback refers to providing information about the employee's job performance. Autonomy refers to the amount of discretion to do a job as desired.

A job containing the five core dimensions leads to critical psychological states including experienced meaningfulness—the importance and value of the job stemming from skill variety, task identity and significance; personal responsibility and accountability that stem from autonomy; and knowledge of results that stems from feedback. These critical psychological states lead to positive work outcomes in terms of high internal motivation, high quality work performance, high satisfaction with the job, and low turnover and absenteeism. According to the job characteristics model, the strength of an employee's growth need determines the extent to which he or she will be motivated by a job having these five core dimensions. Growth need strength describes the extent to which individuals have a high need for personal growth and development. Employees

TABLE 5.1 Motivators and Hygiene Factors

Motivators	*Hygiene Factors*
Achievement	Company policies
Advancement	Salary
Recognition	Supervision
Stimulating work	Colleagues
Responsibility	Interpersonal relations with supervisors
	Working conditions

who are high on growth need strength would be more motivated by the job characteristics model than those who are low on growth need strength.

The job diagnostic survey (JDS, see an abbreviated version in Exercise 5.1) is used to measure the core dimensions present in a given job. The scores on the JDS help determine if an employee is motivated by the job he/she performs. The scores also help compute the motivational potential score (MPS), which represents a mathematical index describing the degree to which a job is designed to motivate people.

$$\text{MPS} = [\text{Skill variety} + \text{Task identity} + \text{Task significance}] \times \text{Autonomy} \times \text{Feedback}$$

There are several techniques to design jobs that motivate employees. Two major techniques include job enlargement and job enrichment. Job enlargement refers to adding tasks to an existing job, whereas job enrichment refers to adding more responsibility and autonomy to an existing job. In job enlargement there is horizontal loading of the job, whereas in job enrichment there is vertical loading of the job. Managers can improve the motivational potential of a job through job enrichment or job enlargement.

Herzberg's Two-Factor Theory

Herzberg identified two types of factors: *motivators* and *hygiene factors*.[18] According to the two-factor theory, job satisfaction results from a set of factors known as motivators. Examples of motivators include advancement, achievement, growth, recognition, responsibility, and the work itself. Another set of factors, called hygiene factors, prevent employees from being dissatisfied. Examples of hygiene factors include company policy, job security, relationship, salary, supervision, status, and working conditions. As you can see, hygiene factors are the conditions surrounding the job the employee performs, whereas motivators are factors related to the job itself. Table 5.1 provides examples of motivators and hygiene factors.

Non-financial incentives affect behavior by increasing motivation, as exemplified in a study of health professionals in Benin and Kenya.[19] Even though hygiene factors do not motivate, they are likely to reduce the level of dissatisfaction associated with the economic, social, and political deprivation of employees. Consequently, employees, particularly those at the lower level, are likely to be motivated by the hygiene factors.

The Group as a Motivator

This section deals with the group or team and organization as contexts of motivation. Teams and organizations represent small and large groups respectively. Even though there are enormous problems with groups (e.g., free riding) that demotivate, groups generally are viewed as social contexts that motivate individuals. The motivation of groups occurs through the social interactions, interpersonal influence, and leadership. Group interactions increase the affective reactions of members which sustains them in assigned tasks. Group members also learn vicariously from other members. For example, if Kolsabilik observes Apusigah executing a task well, he is likely to imitate her, which enables him to improve. Vicarious learning is a way by which individuals are motivated; it excites and sustains them. In addition to this vicarious learning, interpersonal influence can activate the drive and persistence of individuals in task execution. A good friend may persuade Mary not to give up. The persuasion is extrinsic motivation. Leaders can also be a source of motivation in groups. Effective leadership not only activates the key drives of individuals but also sustains those drives through guidance, modeling, and outcomes.

Team Motivation

Teams, like individuals, have needs and goals. Consequently, they can be motivated. Team motivation focuses on the whole set of individuals and how its needs and goals are activated. The motivation of the individual is essential for successful motivation of the team. The intrinsic and extrinsic motivation of the team thus derives from the ability of team members to fulfill their needs and to show commitment to the team. The factors that motivate a team include task, structure, goals, and members.[20] To the extent that the task is challenging, involving, and exciting, it will motivate the team. The way the team is structured can also motivate it. Self-autonomous teams are embedded with participation and responsibility which heightens the drive to achieve team goals. Goals, the objectives to be achieved by the group, also motivate the team, particularly if they are specific, measurable, attainable, realistic, and timely. Knowledge sharing, support, solidarity, and communication also motivate a team.

Group motivation should not be difficult to understand because African culture is group-oriented. Remember, in Chapter 2 we described the African culture as being collectivistic. Managers and supervisors should therefore not have problems motivating teams particularly if they remember that motivation is both process and content-oriented.

Summary

In this chapter we have discussed the various ways by which African workers' purposive drive and persistence are activated and maintained. The constituents (i.e., what is used to drive an individual's behavior) activate the individual. In some instances, some are maintained through a process. The job can also be a motivator because the characteristics of the job activate essential drives of the worker. Finally, the group can motivate individuals and also be motivated.

Exercise 5.1: Self-Assessment Exercise—Job Diagnostic Survey

Purpose

This exercise is designed to help students learn how to measure the motivational potential of jobs and to evaluate the extent to which jobs should be further enriched.

Instructions

Being a student is like being an employee in several ways. You have tasks to perform, and someone (such as your instructor) oversees your work. Although few people want to be students most of their lives (the pay rate is too low!), it may be interesting to determine how enriched your job is as a student.

Job Diagnostic Survey

Circle the number on the right that best describes student work.

	Very Much	*Moderately*	*Very little*
1. To what extent does student work permit you to decide on your own how to go about doing the work?	1 2	3 4 5	6 7
2. To what extent does student work involve doing a whole or identifiable piece of work, rather than a small portion of the overall work process?	1 2	3 4 5	6 7
3. To what extent does student work require you to do many different things, using a variety of your skills and talents?	1 2	3 4 5	6 7
4. To what extent are the results of your work as a student likely to significantly affect the lives and well-being of other people (e.g., within your school, your family, or society)?	1 2	3 4 5	6 7
5. To what extent does working on student activities provide information about your performance?	1 2	3 4 5	6 7
6. Being a student requires me to use a number of complex high-level skills.	1 2	3 4 5	6 7
7. Student work is arranged so that I do not have the chance to do an entire piece of work from beginning to end.	1 2	3 4 5	6 7
8. Doing the work required of students provides many chances for me to figure out how I am doing.	1 2	3 4 5	6 7
9. The work students must do is quite simple and repetitive.	1 2	3 4 5	6 7
10. How well the work of a student gets done can affect a lot of other people.	1 2	3 4 5	6 7
11. Student work denies me any chance to use my personal initiative or judgment in carrying out the work.	1 2	3 4 5	6 7
12. Student work provides me with the chance to completely finish the pieces of work I begin.	1 2	3 4 5	6 7
13. Doing student work by itself provides very few clues about whether or not I am performing well.	1 2	3 4 5	6 7
14. As a student, I have considerable opportunity for independence and freedom in how I do the work.	1 2	3 4 5	6 7
15. The work I perform as a student is not very significant or important in the broader scheme of things.	1 2	3 4 5	6 7

Scoring Core Job Characteristics

Use the following set of calculations to score the core job characteristics for the job of being a student. Use your answers from the Job Diagnostic Survey that you completed above.

Skill variety (SV)	Questions 3 + 6 + 9 / 3 = ...
Task Identify (TI)	Questions 2 + 7 + 12 / 3 = ...
Task Significance (TS)	Questions 4 + 10 + 15 / 3 = ...
Autonomy	Questions 1 + 11 + 14 / 3 = ...
Job Feedback	Questions 5 + 8 + 13 / 3 = ...

Calculating the Motivating Potential Score (MPS)

Use the formula below and the scores above to calculate the motivating potential score.
Note: Notice that skill variety, task identity, and task significance are averaged before being multiplied by the scores for autonomy and job feedback.

$$MPS = (SV + TI + TS)/3 \times autonomy \times job\ security$$

The higher the score, the more motivating the job is.

Exericise 5.2: Case Study

Ama Kwame has just reported to work in the marketing department of a university in Ghana. Her new boss has chatted with her briefly about the nature of the department's work and introduced her to her co-workers and the department's faculty. Ama thought that her co-workers were a likeable group, that they were having a good time even though the workload was heavy. This was important to Ama because at her last job she had no chance to socialize with other workers.

Before leaving Ama by herself, her supervisor takes her aside and tells her that her new job success will depend completely on how well she wants to do; she will be paid according to her productivity and her productivity will be taken into account when raises and promotions are discussed. Shortly after she starts work, Ama is told by her co-workers in no uncertain terms that if she wants to get along she will produce the departmental "norm." No secretary produces more than this. The last secretary who produced more than the norm found life "lonely," and got the "silent treatment" from the rest of the secretaries.

Answer the following questions:

1. How will Ama behave? Will she ignore the group's established "norm" and strive to meet her best productivity? Or, will she bow to the pressure, restrict output, and gain acceptance by the group?
2. Use Maslow's hierarchy of needs to analyze this incident.
3. Report your findings to the class.

Duration: 10 minutes

Exercise 5.3: Case Study

Bridget Ikein graduated last year from Enugu University with a bachelor's degree in accounting. After interviews with a number of organizations on campus, she accepted a position with one of the nation's largest public accounting firms and was assigned to its Lagos office. Bridget was very pleased with the offer she received: challenging work with a prestigious firm, an excellent opportunity to gain important experience, and the highest salary any accounting major from Enugu University was offered last year—$3,000 a month. But Bridget was the top student in her class; she was ambitious and articulate and fully expected a commensurate salary.

Twelve months have passed since Bridget joined her employer. The work has proved as challenging and satisfying as she hoped. Her employer is extremely pleased with her performance; in fact, she recently received a $300-a-month raise. However, Bridget's motivational level has dropped dramatically in the past few weeks. Why? Her employer has just hired a fresh college graduate out of Boston University in the United States, who lacks the one-year experience Bridget has gained, for $5,600 a month, $300 more than Bridget now makes. It would be an understatement to describe Bridget in any other terms than livid. Bridget is even talking about looking for another job.

Discuss this case by answering the following questions:

1. Why is Bridget upset?
2. What should Bridget do?
3. Use equity theory to explain Bridget's situation.

PART II

6

POWER, INFLUENCE, AND POLITICS

Overview

This chapter discusses politics and power in organizations. The chapter is organized around these three topics. First, we discuss power in organizations. Next, we explore the topic of influence in organizations. Third, we analyze organizational politics. By the end of this chapter you should be able to:

- Describe power and its sources in organizations
- Describe influence and influence tactics
- Explain organizational politics and its effects on organizational life
- Recognize the five types of power in organizations

Power in Organizations

Power refers to the capacity to change the behavior or attitudes of others in a desired manner. Power is a function of dependence. The essence of power is control over the behavior of others.[1] Suppose two individuals, A and B, are working together in an organization. A will have power over B when A has something that B desires. B's dependence on A will be contingent on the fact that B really needs the resource controlled by A. Suppose that your parents are paying for your college. Without them, you could not afford to attend college on your own. It is obvious that your parents will have a tremendous power over you.

Sources of Power

French and Raven identify five bases of power: *legitimate power, reward power, coercive power, expert power,* and *referent power.*[2] Legitimate power refers to authority vested in the position. For instance, the CEO of a company has legitimate power by virtue of holding the office. Once his/her term ends and he/she leaves office, he/she no longer holds this power. In the workplace, managers hold legitimate power by virtue of their formal status. Reward power refers to power to control the rewards that others receive. Managers can also have reward power because they make decisions related to allocating resources, promoting employees, or providing pay increases and bonuses. Coercive power refers to power to control punishments that others receive. Managers hold coercive power because they can make decisions related to demotion, firing, or reprimanding employees. Expert power refers to power related to one's knowledge and skills in a specific domain. An employee who has expertise in a particular area has expert power. Finally, referent power refers to power related to the extent to which people like a person and consider him/her as a role model. A manager can have referent power if he/she is admired by employees who strive to emulate his/her behavior.

In addition to these five bases of power, there are two additional bases of power, *information power* and *power by association*. A person has information power when he/she has information that others need. Suppose that an employee has information that is critical for the job of other employees. Because the employee has this critical information, he/she will have power over other employees or even his/her manager. A person has power by association when he/she is associated with a most powerful person in the organization or the community. For instance, the First Lady of the United States has power by association by being the wife of the president of the United States, the most powerful person in the world. In an organization, an employee may have power by association when he/she a relative of the CEO or the friend of a powerful manager. In the African context, an employee may have power by association when he/she is related to a powerful person within or even outside the organization. An employee who has political connections and who was selected in an organization because of these political connections may have power by association. In such conditions, the employee may benefit from privileges and avoid punishments compared to other employees who do not have such connections.

Power in Organizational Sub-Units

Within organizations, power is not always limited to individuals. Organizational units can exercise power over other units. In the following lines, we discuss power held by units within organizations. In so doing, we rely on two theories, Resource Dependence Theory (RDT) and Strategic Contingencies Theory (SCT).

Resource Dependence Theory

Resource dependence theory contends that units within an organization that control critical resources will have more power over those units that need the resources.[3] Take the example of two units, the accounting unit and the marketing unit. Suppose that the accounting unit has resources (money) needed by the marketing unit. According to resource dependence theory, the accounting unit will have power over the marketing unit. Thus, the key determinant of a unit's power in an organization is its degree of control over valued resources. Research has shown that departments within an organization that control valued resources indeed have power over other departments.[4]

Strategic Contingencies Theory

The strategic contingencies theory contends that organizational units acquire power based on the importance of the activities they perform. There are generally three factors that affect the power of an organizational unit: 1) uncertainty, 2) centrality, and 3) nonsubstitutability. A unit can enhance power when: it can reduce the level of uncertainty faced by other units or the organization; it occupies a central position in the organization; and its activities are highly indispensable to the organization.[5] Uncertainty refers to the lack of knowledge about the likelihood of future events. Centrality refers to the degree to which the unit's activities have a key impact on other units or the organization. Substitutability refers to the degree to which the unit is the only one to perform particular duties.

How Can Managers Increase their Power in Organizations?

Even though power may be perceived as a dirty word, it is important to have it to get things accomplished in organizations. Thus, managers and employees alike need to learn about how to increase their power. Strategies that managers can use to increase their power include the following: 1) demonstrate to others that their work unit is relevant to the organization; 2) make job responsibilities unique; 3) expand communication networks; 4) become an internal coordinator; 5) become an external representative; 6) enhance expertise (through training and education); 7) develop political savvy; and 8) enhance likeability.[6]

The most important thing for managers, however, is not to have power but to use power effectively and wisely. David McClelland identified two types of power, *personalized power* and *socialized power*.[7] The former is power used for self-aggrandizement, to advance one's self-interests, whereas the latter is power used to advance the goals of the organization, the community, or even the country. You might have observed around you how people with power may attempt to misuse it. In most African organizations, are managers using power effectively or are they using it to advance their personal interests? There is evidence in some cases that some managers use personalized power to the extent that they use their formal positions to hire their relatives or tribesmen. They could also use their power to engage in actions that could be described as sexual harassment. In most African countries, there are few laws against sexual harassment in the workplace. Thus, managers could engage in such practices without major consequences for their professional careers. Thus, abusing power is using power to influence someone to do something that the person will later regret or that he/she did not want to do in the first place. You have read or heard the following sentence. "Power tends to corrupt and absolute power corrupts absolutely." Because power gives the ability to influence others, it must be used wisely.

Influence in Organizations

The outcome of exercising power is to influence the behavior of other people. Thus, influence can be construed as a behavioral response to the exercise of power. In this section, we describe some of the tactics that employees and managers can use to influence one another. Influence is generally defined as an attempt to affect another in a desired fashion, whether one succeeds or not. For example, someone is influencing you when the person can do or say something that might impact (or not) your behavior. If you act in the way that the person desired, then his/her attempt to affect your behavior would have been successful. If not, the attempt would not have been successful. However, the person might have influenced you because you may be upset by his/her actions even though you did not fulfill his/her wishes.

Influence Tactics

Since power is an act of influence, one must consider the following social influence tactics. These tactics include rational persuasion, inspirational appeal, consultation, and ingratiation. Rational persuasion is based on logical arguments. It involves the use of facts and evidence to influence the behavior of another person. Inspirational appeal consists of appealing to another person's values and ideals. Consultation consists of requesting participation in decision making. Finally, ingratiation refers to putting a person in a good mood before making a request. Other influence tactics include exchange, personal appeal, coalition building, legitimating, and pressure. The success of each tactic depends on the people involved in the process and the nature of the request. The use of these influence tactics could also depend on the status of the person within the organization.

Employees are more likely to use rational persuasion and consultation to influence their managers, whereas managers use a variety of tactics, including rational persuasion, inspirational appeals, pressure, consultation, ingratiation, exchange, or legitimacy to influence employees. Peers are likely to use rational persuasion, consultation, ingratiation, exchange, legitimacy, personal appeals, and coalitions to exercise influence. Some influence tactics tend to be more successful than others. The most popular techniques used to influence people at all levels are consultation, inspirational appeals, and rational persuasion. Consulting with others tends to be appreciated because people like to be involved in decisions affecting their work or lives. Similarly, inspiring people by focusing on their ideals and values tends to motivate them to act in the desired manner. The same is true for rational persuasion. Presenting facts and evidence makes it easier to influence others.

Organizational Politics

Organizational politics are actions not officially approved by an organization that are taken to influence others to meet personal rather than organizational goals. In so doing, the employee places more emphasis on his/her personal interests rather than the organization's interests. Political behavior is inherent to organizational life and takes several forms, such as controlling access to information, cultivating a favorable impression (impression management), aligning oneself to more powerful people within the organization, developing a basis for support, and blaming and attacking others. Both organizational and individual factors influence political behavior in organizations.

Factors Fostering Organizational Politics

Organizational factors leading to political behavior include resource re-allocation, promotion decisions, trust, reputation, and role ambiguity. Political activities are also more likely in the absence of clear policies. Political activity is also related to the life cycle of an organization. Political activity is not particularly likely at the birth stage of an organization. When organizations start, founders and first employees are more preoccupied by ensuring their survival, and less likely to engage in politics. However, as the organization matures (mature stage), there is a full range of political activities. This is so because there are more units and people in the organization. Political activity is intense in organizations that are at a declining stage. This stage is characterized by insecurity throughout the organization. This insecurity prompts intense political activity because everyone is trying to protect his/her personal interests.

Individual factors leading to organizational politics include personality traits such as Machiavellianism, internal locus of control, self-monitoring, personal job alternatives, job involvement, and expectations of success. People high on Machiavellianism have a tendency to manipulate others in order to accomplish their personal goals. For such individuals, the ends justify the means. Likewise, people who have an internal locus of control have a tendency to be manipulative and exploitative. The same is true for those who score high on self-monitoring. A person high on self-monitoring is one who has a tendency to modify his/her behavior to fit a particular situation. Such individuals are good at playing politics, as are those who have fewer alternatives outside their current job.

Political Tactics

Political tactics include controlling access to information, being able to determine who should receive information and who should not, and cultivating a favorable impression. Using this political tactic can help build positive impressions in organizations. For instance, using impression management helps develop a positive reputation. An employee may also use the political tactic of aligning himself or herself with powerful others within the company. Doing so helps acquire some power and protects against backlashes. However, if an employee aligns himself or herself with those who are not powerful or have a bad reputation, he or she may suffer from such an alliance. An employee may play politics by developing a base of support. The employee can do so by interacting with people who have power within the organization or with whom he/she shares similar views and who are ready to defend them. Developing friendship with powerful people within an organization could help build a base of support. Employees may also play politics by blaming and attacking others.

Consequences of Organizational Politics

Although organizational politics is not always bad, it has several negative consequences. It decreases job satisfaction, increases anxiety and stress and turnover, and reduces performance. Employees who witness political behavior in their organizations tend to be less committed and show low levels of job satisfaction. The main reason is that political behavior is viewed as dysfunctional and not serving the organization's objectives. Organizational politics may also lead to job anxiety and undermine trust among employees and between employees and managers. An interesting effect of organizational politics is that it can also enhance political behavior. Suppose an employee was not previously involved in political behavior in the workplace. By observing others play politics in the organization, the employee may attempt to imitate them, especially if such behaviors are rewarded. Regardless of its negative consequences, organizational politics is pervasive in modern organizations. Therefore, managers must ensure that it does not undermine the motivation and productivity of their employees.

Power and Politics in African Organizations

Organizational politics is observed in every organization and in every country. The same is true for African organizations. Organizational members play politics for several reasons. However, the main reasons for playing politics are to acquire power and advance one's personal interests without regard for the interests of the organization. Media reports have also chastised the abuse of power by African leaders, especially political leaders. To discuss the use of power and how it might affect African organizations, we start with two classical studies on obedience conducted in the 1960s by Stanley Milgram at Yale University and Philip Zimbardo in the 1970s at Stanford University. The purpose of Milgram's experiment was to study people's obedience to authority. His findings showed that people have a tendency to obey authorities. He summarized his findings in the following way: Ordinary people, simply doing their jobs, and without any particular hostility on their part, can become agents in a terrible destructive process. Moreover, even when the destructive effects of their work become patently clear, and they are asked to carry out actions incompatible with fundamental standards of morality, relatively few people have the resources needed to resist authority.[8] A similar study was conducted at Stanford University by Philip Zimbardo in his now famous prison experiment.[9] His findings also showed that people have a tendency to obey orders from authority figures. The study demonstrates that people tend to be obedient when provided with a legitimizing ideology, social and institutional support.

In Chapter 2, we indicated that African cultures tend to be high on power distance. One phenomenon in high power distance cultures is respect for authority. Even though it is not necessarily bad, obedience can lead to situations where those who hold power can abuse it. Obedience also stems from the consent of the governed.[10] Chester Barnard coined the term "zone of indifference" to explain the extent to which an employee could obey the order of the manager or a representative of the organization without questioning his/her motives. Respect for authority, hierarchy, and acceptance of traditions and customs could lead to a situation where African employees and managers develop a systematic tendency to follow orders. For instance, in most African cultures, obedience to the elderly and authority figures is considered as a sign of respect and culturally valued. Although not necessarily bad, it could have a negative impact in the workplace where decisions may not be questioned. As employees, people expect to act in certain ways as a result of the psychological contract between them and their employing organization. However, when the demands fall beyond the zone of indifference, then employees may question them and even refuse to obey them.

Resource dependence theory may be particularly relevant not only for African organizations but also for African governments and citizens. As we have explained, the essence of resource dependence theory is control over critical resources. To the extent that a party controls resources that another party desires, it will have control and power over it. Most African countries rely on foreign aid for development programs. To the extent that African countries rely on foreign aid those countries or organizations providing them will have power over African countries. Thus, to reduce dependency, African countries must do better by finding alternate sources of funding or by relying on their own resources and ingenuity.

Summary

In this chapter we have discussed the concepts of power, influence, and politics in organizations. These three concepts are interconnected and part of organizational life. Although power is the ability to influence others to act in a way we want them to, when misused, power can have detrimental consequences for others and the organization as well. Power is not only limited to individuals. Sub-units within organizations can exercise power over units by controlling critical resources or by performing activities that are central to the organization's mission. We have finally described these concepts in regard to the African context.

■ Group Discussion Questions

1. Identify the different sources of power.
2. What is the relationship between power and influence?
3. Is organizational politics necessarily bad?
4. Describe the organizational factors leading to political behavior.
5. Contrast the resource dependence theory and the strategic contingencies model.

Exercise 6.1: Self-Assessment Exercise—What is my Preferred Type of Power?

Instructions

Respond to the 20 statements by thinking in terms of how you prefer to influence others. You have the choice among five alternatives, Strongly Agree (5), Agree (4), Neither Agree nor Disagree (3), Disagree (2) and Strongly Disagree (1).

Items	1	2	3	4	5
To influence others, I would prefer to:					
1. Increase their pay level.	1	2	3	4	5
2. Make them feel valued.	1	2	3	4	5
3. Give them undesirable job assignments.	1	2	3	4	5
4. Make them feel like I approve of them.	1	2	3	4	5
5. Make them feel that they have commitments to meet.	1	2	3	4	5
6. Make them feel personally accepted.	1	2	3	4	5
7. Make them feel important.	1	2	3	4	5
8. Give them good technical suggestions.	1	2	3	4	5
9. Make the work difficult for them.	1	2	3	4	5
10. Share my experience and/or training with them.	1	2	3	4	5
11. Make things unpleasant here.	1	2	3	4	5
12. Make being at work distasteful.	1	2	3	4	5
13. Influence their getting a pay raise.	1	2	3	4	5
14. Make them feel like they should satisfy their job requirements.	1	2	3	4	5
15. Provide them with sound job-related advice.	1	2	3	4	5
16. Provide them with special benefits.	1	2	3	4	5
17. Influence their getting a promotion.	1	2	3	4	5
18. Give them the feeling that they have responsibilities to fulfill.	1	2	3	4	5
19. Provide them with needed technical knowledge.	1	2	3	4	5
20. Make them recognize that they have tasks to accomplish.	1	2	3	4	5

Source: Hinken & Schriesheim (1989).[11]

Scoring Key

Calculate your scores as follows:

Reward Power: Add your responses to items 1, 13, 16, 17; then divide by 4.
Coercive Power: Add your responses to items 3, 9, 11, 12; then divide by 4.
Legitimate Power: Add your responses to items 5, 14, 18, 20; then divide by 4.
Expert Power: Add your responses to items 8, 10, 15, 19; then divide by 4.
Referent Power: Add your responses to items 2, 4, 6, 7; then divide by 4.

Analysis and Interpretation

A high score (4 or above) indicates that you prefer to influence others by using this particular type of power. A low score (2 or below) indicates that you prefer not to use this type of power.

Exercise 6.2: Case Study

David Mbula (name disguised) was appointed CEO of the national utility company in an African country a decade ago. The company controls both running water and electricity distribution in the country. It is a state monopoly that has been recently partially privatized. The state owns 60 percent of the company and foreign and local investors retain the remaining 40 percent. However, the national government is the powerful owner and generally appoints the CEO as well as board members. Mr. Mbula is a powerful person who has a lot of political connections in the country. He is also the mayor of his home town, a city of 135,000 inhabitants. He is the friend of the president of the country and part of the ruling elite. He is so powerful that employees and managers refer to him as "The Boss." He expects managers to respect his title and very often these managers are required to attend private events at his home in the capital city as well as in his home town. For instance, when there are funerals or weddings in his family, the Boss expects his managers to attend.

This has become a tradition, so much so that failure to attend such events and make oneself visible can lead to detrimental consequences, such as stalling one's promotion. Kone, a new hire from the local university, refused to attend such events. He was heard complaining that attendance of private events was not part of his job description. Moreover, he complained about the Boss running the company as a family affair or a political party by distributing favors to those loyal to him and attempting to blackmail those who dare to think freely. Shortly afterward, Kone was re-assigned to another position in a small town. Seeing this re-assignment as a demotion, Kone refused to make the move. Because of his refusal to relocate to the small town and perform a job that was less than his current job, he was dismissed from the company. He filed a lawsuit alleging abusive treatment and firing but to no avail. He did not even have the chance to have his case heard in court.

Discussion Questions

1. Based on your understanding of the different sources of power, what type of power did the Boss have?
2. Did the Boss have referent power?
3. How did the boss use his power toward his managers and Kone?
4. Did the demands of the Boss fall within Kone's zone of indifference?
5. Give an example of a situation where you think a person has abused his/her power.

7

LEADERSHIP IN AN AFRICAN CONTEXT

Africa has a serious leadership deficiency. A new wave of ambitious, critical and perhaps more open politicians are clamoring for change.

Time Magazine

Overview

By the end of this chapter you should be able to:

- Explain the nature of leadership
- Explain contingency models of leadership
- Explain charismatic leadership
- Explain transformational and transactional models of leadership
- Describe emerging theories of leadership
- Discuss the extent to which leadership theories can be applied to African organizations

The Nature of Leadership

Who is a Leader? What is Leadership?

A leader is a person in a group, an organization, or a society who exercises the most influence over others. Leadership is a process of influence. If leadership is a process of influence, then there is no leader without followers. Leaders and followers mutually influence each other. Leadership takes place in a social context. Consequently, the behaviors, attitudes, and cognitions of the leader and follower during the influence exchange indicate the submission or resistance of either but particularly the followers. To better understand the leadership process, we use an interactional framework.

An Interactional Framework of Leadership

In order to appreciate leadership we have to understand the interactional framework which describes the interplay between leader characteristics, follower characteristics, and situational characteristics. It is a useful aid that facilitates comprehension of leadership as a process. The inter-actional framework specifies three elements: 1) the leader, 2) the followers, and 3) the situation in which leadership takes place.

Leader

The focus here is on the characteristics of the leader. What are the individual characteristics that influence a leader's behavior? These personal characteristics include personality traits, attitude, and competence. The leader's personality influences his/her reactions toward specific situations and followers. Examples of personality traits include emotional stability, assertiveness, risk-prone (risk aversion) behavior, open-mindedness, and so on. In addition to personality traits, the leader's cognitive abilities shape his/her behavior, for example, factors such as intelligence, creativity, and self-monitoring. Cognitive abilities are also related to level of education and knowledge. How-ever, leaders' characteristics alone are not enough to explain the leadership process. We need to consider the followers' characteristics as well as the characteristics of the situation.

Followers

The followers' characteristics—personality, attitude, and competence—are similar to those of the leader. A follower's personality and cognitive abilities can affect the behavior and relation with the leader. For example, followers who are open to experience are likely to embrace change more than those who are not open to experience. Intelligent, educated, and knowledgeable followers may require leadership styles that are different from those followers who do not exhibit such cog-nitive resources. When followers are highly educated and knowledgeable, there is often no need for an autocratic (or directive) leadership style. The number of followers a leader oversees can also impact the leader's behavior. Finally, we consider the followers' level of maturity. Mature fol-lowers tend to require leadership styles that differ from that of non-mature followers. The key idea here is that followers' characteristics shape the different styles a leader uses.

Situation

The situation includes both a specific task and the social context in which leadership takes place. A situation may be simple (all parameters are known) or complex (some key parameters are unknown or are many). Such characteristics affect how the leader interacts with the followers. For instance, in a situation of downsizing, a leader may behave quite differently than in a situation of performance appraisal.

Contingency Theories of Leadership

As we discussed above, the situation is a leadership context. As a result, scholars have identified influence behaviors that are based on the situation a leader encounters. We elaborate on them below.

Fiedler's Contingency Model

According to F. E. Fiedler,[1] the performance of a leader depends on two interrelated factors: 1) the degree to which the situation gives the leader control and influence—that is, the likelihood that the leader can successfully accomplish the job; and 2) the leader's basic motivation—that is whether the leader's self-esteem depends primarily on accomplishing the task or on having

TABLE 7.1 The Least-Preferred Co-Worker Scale

Describe the person with whom you can work least well. Describe this person on the following scale by circling the appropriate number. Do not omit any items, and mark each item only once.

Pleasant	8	7	6	5	4	3	2	1	Unpleasant
Friendly	8	7	6	5	4	3	2	1	Unfriendly
Rejecting	8	7	6	5	4	3	2	1	Accepting
Tense	8	7	6	5	4	3	2	1	Relaxed
Distant	8	7	6	5	4	3	2	1	Close
Cold	8	7	6	5	4	3	2	1	Warm
Supportive	8	7	6	5	4	3	2	1	Hostile
Boring	8	7	6	5	4	3	2	1	Interesting
Quarrelsome	8	7	6	5	4	3	2	1	Harmonious
Gloomy	8	7	6	5	4	3	2	1	Cheerful
Open	8	7	6	5	4	3	2	1	Guarded
Backbiting	8	7	6	5	4	3	2	1	Loyal
Untrustworthy	8	7	6	5	4	3	2	1	Trustworthy
Considerate	8	7	6	5	4	3	2	1	Inconsiderate
Nasty	8	7	6	5	4	3	2	1	Nice
Agreeable	8	7	6	5	4	3	2	1	Disagreeable
Insincere	8	7	6	5	4	3	2	1	Sincere
Kind	8	7	6	5	4	3	2	1	Unkind

Scoring and Interpretation: To calculate your score, add the numbers. If you scored 64 or higher, you are a high LPC leader (relations-motivated). If you scored 57 or lower, you are a low LPC leader (task-motivated). If your score falls between 58 and 63, you are a socio-independent leader.

close supportive relations with others. Fiedler identifies two classifications of leadership styles, *relationship-motivated* and *task-motivated* based on the LPC (Least-Preferred Co-worker scale, see Table 7.1). Fiedler argues that a leadership style is permanent and difficult to modify. Therefore, what needs to be modified is the situation. To be effective, leaders should work in situations that match their style. A key concept in Fiedler's contingency model is the leader-match concept. Effectiveness depends on matching leaders to situations. Task-motivated leaders are effective in situations of both high control and low control, whereas relationship-motivated leaders are effective in situations of moderate control.

Path-Goal Theory

The path-goal theory of leadership specifies what a leader must do to achieve high productivity and morale in a given situation.[2] The leader must clarify the path, set goals, and provide information related to how to accomplish those goals. In any organization, there are factors beyond the control of group members that influence task and satisfaction. These factors include group members' tasks and the authority system within the organization. Effectively using path–goal theory requires assessing the relevant environmental variables and selecting one of the four leadership styles: directive, supportive, participative, and achievement-oriented. Table 7.2 helps you assess your leadership style based on the path–goal theory.

TABLE 7.2 Path–Goal Leadership Questionnaire

Instructions:

This questionnaire contains questions about different styles of path-goal leadership. Indicate how often each statement is true of your own behavior.

Key:
1 = Never, 2 = Hardly ever, 3 = Seldom, 4 = Occasionally, 5 = Often, 6 = Usually, 7 = Always

_____   1. I let subordinates know what is expected of them.

_____   2. I maintain a friendly working relationship with subordinates.

_____   3. I consult with subordinates when facing a problem.

_____   4. I listen receptively to subordinates' ideas and suggestions.

_____   5. I inform subordinates about what needs to be done and how it needs to be done.

_____   6. I let subordinates know that I expect them to perform at their highest level.

_____   7. I act without consulting my subordinates.

_____   8. I do little things to make it pleasant to be a member of the group.

_____   9. I ask subordinates to follow standard rules and regulations.

_____ 10. I set goals for subordinates' performance that are quite challenging.

_____ 11. I say things that hurt subordinates personal feelings.

_____ 12. I ask suggestions from subordinates concerning how to carry out assignments.

_____ 13. I encourage continual improvement in subordinates' performance.

_____ 14. I explain the level of performance that is expected of subordinates.

_____ 15. I help subordinates overcome problems that stop them from carrying out their tasks.

_____ 16. I show that I have doubts about their ability to meet most objectives.

_____ 17. I ask subordinates for suggestions on what assignments should be made.

_____ 18. I give vague explanations of what is expected of subordinates on the job.

_____ 19. I consistently set challenging goals for subordinates to attain.

_____ 20. I behave in a manner that is thoughtful of subordinates' personal needs.

Scoring:

1. Reverse the scores for items 7, 11, 16, and 18.

2. Directive style: Sum of scores on items 1, 5, 9, 14, and 18.

3. Supportive style: Sum of scores on items 2, 8, 11, 15, and 20.

4. Participative style: Sum of scores on items 3, 4, 7, 12, and 17.

5. Achievement-oriented style: Sum of scores on items 6, 10, 13, 16, and 19.

Scoring Interpretation:

Directive style. A common score is 23; scores above 28 are considered high and scores below 18 are considered low.

Supportive style. A common score is 28; scores above 33 are considered high and scores below 23 are considered low.

Participative style. A common score is 21; scores above 26 are considered high and scores below 16 are considered low.

Achievement-oriented style. A common score is 19; scores above 24 are considered high and scores below 14 are considered low.

TABLE 7.3 Strategies for Making Decisions

Autocratic I (AI)	Leader solves problem alone, using information that is readily available.
Autocratic II (AII)	Leader obtains additional information from group members then makes decision alone. Group members may or may not be informed.
Consultative I (CI)	Leader shares problem with group members individually, and asks for information and evaluation. Group members do not meet collectively, and leader makes decision alone.
Consultative II (CII)	Leader shares problem with group members collectively, but makes decision alone.
Group II (GII)	Leader meet with group to discuss situation. Leader focuses and directs discussion but does not impose will. Group makes final decision.

Source: Vroom, V. H., & Jago, A. G. (1988). *The new leadership: Managing Participation in organizations*. Englewood Cliffs, NJ: Prentice Hall.

The Normative Model

The normative model of leadership is mostly a decision-making model of leadership.[3] It assesses the contingencies that a leader considers in making a decision. Two criteria are important in judging decision effectiveness: *decision quality* and *decision acceptance*. Decision quality means that if the decision has a rational or objectively determinable "better or worse" alternative, the leader should select the best alternative. Decision quality would apply when it is possible to quantify the decision outcomes. Decision acceptance implies that followers accept the decision as if it were their own and do not merely comply with the decision. Acceptance of the decision outcome may be critical, particularly if followers are responsible for implementing the decision. The factors that may affect decision acceptance include the type and complexity of the decision and feelings of having too much power from the leader.

Other factors such as time may play an important role in making the decision. If the leader feels he/she does not have time and needs a faster decision, he/she may use an autocratic leadership style. After all, it takes less time to make an autocratic decision than a participative one. The leader may also consider a follower's level of development. After decision quality and acceptance have been assessed, and if the leader has determined that time is not a critical issue, he/she may follow a decision process more apt to allow the follower to develop his/her own decision-making style. The leader may also develop a style that best meets his/her needs (i.e., the process with which the leader is more comfortable). Based on these contingencies, the decision maker may use one of the following styles: Autocratic I, Autocratic II, Consultative I, Consultative II, or Group II (See Table 7.3).

Situational Leadership Model

P. Hersey and K. H. Blanchard,[4] two prominent leadership scholars, developed the situational leadership model. This model considers two leadership dimensions: *task behavior* and *relationship behavior*. Task behavior refers to the extent to which the leader spells out the responsibilities of an individual or a group. Relationship behavior, however, refers to friendly relationships with group members. The relative effectiveness of these two dimensions often depends on the situation. The authors developed several combinations of these two dimensions. They believe that some combinations are more effective than others. They also considered some characteristics that followers should have for a particular leadership style to be used. Among these characteristics are job maturity and psychological maturity. Job maturity refers to the amount of task-relevant knowledge,

TABLE 7.4 Leadership Styles and Behaviors

Styles	*Behavior*
Telling style (HiT/LR)	Leader is directive
Selling style (HiT/HiR)	Directive but in a more persuasive way
	Leader emphasizes both task and human considerations
Participating style (HiR/LT)	Less direction and more collaboration between leader and followers
Delegating style (LR/HiT)	Leader delegates responsibility and is only informed of progress

experience, and skills. Psychological maturity refers to a follower's self-confidence, commitment, motivation, and self-respect relative to the task.

To effectively use the situational leadership model, leaders should first assess a follower's maturity level relative to the task to be accomplished. According to this model, a leader may implement a series of developmental interventions to help boost followers' maturity levels. This process would begin by assessing a follower's current level of maturity and then determining the leader behavior that best suits that follower in regard to the particular task. A leader should assess a follower's readiness to determine the style to use. Follower readiness includes ability and willingness to perform a given task. Based on this, the authors developed four leadership styles: telling, selling, participating, and delegating. The appropriateness of each style depends on a follower's readiness (See Table 7.4).

Leaders Exchange Model (MX Model)

According to this model, the type of exchange between the leader and follower determines group effectiveness.[5] The model contends that leaders have special relations with their subordinates and these relationships shape the outcomes of the exchange. There are two types of group members, the "in-group" members and the "out-group" members. There is more trust between the leader and in-group members. Those members receive better rewards, have frequent interactions with the leader, and develop high levels of performance and satisfaction. In contrast, out-group members have fewer interactions with the leader and their interactions are more formal with the leader. There is also less trust between the leader and the out-group members. These members have lower levels of satisfaction and performance and receive fewer rewards from the leader. The leader therefore influences in-group and out-group members differently as a result.

Contemporary Theories of Leadership

All the above theories are traditional; for a long time our understanding of leadership focused on those theories. More recently, there has been an interest in other ways of influencing followers. These ways are often termed contemporary theories of leadership. They include charismatic, transformational, and transactional leadership.

Charismatic Leadership

Charismatic leadership is another way of saying that traits do matter for effective leadership. Charisma refers to extraordinary abilities that followers attribute to leaders.[6] Charisma is not a physical trait that a leader possesses per se; it is an attribution that followers make about the leader. These followers think that the leader has exemplary qualities. As beauty lies in the eye of the beholder, charisma lies in the eye of the follower. Charisma helps create an emotional bond between the leader and his/her followers. And because followers "like" the leader, they are likely to follow him/her and obey his/her orders. Leaders considered as charismatic are visionary, inspire trust, and possess excellent communication skills. Charismatic leaders also have strong convictions about the vision and show emotional expressiveness and warmth. In addition to using unconventional strategies, they tend to be self-confident.

Transformational Leadership

Whereas charismatic leadership deals with the leader's personal attributes, transformational leadership deals with what the leader does, what types of changes the leader brings to the follower, group, organization, or the community. Transformational leadership requires four key characteristics: charisma, inspirational leadership, individualized consideration, and intellectual stimulation.[7] By being charismatic, the transformational leader has a vision and a sense of a mission. This helps him/her gain respect and loyalty from followers. By practicing inspirational leadership, the leader communicates the vision to followers. Transformational leaders use emotional appeals to inspire followers. By providing intellectual stimulation, the leader encourages followers to analyze problems in new ways, creates an atmosphere conducive to creative thinking, and emphasizes the use of methodical problem solving and reasoning. Finally, by providing individualized consideration, the leader pays personal attention to employees and uses a one-on-one communication style. He/she also emphasizes personal development of group members.

Transactional Leadership

Transactional leadership is characterized by a contractual relationship between the leader and followers. This contractual relationship may be explicit or implicit. An explicit contractual relationship is a relationship based on formal authority. It tends to be spelled out in a formal contract such as the one existing between an employee and his/her supervisor. An implicit contractual relationship is a *de facto* relationship between a leader and a follower, which is not based on a written contract.

The leader's behavior is associated with constructive and corrective transactions. This transactional relationship implies that subordinates will work in exchange for rewards. A transactional leader can use a constructive style or a corrective style. When the leader uses a constructive style, he/she makes rewards contingent on performance. Followers are rewarded when they accomplish the objectives. In a corrective style, the leader manages by exception. The leader may manage by exception passively or actively. In managing by exception actively, the leader intervenes to criticize employees when mistakes are made. In managing by exception passively, the leader does not intervene unless he/she is required to do so. When the leader intervenes, he/she will point out mistakes and wrongdoings. The relationship between the leader and follower is based on exchange transactions—whether the leader has to straighten out a follower or not.

Emerging Theories of Leadership

Recently there has been interest related to novel theories of leadership, such as servant leadership,[8] Level 5 leadership[9] and crisis leadership.[10] Servant leadership deals with the leader being in the service of his or her followers. A servant leader is self-effacing and tends to focus on serving followers. Servant leaders go beyond their own self-interest and focus on opportunities to help followers grow and develop. The behaviors characterizing servant leadership include: listening, empathizing, persuading, accepting stewardship, and actively developing followers potential. Recent research has also identified Level 5 leadership that focuses on building a trustful relationship between the leader and his/her followers. Level 5 leaders are leaders who focus on the following four characteristics: 1) individual competency, 2) team skills, 3) managerial competence, and 4) ability to stimulate others to high performance. A blend of personal humility and professional will characterizes Level 5 leaders. In this type of leadership, personal ego needs are focused toward building a great company. Level 5 leaders take responsibility for failures and give credit to others for successes.

Finally, recent events, such as the September 11, 2001 terrorist attacks in the United States and the economic crisis of 2008 have called attention to a new form of leadership, crisis leadership. How do leaders react in situations of crisis? Are there particular behaviors that must be displayed when the company, the group, the community, or even a nation faces a situation of crisis? Very often, in such situations, followers look up to the leader for guidance and reassurance. Meeting the challenges of a critical situation is the very essence of leadership in crisis situations. Imagine that you are the captain of a boat that is dangerously drifting. How do you assure your crew members that they will be safe and all will be ok? It takes courage and stamina to ride the storm and reassure followers when facing a crisis. Crisis leadership has two distinct phases. First there is an emergency phase. The task of the leader is to stabilize the situation and buy time. The second is the adaptive phase. Here the leader tackles the underlying causes of the crisis and builds the capacity to thrive in a new reality. During the adaptive phase the leader faces enormous pressure to respond to the anxieties of stakeholders with authoritative certainty, even if doing so means overselling what the leader knows and having to discount what he/she doesn't know. Little is known of this type of leadership in Africa even though a number of countries face various crises.

Applying Leadership Theories in an African Context

The epigraph to this chapter shows that there is a great need for leadership in Africa. Indeed, Raila Odinga, Prime Minister of Kenya observed that there is "mediocrity of African leadership."[11] How can leadership in Africa be optimal or excellent? First, some of the leadership principles discussed here which have relevance in Africa can be adopted. A legitimate question to ask is whether all these leadership theories apply in an African context. To address this question, we look at some of the leaders in the political and business arenas who have marked the African continent. Most people across the globe admire and even venerate African leaders, such as Nelson Mandela. But why is Mr. Mandela considered a leader and an icon for South Africa's str uggle for freedom and democracy? To answer this question, one has to look at his accomplishments. First, Nelson Mandela had a vision for a free and democratic South Africa. This vision was conveyed to other members of the struggle against apartheid. Nelson Mandela also had a strong conviction that fighting the then oppressing apartheid regime was the right thing to do. He never wavered regardless of the hardship he endured (27 years in the Roben Island prison). Such leaders certainly exist in other African countries and organizations. Other political leaders include Kwame Nkrumah of Ghana, Julius Nyerere of Tanzania, Jomo Kenyatta of Kenya. These leaders put country ahead of self-interest.

Every community and organization has leaders. The same is true for African communities and organizations. Thus, the theories discussed in this chapter could easily apply to African organizations. For instance, the contingency theories of leadership indicate that leaders could focus on tasks or human relations depending on the situation. We may argue that because the African culture emphasizes collectivism and the importance of group success over individual achievement, leaders in African organizations should strive to strike a balance between concern for production (or a focus on the task) and concern for people. Specifically, Africans tend to be sensitive to interpersonal treatment. Thus, a leader who uses a style in which followers perceive that their personal interests are considered would be more likely to be effective in an African context.

Leaders in African organizations tend to be directive and autocratic because to some extent African cultures are conducive to such styles. The chieftaincy systems which confer authority to the chiefs and council of elders may be considered hierarchical and therefore less involving. Hofstede's study of culture generally considered African culture as high on power distance. Thus, most Africans may tend to expect the leader to provide guidance and instructions. Some employees may see a more participative style from a leader as a sign of weakness or a lack of knowledge. However, as more and more African employees become better educated, a participative leadership style that encourages empowerment and employee involvement could be more appealing than an autocratic style.

Summary

We have discussed leadership as it relates to Africa. It affects employee behaviors in organizations.

■ Group Discussion Questions

1. Do you think that most theories of leadership could be applied to the African context? Explain your answer.
2. Give examples of leaders you consider charismatic or transformational and give an example.
3. Would you consider leaders such as Nelson Mandela to be charismatic? Yes or No? Explain Why.
4. Can leadership be taught?
5. Are leaders born or raised?

Exercise 7.1

1. Draw a picture of a leader.
2. Identify 10 adjectives that describe an effective leader.
3. Formulate your personal leadership philosophy. In other words, explain how you think people should be led.

Exericse 7.2: Case Study

IMPRODAPIM[12] is an institution focused on human capability management. Due to economic liberalization and structural adjustment programs initiated by the government in the 1980s through the 1990s IMPRODAPIM was converted to a university with extended privileges to run as a quasi-private, semi-autonomous institution. IMPRODAPIM's vision was to be a world class center of excellence for training, consultancy, and research in leadership, management, and administration consistent with the economic and development objectives of the country. This was to be achieved through the training, research, and consultancy expertise of the institution in line with its core values of academic excellence, superior professional standards, speedy response to clientele and stakeholders, purposefulness in national character, conformity to global organizational standards, honesty, hard work, integrity, transparency, innovation, and accountability.

IMPRODAPIM adopted a two-tier (graduate and undergraduate) and four semi-autonomous unit structure. The units included a public services unit focusing on training of civil and other public servants; governance, leadership, and public management which is a graduate school; a business school; and a technology school.

Political (frequent military actions and lack of viable regulatory controls), economic (low productivity, lack of foreign investment, underperforming state-owned enterprises (SOEs), poor agricultural performance, and natural environmental disasters including drought and deforestation that worsened economic performance), cultural (festering national schisms and tribalism), and educational (introduction of private universities and tertiary institutions) factors were threatening the viability of IMPRODAPIM. In addition, internal factors in IMPRODAPIM such as deterioration of physical facilities which discouraged young professionals with business qualifications from joining the institution, guaranteed incentives, dependence on government subventions, aging professoriate, and lack of a research were also undermining the vision of the organization.

In order to help IMPRODAPIM achieve its objectives and to function effectively the government appointed a new CEO who had studied both in the country and abroad. His academic credentials suggested strong capabilities and his cross-cultural experience from sojourning in Europe, America, and other African countries, as well as work with both private and public international institutions (e.g., Commonwealth Secretariat) indicated the New President had strong leadership abilities and competence. His appointment was therefore viewed positively by several stakeholders including the government and employees.

The new leader was expected to transform IMPRODAPIM. The government, faculty, and students all had different expectations. How to meet those expectations was one challenge among others, such as the lack of human capital to build a center of excellence for knowledge exploration, how to implement whatever changes he envisioned, retention of human resources, and adoption of a leadership style that could facilitate a culture of excellence. After several weeks of critical reflection the new CEO began to establish structural changes by advocating for legislative changes that would enable the institution to support itself financially by charging fees, power to train public servants, and authority under an 11-member Governing Council to develop programs and services consistent with its university status (i.e., leadership, management, and administration) for both the public and private sectors. He also brought in foreign faculty from all regions of the globe (e.g., Asia, Europe, America, Africa, and South America) to teach, set up new schools—business, technology, governance—and hired qualified faculty to help run them. With these programs, the institution improved its image from one of low quality to a center of excellence. Press reports suggested IMPRODAPIM was being transformed.

Other changes included programs to enhance human resources within the institution through improved working conditions, performance management in which staff were evaluated for attendance, punctuality, and productivity, a performance-based reward system, employee involvement through durbars, communication systems, and retention based on performance.

Shortly after the changes were initiated problems began to emerge. The style of leadership of the New President, though results-laden, was disapproved by some employees. First, he was perceived as dictatorial. The grapevine indicated that any employee who dared to question a policy, initiative, or program was summarily dismissed, punished, or disparaged publicly. Several faculty members were victimized as a consequence. This style seemed to invalidate the transformation initiatives. Staff and faculty began to question the value of suggestions if they could be victimized as a consequence. It seemed conflicts could not be amicably resolved. As a result, dissatisfied employees explored alternative mechanisms of conflict resolution: legal action. Among others, the CEO was accused of tribalism, autocratic rule, and dishonesty. His leadership was also perceived to create a hostile work climate. His attitude toward staff and faculty, including visiting professors and students, was very abrasive, insensitive, and condescending. His distrust intensified. As a result, he resorted to threats of arbitrary dismissal of staff. Staff and faculty were uncertain of the future of the institution and their own careers. The climate was so toxic that productivity was diminishing. Given that environment, the CEO could not but resign before his vision was achieved. Even though the government appointed a successor, IMPRODAPIM no longer enjoys the reputation it had during the old CEO's initial tenure.

Questions for Group/Class Discussion:

1. How did leadership help IMPRODAPIM?
2. How would you describe the leadership style of the CEO?
3. How did the leadership style of the CEO negatively affect the institution?
4. Overall, was the leadership style facilitative or inhibitive to the mission of the organization?

8

GROUPS AND TEAMS

Overview

In this chapter we examine groups and teams. We discuss differences between groups and teams. In addition, we discuss the model of team effectiveness. By the end of this chapter you should be able to:

- Explain groups and teams
- Explain the stages of group formation
- Discuss the importance of groups in organizations
- Differentiate groups from teams
- Explain the team effectiveness model

Nature of Groups

Groups are based on collaboration and collective execution, an idea that is not foreign to the collectivistic cultures of Africa. In the rural areas, houses or compounds are built through group activities; members of the village help one another in expectation of others helping them in the future when needed. What then is a group? A group is defined as a collection of individuals (two or more) with a common purpose, whose members see themselves as members of a group. For a group to be recognized as such, we need three elements. First, there should be more than one individual in it. Second, they should have a common purpose. Third, the members should see themselves as a group.

To better understand the notion of group in organizations, you have to make the distinction between formal groups and informal groups. A formal group is one that is created for a specific purpose—to perform a specific task. Organizations often create groups to resolve crises. An informal group is one that is spontaneously created not for a particular job but because its members have some common interest. Informal groups are based on friendships and common interests. We may ask ourselves why people join groups. People join groups for different reasons some of which include status, security, power, prestige, affiliation, self-esteem, and achievement.

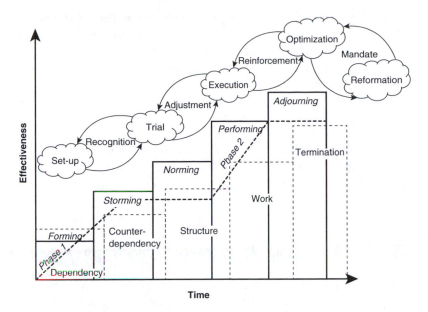

FIGURE 8.1 Models of Team Development

Stages of Group Formation

Groups develop over time because they are composed of individuals who need to cohere, know one another, and understand each other's capabilities. Three major models of group development include Tuckman's 5-stage model,[1] Gersick's punctuated equilibrium model (PEM),[2] and Wheelan's integrated model of team development.[3] Tuckman's model identifies forming, storming, norming, performing, and adjourning stages. In the forming stage, group members are selected, tasks specified, and goals assigned. In the storming stage, the members "fight" over control of group activities. Some may emerge as leaders. In the norming stage, the group develops acceptable standards of behavior. The group also demonstrates cohesiveness. Group members assimilate some common expectations. After this stage, the group moves to the performing stage where the group does the work for which it was established. Temporary groups have an adjourning stage where members disband and the group ceases to exist. The model specifies successive stages of development.

In contrast, the punctuated equilibrium model (PEM) proposed by Gersick suggests that teams or groups go through long periods of equilibrium punctuated by periods of radical change and reorientation. Gersick studied naturally occurring groups and found that they depart from the traditional linear models of group development.[4] She found that groups develop through the sudden formation, maintenance, and sudden revision of a "framework for performance." In Phase I (see Figure 8.1) a framework of behavioral patterns and assumptions through which a group approaches its project emerges. The group stays with that framework through the first half of its life. At the midpoint groups experience transitions defined as paradigmatic shifts in their approaches to their work. In Phase 2, the group takes its direction from plans crystallized during the transition which guide them toward completion. At completion, when a team makes a final effort to satisfy outside expectations, it experiences the positive and negative consequences of past choices. The pause breaks the successive stages of PEM.

Wheelan's "integrated" model of group development has five stages. In stage I, dependency and inclusion, members depend on the designated leader, express concerns about safety, and seek to be included in almost all discussions. In stage II, counterdependency and fight, disagreement among members with regard to group goals and procedures emerges as the group strives to develop a unified set of goals, values, and operational procedures to guide them. Stage III is defined as trust and structure. The group establishes a structure of work and interactions; develop trust in one another, and show increased commitment to the group, willingness to cooperate, and greater open and task-oriented communication. In stage IV, work and productivity, team members expend greater energy and focus on the purpose for which they were constituted: work and productivity. They strive to achieve the goals of the task and group. In the final stage, the group finishes its task and is disbanded. The three models are summarized in Figure 8.1.

In addition, we propose a dynamic model that combines the linear and non-linear characteristics of groups. The model is depicted as fuzzy to reflect naturalistic group processes. It has five major states—set-up, trial, execution, optimization, and reformation—and four transitions—recognition, adjustment, reinforcement, and mandate. The back and forward arrows (see Figure 8.1) reflect feedback and feedforward team orientations and decision-making. Teams are set-up before they try out (pilot) the task they are assigned to perform. Between the two states is recognition of team members' capabilities, personalities, achievements, potentials, and idiosyncracies. The trial period is followed by full execution of the task. Adjustment to roles, norms, procedures are made to facilitate unfettered execution. The execution is optimized with reinforcements. Teams reform (i.e., disband or reconstitute) based on a mandate after achieving their goals.

Differences Between Groups and Teams

Before we explain the concept of teams, let's compare groups and teams. This comparison is made on four factors: performance, accountability, team member commitment to the goal, and team member responsiveness. In a team, performance depends on team contributions and collective products, whereas in groups, performance depends only on individual contributions. This is why in groups, we talk about social loafing—some group members fail to put in much effort. In teams, accountability for outcomes rests on mutual outcomes, whereas in groups, it rests on individual outcomes. In teams, all members are committed to the common goals and have a commitment of purpose, whereas in groups, members are only interested in common goals. The identification with the common goal is more intense in a team than in a group. Finally, team members are responsive to self-imposed demands, whereas group members are responsive to management demands.

Nature of Teams

Teams are an important component of today's work environment. A team is a special form of group; it is defined as a group whose members have complementary skills and are committed to a common purpose or set of performance goals for which they hold themselves mutually accountable. Most jobs are organized around teams. Why do companies organize work around teams? First, some tasks are more effectively and efficiently accomplished through teams. Second, teams enable organizations to take advantage of various talents of employees. Teams can enhance creativity and innovation in organizations.

Team Roles

Explicit in the group development models above is the idea that team effectiveness depends on role allocation, execution, and management. Role allocation refers to the distribution of roles among team members. Team members tend to assume different roles; some may be leaders, others clerks and still others evaluators or monitors. Others may simply be members. Some scholars classify roles into action-oriented roles (e.g., implementer), people-oriented roles (e.g., coordinator), and thought-oriented roles (e.g., monitor-evaluator).[5] Regardless of rank, each group member is expected to contribute in some way to the group's well-being. Role execution, team members' enactment of their roles, enables teams to achieve their goals. Role management refers to the process by which teams manage the roles of members. Some members either do not enact their roles at all or do so passively. These individuals are sometimes termed free riders or social loafers because they rely on other team members, rather than themselves, to execute their roles. Role management ensures that all team members are enacting their roles consistent with the norms, times, and expectations.

Types of Teams

In today's organizations, there are various types of teams, including work teams, cross-functional teams, self-managed teams, and permanent teams, to name just a few. Work teams are concerned with products and services. Cross-functional teams are composed of employees from different departments within the company, whereas functional teams are composed of employees from the same department. Self-managed teams are free to make key decisions. Permanent teams remain intact as long as the organization exists, whereas temporary teams exist for a finite period of time. The introduction of the Internet has resulted in the establishment of virtual teams. These are teams that use computer technology to interact and execute tasks even though the members are dispersed over different locations. The poor state of technology in most Africa countries limits the use of these teams. Imagine how frustrating it is to have a meeting through dial-up phones!

Team Effectiveness

Organizations set up teams to achieve specific goals. Achievement of team goals is therefore one criterion. However, effectiveness is multidimensional. As a result, team effectiveness has many components, some cognitive and affective, and others behavioral. Further, psychological outcomes differ from economic, social, and political outcomes of teams. Team effectiveness as a *system* encompasses the inputs, processes, outcomes, and controls of teams. The system facilitates achievement of the individual, team, and organizational outcomes. As a *criterion*, team effectiveness may be internal to the team when individual members learn and the team grows or becomes viable. External effectiveness manifests when the team generates outcomes for clients, including the organization. Productivity, innovation, profit or sales, as well as customer satisfaction, learning and creativity are examples of external team effectiveness. Figure 8.2 depicts an ecological model of team effectiveness. It proposes that team effectiveness is a function of the ecology of teams. The internal, organizational, and external environments influence team effectiveness differently.

Team Performance

Team performance refers to the outcomes of teams. As shown in Figure 8.2, team performance comprises internal and external outcomes. Internal outcomes focus on the team as a whole and its members. The extent to which team members learn and the team grows or is viable are performance outcomes. External outcomes focus on clients, including the organization. Examples include productivity, innovation, customer satisfaction, and organizational learning. What factors influence internal and external performance? The outcomes depend on context or environment, tasks, conditions, internal team dynamics, and team and member characteristics.

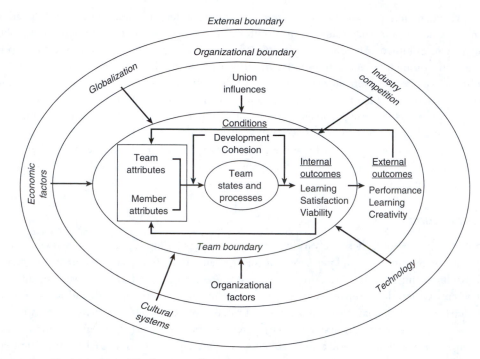

FIGURE 8.2 Ecological Model of Team Effectiveness

Context

Team context refers to the environment of teams. Generally there are two types of environments: internal and external. The internal environment refers to the contextual influences within the team. This context can be nominal (e.g., the room setting in which teams meet) or psychological (the perception of team members about the interactions of team members). Both have the potential to influence team tasks. The external environment is the setting surrounding the internal context of teams. That includes the organizational context and the broader industry, economic, and global environments. What happens in the external context affects not only interactions but also the outcomes of teams.

Team Tasks

Teams are purposeful; they are always set to execute a specific task. There are several tasks that teams usually execute. They have been categorized into eight major types based on generation, choice, negotiation, and execution functions.[6] Generation tasks include planning and creativity where teams come up with plans and ideas. Choice tasks include intellective and decision-making where teams solve problems with correct answers or decide issues with no correct answer. Negotiation tasks include cognitive conflict which involves resolving conflicts of viewpoints, and mixed-motive which involves resolving conflicts of interest. Contests or competitive tasks include resolving conflicts of power while psycho–motor or performance tasks include executing performance tasks.

Conditions

Conditions are situations that affect team effectiveness.[7] Five major conditions include the extent to which the team is *real* (i.e., there are tasks, clear boundaries, clearly assigned authority to make team decisions, and membership stability); has a *compelling direction* (clear, challenging, and conse-quential goals that focus on the ends to be accomplished); has an *enabling structure* (the team's task, composition, and norms of conduct enable rather than impede teamwork); has a *supportive organi-zational context* (whether the team receives adequate resources, rewards, information, education, intergroup cooperation, and support that members need to accomplish their tasks), and has *expert coaching* (availability of a competent coach to help team members deal with potential issues or existing problems). These conditions determine the degree to which a team achieves its goals. They also affect the dynamics of the team.

Team Dynamics

Changes in the internal and external environments of teams also affect team interactions and task execution. The development of teams discussed above reflects changes in team interactions. There are therefore developmental and environmental dynamics. As we discussed above, the transitions affect team interactions and tasks. When there are organizational or other changes, the performance of teams can also change. Team dynamics may be natural or ascribed. In the former, exit and entry of team members affects the progression of teams. In the latter, teams deliberately examine the factors (inputs and process) that either inhibited or enhanced their effectiveness. This is sometimes called feedback or control. Ascribed dynamics are internal when they occur within the internal environment but external when they occur within the external environment. The ecological dynamics are shown by the feedback loops in the external and internal environments.

Determinants

There are a number of factors that influence team effectiveness (see Figure 8.2). The major ones are team member characteristics and team characteristics. Team member characteristics focus on the attributes of individual team members. For example, the personality of team members can affect team performance. Teams composed of emotionally unstable individuals tend to have different outcomes from those composed of conscientious individuals. Attitudes (e.g., commitment, involvement, satisfaction, and identification) of team members also affect performance of teams. Third, the skills or competencies of team members which are instrumental to task execution also affect performance. Teams composed of more competent individuals are likely to have increased productivity, creativity, and innovation in contrast to those composed of less competent indivi-duals. Finally, demographic characteristics such as gender, age, and education influence team performance.

The characteristics of teams that affect performance include size, structure, and leadership. Diverse teams perform differently and sometimes more effectively than homogeneous teams. Small teams also tend to be more effective than large teams. Using small teams, generally between 10 and 12 members, will help ensure success because coordination, cooperation, and communication are easier. Teams with flexible or organic structures also differ in performance from inorganic or rigid teams. Finally, leaderless or self-autonomous teams interact differently and therefore yield out-comes that arguably are less than those with leaders. As discussed above, leadership is a condition that facilitates team effectiveness. It must be noted that environmental factors—unions, organiza-tion, economic state, globalization, technology, and industry can also influence team effectiveness.

Building High Performance Teams

Since most work is organized around teams, it is important that these teams perform very well. Organizations diversify team membership to harness the advantage of heterogeneity and to build high performance teams. Having members with different backgrounds can help improve team effectiveness because people bring varied expertise and different viewpoints. One should remember that the number of people in the team depends also on the nature of the tasks. But generally, a small number may ensure the critical mass for effectiveness. The right people should also be selected, trained, and properly compensated. Goals should be clear and communication should be fostered. Providing teams with challenging assignments is often stimulating and can lead to high performance.

Teams and African Organizations

Teams are important devices for African organizations for two major reasons. First, their productivities are not as high as competitors from Europe, America, and Asia. By harnessing the talents of employees in teams, African organizations can increase creativity, innovation, and performance. For example, customer service which seems "alien" to African organizations can be enhanced through customer service teams. The second reason is that African organizations would not have difficulties adopting team-based structures. Teams are collectivistic. Their structures therefore fit with the culture of African countries. Using teams should therefore be easy; it simply requires establishment of team structures. It also requires managing the negatives of teams such as free riding and social loafing.

Summary

In this chapter we have discussed groups and teams. We defined and differentiated both. In addition, we identified the types of teams that are observed in African organizations. Further, we discussed the effectiveness of teams by considering the antecedents, processes, outcomes, and contingencies or moderators. The dynamics of teams including development process were also discussed.

■ Individual Learning Questions

1. What is the difference between teams and groups?
2. What are the elements of the team effectiveness model?

■ Group Discussion Questions

1. Using the systems view, discuss the types of effectiveness of teams you have encountered.
2. What were the dynamics of teams you may have experienced?
3. How can team effectiveness be improved?
4. What types of teams would you recommend for your organization?

Exercise 8.1: Case Study

LIQUORIDE, a progressive company with a reputation for seeing projects through, and a market leader in the liquor industry in an East African country, wanted to establish a new team-based organization on the assembly line of one of its plants. The decision was based on benchmarking which indicated that a better level of performance could only be achieved with people with higher skill levels and a team-based work organization. After negotiations with the union, solicitation of suggestions, establishment of structural changes, allocation of resources for training, and a competency audit that identified high-skilled individuals from the shop floor, the company selected some individuals to pilot the new team-based form of work organization on one of the assembly lines before all the other lines were also re-organized into teams. The selected individuals were taken off normal production for several months and given extensive training in machine operation, process quality and performance maintenance, interpersonal skills, and the principles of world class manufacturing. The selected individuals were rewarded as individuals for their pilot roles. As part of the team-based structure, they were expected to be rewarded as teams.

The 80 employees on the pilot line were divided into five shift-based teams to run the line on a 24/7 schedule. Maintenance and quality staff were incorporated into the shift teams, and problem-solving as well as shift hand-over meetings were introduced. Team members were certified to run all the machines according to the operating procedures, as well as to perform basic quality and maintenance checks in their section. The teams themselves determined their work allocation. The teams dealt with any production problems that occurred on the spot, if possible. Problems that could not be resolved immediately were resolved at team meetings. Improvement recommendations were logged and followed up until implemented or escalated up to a multidisciplinary team at the next higher level of management for resolution.

Team leadership which initially was executed by the line manager was now determined by the teams. Shift hand-over meetings between team leaders were instituted to facilitate communication between teams. The team members and work processes took time to flow and naturally disagreements and conflicts within and outside of the teams seemed common. However, when they resolved the conflicts, the team members assumed their new responsibilities with grace. Regular team meetings were held to discuss performance review and process improvement. The teams identified performance "gaps" and proposed solutions or the need for more information. The responsibility for resolving each gap was assigned to team members, with the status discussed at further meetings until it was resolved. After a year of establishing the new team-based organization, plant efficiency and other indicators of effectiveness had improved substantially.

Questions

1. What types of teams were set up at Liquoride Company Ltd?
2. How did the teams develop?
3. Using a systems view, discuss the effectiveness of Liquoride's teams.
4. What role would organizational systems (e.g., HR) play in enhancing the effectiveness of the teams?

Exercise 8.2: Self-Assessment Exercise

Purpose

This self-assessment exercise is designed to help you identify your preferred roles in meetings and similar activities.

Instructions

Read each statement below and circle the response that you believe best reflects your position regarding that statement. When you have finished, use the scoring key to calculate your results for each team role. Choose among five categories: Does not describe me at all (1); Does not describe me very well (2); Describes me somewhat (3); Describes me well (4); Describes me very well (5).

Team Roles Preferences Scale

1. I usually take responsibility for getting the team to agree on what the meeting should accomplish.   1   2   3   4   5
2. I tend to summarize to other team members what the team has accomplished so far.   1   2   3   4   5
3. I am usually the person who helps other team members overcome their disagreements.   1   2   3   4   5
4. I try to ensure that everyone gets heard on issues.   1   2   3   4   5
5. I am usually the person who helps the team determine how to organize the discussion.   1   2   3   4   5
6. I praise other team members for their ideas more than do others in the meetings.   1   2   3   4   5
7. People tend to rely on me to keep track of what has been said in the meetings.   1   2   3   4   5
8. The team typically counts on me to prevent debates from getting out of hand.   1   2   3   4   5
9. I tend to say things that make the group feel optimistic about its accomplishments.   1   2   3   4   5
10. Team members usually count on me to give everyone a chance to speak.   1   2   3   4   5
11. In most meetings, I am less likely than others to put down the ideas of teammates.   1   2   3   4   5
12. I actively help teammates resolve their differences in meetings.   1   2   3   4   5
13. I actively encourage quiet team members to describe their ideas on each issue.   1   2   3   4   5
14. People tend to rely on me to clarify the purpose of the meeting.   1   2   3   4   5
15. I like to be the person who takes notes or minutes of the meeting.   1   2   3   4   5

Scoring Key for Team Roles Preferences

Write your circled score for each statement on the appropriate line below (statement numbers are in parentheses), and add the numbers for each role category.

Encourager   _____ + _____ + _____ = _____
           (6)   (9)   (11)

Gatekeeper   _____ + _____ + _____ = _____
           (4)   (10)   (13)

Harmonizer   _____ + _____ + _____ = _____
           (3)   (8)   (12)

Initiator   _____ + _____ + _____ = _____
           (1)   (5)   (14)

Summarizer   _____ + _____ + _____ = _____
           (2)   (7)   (15)

Encourager. People who score high on this role (10 points or above) have a strong tendency to praise and support the ideas of other team members.

Gatekeeper. People who score high (10 points or above) have a strong tendency to encourage other team members to participate in discussions.

Harmonizer. People who score high (10 points or above) have a strong tendency to mediate intragroup conflicts and reduce tension.

Initiator. People who score high (10 points or above) have a strong tendency to identify goals for meetings, including ways to work on goals.

Summarizer. People who score high (10 points or above) have a strong tendency to keep track of what was said in meetings (act as the team's memory).

9

DECISION MAKING

Overview

By the end of this chapter you should be able to:

- Explain the decision making process
- Describe the rational decision making model
- Describe the bounded rationality model
- Explain decision heuristics and errors
- Describe group decision making techniques
- Explore the role of culture in decision making

Nature of the Decision-Making Process

Decision making pervades everyday life. We make decisions concerning when to get out of bed, when to eat, when to watch TV or use our home computer. In organizations, managers and employees make decisions constantly. Thus, decision making is considered as the essence of the manager's job. A decision is defined as a choice between two or more alternatives.[1] Any time a person selects between two or more alternatives, he/she is making a decision. To better understand this process in organizations, we will start with the notions of *objectives* or *standards* and *problems*. In organizations, decisions are often made to solve problems.[2]

Defining a Problem

Several conditions must happen for a manager to have a problem. First, there should be a standard or a norm. Second, there should be a difference between the actual performance and the standard. Third, the person should be aware of this gap. Fourth, the person should be motivated to reduce the gap. If these four conditions are met, then the person has a problem. Let's assume that there is a gap between the norm and the actual result, but the person is not motivated to reduce it. Then, we assume that the person does not face a problem. In work settings, managers encounter problems when they observe a gap between actual results and expected results. They should also have the resources to reduce the gap and be under some time pressure to do so. Managers cannot solve a problem unless they have the resources to do so. Asking managers to solve a problem without giving them the resources needed to solve it is like putting them under undue pressure to perform.

Types of Problems

Managers encounter several types of problems. The types of problems managers face determine the type of decisions they make. Generally, problems are either well structured or poorly structured. Each type of problem calls for different types of decision.

Well-Structured Problems and Programmed Decisions

Well-structured problems are those for which the existing state and desired state are clearly identified, and the methods to reach the desired state are fairly obvious. When problems are well structured, managers make programmed decisions.[3] Decisions are programmed to the extent that they are repetitive and routine and a definite approach has been worked out for handling them. There are three guidelines that help to solve well-structured problems. They include procedures, rules, and policies. A procedure is a series of interrelated sequential steps that can be used to respond to a well-structured problem. A rule is an explicit statement that tells managers what they can or cannot do. A policy is a guideline that establishes parameters for making decisions. These guidelines enable managers to easily make decisions involving structured problems.

Poorly-Structured Problems and Non-programmed Decisions

Poorly-structured problems are problems that are new or unusual and for which information is ambiguous or incomplete. When problems are poorly structured, managers rely on non-programmed decisions.[4] Non-programmed decisions are unique and non-recurring. The ambiguity suggests that managers make decisions in one of three conditions: certainty, risk, or uncertainty. A condition of certainty refers to a situation in which a manager can make accurate decisions because all outcomes are known. A risky condition involves those decisions in which the decision maker is not able to estimate the likelihood of the decision outcomes. An uncertain condition refers to a situation in which a decision maker has neither certainty nor reasonable probability estimates available. We discuss two models of the decision-making process: the rational model and the bounded rationality model.

The Rational Model of Decision Making

The rational model proposes that decision makers attempt to optimize solutions.[5] The best solution is the one that maximizes the outcome. Under this model, decision makers have all information needed and all alternatives are available. A rational decision therefore is one that yields the maximum payoff for the decision maker. In using the rational decision making model, the decision maker seeks to optimize by following a series of steps (see Table 9.1). The rational model considers the decision-making process as a six-step process.[6]

The decision making process begins with the existence of a problem. As stated earlier, a problem is a discrepancy between a desired state and an existing state. The person should be aware of the discrepancy and be willing to do something about it. In management, managers and

TABLE 9.1 Steps in the Rational Model of Decision Making

1. Define the problem.
2. Identify the decision criteria.
3. Allocate weights to the criteria.
4. Develop the alternatives.
5. Evaluate the alternatives.
6. Select the best alternative.

employees alike can identify problems. For instance, when managers realize that there is a discrepancy between what was expected and the actual results, they may consider this as a problem. Problem identification is also subjective. What one manager considers as a problem may not be considered as such by another manager. The problem identification step is important because "an excellent solution to a false problem is a false solution."

Once the decision maker has identified the problem, he/she must identify the decision criteria. The decision criteria are the parameters that the decision maker will consider when making a choice. For instance, he/she must decide what is important and relevant in selecting a given alternative. In buying a new laptop, an example of criteria could include the brand, the capacity of the laptop, or the model. Once the criteria have been identified, the decision maker will assign weight to each of them. Some criteria may carry more weight than others depending on the expectations and situation of the decision maker. The decision maker will then develop several alternatives or options or potential choices. He/she will evaluate these alternatives to determine which one to select. The final step in the decision-making process according to the rational model is to select the best alternative, that is the option that yields the maximum payoff for the decision maker.

The rational model of decision making relies on several assumptions. It assumes that the decision maker has complete information. It also assumes that the decision maker is able to identify all the relevant options, is not biased, and is able to select the alternative that has the highest utility.[7] The rational model also assumes that the decision maker's preferences are clear and do not change over time and he/she is not under time constraints. Despite these assumptions, we all know that in "real life" people do not always follow the rational model of decision making. Very often, people make decisions based on limited information and under severe time and resource constraints. The rational model of decision making is limited in that decision makers have vested personal interest in the decisions they make, they can block out negative information. In addition, mental models blind people from seeing opportunities over weighing alternatives objectively. People also may suffer from a lack of motivation to diagnose problems, and may have a tendency to define problems in terms of their solutions. Thus, decision makers tend to rely on the bounded rationality model.

The Bounded Rationality Model

Herbert Simon,[8] who won the Nobel Prize in Economics in 1978, introduced the construct of bounded rationality to explain the extent to which human nature limits our ability to make rational decisions. According to the bounded rationality model, because decision makers cannot have all the information needed, they tend to select the alternative, which is good enough. Because of people's limited ability to process information, they work within a simplified model.

According to Simon, decision makers make *satisficing* decisions instead of optimal decisions. He further argues that satisficing can be increased by setting higher standards, by personal determination, and by the availability of sophisticated management and computer tools. The bounded rationality model is a descriptive model insofar as it describes how people actually make decisions. When confronted with complex choices, people tend to reduce this complexity into a manageable set of options and criteria that they can understand and use to make a decision that is acceptable. The goal in the bounded rationality model is not to optimize but to make a decision that is good enough and that can be accepted. The bounded rationality model describes not only how we make decisions as individuals but also how managers make decisions in organizations.

Decision Making Styles

Individuals tend to use four types of styles in making decisions. They include directive, analytical, conceptual, and behavioral.

Directive Style

A directive style is a decision style characterized by low tolerance for ambiguity and a rational way of thinking. People with this style are efficient and logical. They make fast decisions and focus on the short term. They use minimum information and assess few alternatives.

Analytical Style

This is a decision-making style characterized by a high tolerance for ambiguity and a rational way of thinking. People with analytical styles prefer to have more information before making a decision and consider more alternatives than a directive-style decision maker does. They are careful decision makers who are able to cope with unique situations.

Conceptual Style

Individuals with the conceptual decision-making style tend to be broad and look at many alternatives. They focus on the long run and tend to be good at finding creative solutions to problems.

Behavioral Style

Individuals with this decision-making style tend to work well with others. They are receptive to suggestions from others. They tend to be concerned about the acceptance of the decision by others.

Group Decision Making

Groups also make decisions. What then is group decision making? It refers to the process by which two or more people working together on a problem make a decision. Teamwork, an important means for increasing productivity and innovation in organizations, involves group decision making. What are the advantages of group decision making? One advantage is pooling of resources. The capabilities of group members are harnessed to optimize resolution of a problem. Group decision making also profits from specialization of labor. When decisions are made in groups, there is a greater chance for the decision to be accepted by members. However, group decision making has some disadvantages. First, it is time consuming. Second, sometimes the decision reflects the will of the dominant members even though they may be the minority. In a group, there may also be some pressure to conform (groupthink) and responsibility may be ambiguous. There may also be intimidation from group leaders. The recommended techniques below help to minimize the problems in group decision making.

Brainstorming

Brainstorming is a group decision-making technique in which 6 to 12 people meet together. It is an idea generating technique.[9] The process involves three stages. First, each member's ideas are recorded. Each group member is required to generate as many ideas as possible. There is no criticism of the ideas generated and each member is encouraged to participate. Second, the generated ideas are recorded by a team member, sometimes the team leader. Third, members build on the ideas that are generated to increase the pool. The goal is to generate as many ideas as possible. Although brainstorming helps generate many ideas and requires participation from group members, those group members who are shy may not participate as much. To encourage everyone therefore, some authors prefer the nominal group technique.

Nominal Group Technique

The nominal group technique is used to generate ideas. Members meet as a group and are presented with a problem. Each member presents one idea on a piece of paper. The group discusses the ideas and evaluates them. The group ranks the ideas. The idea with the highest rank is selected.[10] The nominal group technique helps everyone to participate in generating ideas. Even group members who are shy can contribute. However, since group members are not identified when they generate ideas, it is not possible to reward outstanding contributions.

Delphi Technique

The Delphi technique improves upon the brainstorming and nominal group techniques by using expert opinions.[11] Expert opinions are solicited by mail and the answers are analyzed. Usually, a consensus from the experts serves as a basis for the final decision. In applying the Delphi technique, the problem should first be identified. Then a questionnaire is developed and mailed to experts. This implies that the decision makers know who the experts are or can identify them. The experts complete the questionnaires and return them. The results are analyzed. Group members receive copies of the results. When a consensus is reached among the experts, then group members make a decision based on the consensus. However, if there is no consensus among the experts, the process starts over.

Electronic Meeting

The electronic meeting is a modern version of the nominal group technique.[12] Individuals from different locations meet together via telephone or satellite transmissions. They may use a shared space on a monitor screen. In this type of meeting, up to 50 people sit around computer terminals. Responses to issues are typed on computers and projected on a screen. The advantages of the electronic meeting include anonymity, honesty, and speed. One of the disadvantages of electronic meetings is the inability to reward participants for their ideas. This limitation also occurs in the nominal group technique.

Errors and Biases in Decision Making

Human decisions are subject to errors. Potential causes of errors in decision making include decision heuristics. A heuristic is a short cut. In making decisions, humans tend to use short cuts. These short cuts in fact bias the decisions.

Availability Heuristic

Availability heuristic refers to the tendency for individuals to base their judgments on readily available, though potentially inaccurate, information.[13] By focusing on readily available information, we ignore potentially important information that may affect the decision. For instance, if we hear about a plane crash, we are afraid of flying because we assume that a future plane crash is likely. This bias occurs because it tends to arouse some types of emotional reactions. The psychology of human emotions teaches us that events that evoke emotions tend to be vivid in our memory compared to those that do not evoke emotions. Similarly, events that are more recent tend to be readily available in our memory. This short cut, however, does lead to errors.

Representativeness Heuristic

Representativeness heuristic refers to the tendency to perceive others in stereotypical ways.[14] When a negotiator compares two conflicts or parties perceived to be similar, they are using one to represent the other. The problem with this is that no two conflicts or parties are the same or similar in all characteristics. For example, when a negotiator perceives a Nigerian to be similar to a Kenyan merely because they are both Africans, he/she ignores differences such as backgrounds, socializations, and motivations.

Escalation of Commitment Heuristic

Escalation of commitment is the tendency to increase commitment to a decision in spite of evidence that it is wrong.[15] It consists of sticking to a decision even though the evidence shows that it is wrong. An interesting question then is why do people engage in escalation of commitment? The simple answer is that people escalate their commitment to a given course of action that is arguably failing to preserve their self-esteem and to convince themselves that they made the right choice in the first place. Imagine that you are a manager in a reputable organization. You decide to pour your unit's resources into a new project. Of course, you would be personally attached to the project because it is your pet project. Despite the lack of success, your initial reaction would be to continue the project. Discontinuing it would make you look bad in the eyes of your boss. Other reasons for escalation of commitment include vested resources, such as time, money, and personnel; hope of future validation; tacit constituent prods; leadership, culture, and organizational processes.

Anchoring Bias

The anchoring bias consists of using early, first received information as the basis for making subsequent judgments.[16] This is considered a heuristic that helps the individual reduce the cognitive effort involved in the decision-making process. For instance, a manager would make an anchoring bias when he/she uses the previous pay of a job applicant to set his/her future pay. It occurs because the human mind tends to give a disproportionate amount of emphasis to the first information it receives than to the later.

Confirmation Bias

Most people tend to think that they are rational decision makers. Research and experience show that this is far from true. Most of the time, when we make decisions or weigh alternative courses of action, we have a tendency to favor some over others. Thus, we tend to look for additional information that could confirm our favorite choice.[17] In the confirmation bias we seek information that confirms our previous choice and tend to discount information that disproves or contradicts it.

Hindsight Bias

The hindsight bias occurs when after an outcome is already known, we believe that it could have been accurately predicted beforehand.[18] You may be familiar with people who tend to affirm that they knew that something that has already happened was meant to happen. Very often, the hindsight bias prevents people from learning from the past. When people believe that they would have predicted the future, this helps them think that they are better predictors of future events than they actually are.

Overconfidence Bias

Most people believe that they are good at what they do and cannot sway. They tend to overemphasize the quality of their decisions, so much so that they are rarely open to criticism or advice from others. According to Plous, "no problem in judgment and decision making is more prevalent and more potentially catastrophic than overconfidence."[19] In making decisions, people have a general tendency to think that they know the answer or that they have the right information. The overconfidence bias often affects the behaviors of entrepreneurs and the outcome of their ventures. Research has shown that entrepreneurs who are overly confident about the success of their new ventures tend to perform poorly.[20] In fact, the tendency to be overly confident may prevent them from anticipating obstacles and problems that might arise.

Heuristics are a major source of flawed judgments and decision making. In a conflict situation, for example, negotiators have to make quick decisions using multiple and varied information from contexts, parties, and processes so as to prevent escalation of the conflict.

Cultural Differences in Decision Making

Although the decision-making process itself is quite universal, the way people make decisions can vary from culture to culture. The way Africans make decisions may be quite different from that of Americans, Asians, or Europeans. In some cultures, making a decision may require that people take time or consider the interests of those who would be affected by the decision. In other cultures, managerial efficiency would dictate that managers make decisions based on the extent to which such decisions advance the interest of the organization. The cultural background of decision makers can significantly affect their decision-making process or style. It can affect the selection of the problem, the depth of analysis, the importance placed on logic and rationality, and whether decisions should be made autocratically by an individual manager or collectively in groups. For example, managers in Egypt have a tendency to make decisions at a slower and more deliberate pace than managers in the United States. In general, traditional African systems are geared toward consensus decision making. The chieftaincy systems and council of elders often make decisions based on collective agreement of all elders with deference to the chief.

Summary

In this chapter, we have explored the decision-making process and discussed two popular models of decision making, the rational model and the bounded rationality model. We have also discussed the individual styles of making decisions and group decision making. In making decisions, people often rely on heuristics that affect the quality of their choices. Such heuristics were explained as errors in the decision-making process. We concluded the chapter by acknowledging the role of culture in the decision-making process.

■ Group Discussion Questions

1. Describe the decision-making process and give an example.
2. Contrast the rational model and the bounded rationality model.
3. Explain why people rely on heuristics in making decisions.
4. Explain how you think Westerners differ in their decision-making process compared to Africans.

Exericise 9.1: Case Study

You are the country director for an antiretroviral therapy (ARV) program. Your country has been providing for people living with HIV/AIDS for the past 10 years. Initial negotiations with drug manufacturers resulted in a significant discount in the cost of ARVs. However, the resources needed for ARVs have begun to rise, in large part because of the high cost of second line therapy. As first line therapy has failed for many people living with HIV/AIDS, you have had to purchase brand name second line therapy, at a cost of $10,000 per person per year. Meanwhile, the country's primary source of external funding for its antiretroviral program has recently announced that it is planning to withdraw all of its funds from your country within the next two years, due to its greater emphasis on the HIV/AIDS epidemic in other emerging countries. As a result, the sustainability of your program is in danger.

As the director, you are responsible for developing a presentation which defines the problem and provides clear solutions to the country's problems. You should present data, if possible, regarding the current situation. You should also present the information that your country will need to collect over the next two years in order to ensure that you are achieving your goals. Finally, you should present options for assuring the sustainability of ARVs in your country.

Questions

1. What is the problem?
2. What are the alternatives?
3. Outline your plan to sustain the country's HIV/AIDS program.

Exercise 9.2: Nuclear Catastrophe

Imagine that you are involved in a nuclear catastrophe. There is a fallout shelter but it will only support life for **six** people over the required length of time. There are 10 people in the group. Your task is to first choose the **six** people who will probably be the sole survivors of this tragedy and will start a new civilization. After reading the list of the 10 people, do the following:

1. Individually select six people to save.
2. Form a group of three participants and make a *final selection* of six people. If your initial selection does not agree with that of your group members, negotiate with them to come to an agreement.
3. Report your findings to the class.
4. Discuss the implications of this exercise for project management.

The 10 People

1. A 78-year-old Rabbi. He is a venerable old man who is healthy despite his age.
2. A 28-year-old ex-policeman who was dismissed from the police for using excessive brutality.
3. A 17-year-old female high school dropout. She has been diagnosed as marginally retarded. She is two months pregnant.
4. A 37-year-old violinist. It has been rumored that he is homosexual, but this is not definitely known.
5. A 33-year-old female who is a retired prostitute.
6. An 18-year-old male activist college student.
7. A 39-year-old female medical doctor. For medical reasons, she is unable to have children.
8. A 25-year-old male law student who is married.
9. A 23-year-old female teacher. She is married to #8. She has been diagnosed with terminal leukemia, which is presently in remission. She and her husband have agreed that one will not go into the shelter without the other.
10. A 35-year-old male architect who has been charged but not convicted of selling drugs.

Duration: 15 minutes

10

UNDERSTANDING CONFLICT IN AFRICAN ORGANIZATIONS

Overview

In this chapter we examine conflict in the workplace. We discuss the antecedents, processes, and consequence of workplace conflict. We also discuss the various ways by which conflict is often managed in organizations. By the end of this chapter you should be able to:

- Explain the nature and causes of conflict
- Describe the consequences of conflict
- Identify your own conflict resolution style
- Describe different conflict resolution strategies

Nature of Conflict

Conflicts are so pervasive in African societies that it can be confusing to understand workplace conflict which centers on interpersonal relations between employees. A conflict is a process in which one party perceives that another has (or is about to take) some action that will exert a negative effect on its major interest.[1] Characteristics of a conflict include opposing interests between individuals or groups, recognition of such opposition, belief by each side that the other will take detrimental actions, and actions that produce detrimental effects. There are different types of conflict as well as various causes of conflict. The relationship between the levels and types of conflict are summarized in Figure 10.1 below. Within the internal and external environments are different levels of conflict that relate to African organizations. Across those levels are three major types of conflict.

Types of Conflict

Due to the diverse interests, perceptual errors, and limited cognitive capacity of individuals conflicts occur every time and everywhere.[2] Within organizations, there are conflicts between employers and employees; producers and suppliers; retailers and customers; and investors and entrepreneurs. For example, conflicts between employers and employees may be over compensation, health benefits, working conditions, motivational incentives, productivity, promotion, and

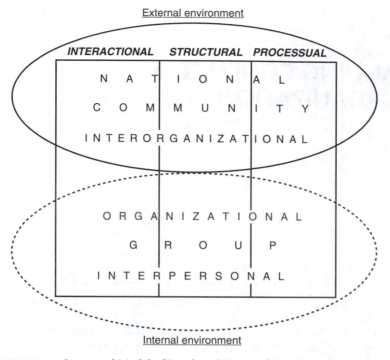

FIGURE 10.1 Integrated Model of Levels and Types of Conflict Related to African Organizations

career. Conflicts between producers and suppliers may focus on quality of raw materials supplied, late delivery of raw materials, and late payments for materials received.

Organizational conflicts are described as structural, interactional, and processual.[3] *Structural conflict* refers to disagreements that result from the structural characteristics of organizations (e.g., who has authority, power, resources, responsibility, accountability; how work is done and how often). In these types of conflicts, one party (usually an employee) perceives that the structure of the organization constrains his/her aspirations or goals. Instead of working with a manager that has interest in his/her career, he/she is assigned to a manager who instead may hurt his/her career. Role and task conflicts also fall within this category. *Interaction conflicts* refer to all conflicts that arise from interactions of employees. The status differences which specify interaction patterns may lead to interpersonal, intragroup, and intergroup conflicts between employees. Behaviors and attitudes which derive from employee interactions (e.g., attendance, commitment) also create interpersonal and intergroup conflict between employees.

Process conflict relates to conflict that arises from business processes of organizations (management, operations, and support). Business processes are embedded with interdependencies, resource limitations, and differentiation. Conflicts related to effective governance of organizations often exist between executives and board members. Conflicts on appropriate strategies are common in organizations. Purchasing conflicts (types, quality, and time of materials to purchase) are also very common within organizations. Supporting business processes such as accounting and human resources are also embedded with conflicts. Accounting conflicts on what to report and not report as well as how to report are often negotiated between executives and accountants. What type of talent to acquire and how to reward the talent are conflicts that human resource managers have to negotiate with executives or other managers. Procedural conflicts (i.e., how to execute a task or project) fall within this category.

Levels of Conflict

Organizational conflict has different levels categorized as internal and external.[4] Conflicts within the internal environments occur at the intrapersonal, interpersonal, intragroup, and intergroup levels while those that occur in external environments include interorganizational, community, tribal, ethnic, and national levels. *Interpersonal* conflict occurs between individuals (e.g., workers, spouses, siblings, roommates, or neighbors). Unlike individualist cultures where people can isolate themselves from society or the community, collectivist cultures such as those of Africa are characterized by high levels of interaction; members cannot isolate themselves from others. Thus perceived cognitive, affective, and behavioral differences are likely to be high.

Intragroup conflict at this level occurs *within a group* (i.e., among members of a work group or team and within families, classes, and networks). It differs from interpersonal conflict in that it does not extend beyond members of the group (i.e., interconnected and interdependent members who have a common purpose). Too often the ability of a group to work effectively, achieve goals, make decisions, resolve differences, develop and promote each other, and share resources is negatively affected by intragroup conflict.

Intergroup conflict occurs between groups (e.g., departments, divisions, and subsidiaries) within an organization. Some experts include organizations, nations, ethnic groups, and communities within this level. However, conflict here is viewed as between small groups within organizations. Disagreements between functions and divisions often arise as a result of differentiation of expertise, roles, and goals as well as resource scarcity.

Functional and Dysfunctional Conflicts

Organizational conflicts can be functional or dysfunctional.[5] *Functional* conflict yields positive outcomes for organizations. To some extent, functional conflicts can contribute to employee self-development (they learn to devise solutions or problem-solving skills; recognize their weaknesses, and control their own lives), group creativity, shared understanding, cohesion, and leadership; and organizational innovation, learning, change, and adaptation. *Dysfunctional* conflict refers to disagreements that yield negative outcomes such as chaos, insecurity, and hostility. Dysfunctional conflicts slow workflow because of delays in production. They also affect quality of products, limit creativity and innovation, and tend to be costly. Anecdotal evidence suggests that conflict in Africa is likely to be skewed toward dysfunctionality. Traditional societies do not use conflict as a means of development; rather, they view it as integral to interactions.

Conflict Process

How does conflict emerge? A model of the conflict emergence process is shown in Figure 10.2. Conflict is a process that begins with the characteristics of conflicting parties (personality, attitude, behaviors, as well as interests, motivations, and goals).[6] These characteristics influence perceptions (individual and group) which in turn affect the reaction of the parties. The reactions also determine escalation (increase or decrease) of the conflict. De-escalated conflicts are resolved whereas escalated conflicts spiral. Resolutions often emerge after escalation.

Party Characteristics

The cognitive, affective, and behavioral tendencies of individuals and groups often serve as the foundation for conflict emergence. The thinking, knowledge, expertise, mental models, of individuals not only influence how they perceive others but also how others perceive them.

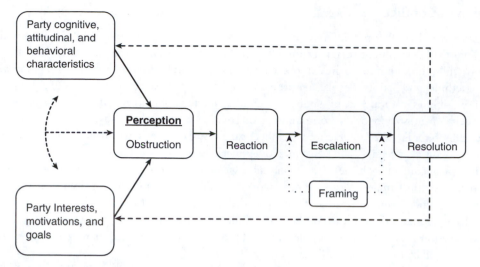

FIGURE 10.2   Conflict Process

In addition, their likes and dislikes as well as emotional involvement in tasks, roles, groups, and processes also influence how they perceive others. Third, what parties do can also initiate conflict. For instance, if a subordinate comes to work late when punctuality is critical, that behavior might be perceived as obstructing the goals of the department or organization.

Interests, Motivations, and Goals

Individuals, groups, and organizations usually have interests, motivations, and goals (IMGs) the pursuit of which is often viewed as central to self-enhancement. These IMGs tend to drive the attitudes and behaviors of individuals and groups; they act to fulfill them. As a result, IMGs influence how employees view relations or interactions with others as well as tasks they have to accomplish, processes they must endure, and procedures they have to follow. IMGs are so fundamental to individuals and groups because they are associated with self-identity and self-development.

The IMGs of Africans tend to be collective because members are part of the community to which they belong. They see their identities and development as integrally linked to those of the collective. Consequently, they think, behave, and orient themselves toward collective goals and interests.

Perception

The process of acquiring, interpreting, selecting, and organizing sensory information about characteristics (attitudes, personality, and goals), interests and goals of individuals, groups and organizations, is critical to conflict. We saw in chapter 3, on perception that perception is related to the motivations, attitudes, and behavior of individuals. It also affects how individuals relate to tasks, other employees, and groups as well as assessment of obstruction (and therefore conflict) and facilitation. Perception determines how individuals react to a situation, event, or person.

Reaction

Reaction refers to the response of an individual or group to a perceived threat. Typical reactions include leaving things as they are (i.e., status quo), ignoring the conflict, and resisting or challenging the threat. Thus, reaction ranges from passive to active forms and may be positive (i.e., viewing the threat favorably) or negative (viewing the threat unfavorably). Unlike positive reactions, negative reactions aggravate the conflict. Neutral (indifference) reactions are also possible. Traditional African behaviors often influence how individuals react to conflict. For example, chiefs and elders (supervisors, managers, and executives in an organization) are often slow to react because of the socialization that requires seniors to be less impulsive.

Escalation

Escalation refers to the tendency of a conflict to aggravate as a result of entrenched positions of disagreeing parties.[7] It includes situations where a conflict does not worsen but rather ebbs. Thus, it ranges from de-escalation to escalation. When both parties react positively to perceived obstruction, a conflict de-escalates immediately as a consequence. When one party reacts negatively to the obstruction and the other party reacts positively the conflict also de-escalates. However, the conflict escalates when both parties react negatively; it spirals in that situation. Spiraling conflicts are difficult to resolve.

Resolution

When conflict emerges and is not dowsed immediately, it has to be resolved before it becomes a dispute.[8] Conflicts can be resolved by the parties through one of several mechanisms including mediation, arbitration, negotiation, and court action. Their resolution depends on what the parties want: immediate outcomes or building relationships. Parties who prefer outcomes approach conflict resolution differently from those who prefer relationship building. Conflict resolution is therefore one aspect of conflict management; it involves understanding the causes and outcomes in addition to the process discussed here.

Causes of Workplace Conflict

There are several factors that can lead to conflict within organizations. Such factors include the task, the individual, the group as well as the organization. We explore the role of each of these factors in the occurrence of organizational factors.

Organizational Causes of Conflict

Organizational factors that lead to conflict include competition over scarce resources, ambiguity over responsibility, uncertainty about tasks, ambiguity over jurisdiction, and uncertainty about authority.[9] These factors lead employees and managers alike to experience conflict. When an employee lacks clear information about his/her responsibility within the company, this may create a conflict not only at the employee's level but also with colleagues. The organization or management may be the target of such conflict. The structure, culture, strategy, and change processes of organizations lead to conflict among operatives, managers, or both.

Group Causes of Conflict

Conflict is integral to teams, as indicated by team development models. For example, Tuckman's model of team development has a storming stage that is characterized by conflict. Conflict is not limited only to the development process; it pervades and emerges from all aspects of group activities, states, and processes including member attributes, team processes, and contextual factors. With regard to member attributes, personality, worldview, and mental programming differences, as well as experiences and biases, affect conflict emergence. Team processes such as communication, cooperation, and coordination are also sources of conflict. Some members' style of communication, cooperation patterns, and coordinative skills tend to conflict with those of other team members. The inability of teams to cohere and to have common understanding constrains team performance, which frustrates some members. Team leadership characterized by ingroup–outgroup tendencies (e.g., the least preferred co-worker approach) also alienates some members and creates intragroup friction. Lastly, the group context tends to create disagreements particularly for members who are either not used to or prefer not to work in groups.

Interpersonal Causes of Conflict

Interpersonal causes of conflict refer to factors related to individuals that lead to conflict. Such factors include faulty attributions, faulty communication, destructive criticism, and naïve realism. Faulty attributions are errors concerning the causes attributed to others' behavior, whereas faulty communication is communication that unintentionally angers or annoys another person. Destructive criticism is negative criticism of others' ideas and naïve realism is a tendency to perceive one's ideas as being more objective than others' ideas. All these affect social exchange in ways that lead to conflict.

Task and Conflict

As we indicated above, teams are purposive; they are formed to execute tasks in a more efficient and effective way. Conflicts usually arise about the tasks either due to ambiguous instructions, mismatch between the demands of the tasks and the team members' capabilities; lack of resources (including time), differences in opinion, viewpoints, and ideas about how and when to accomplish a task. Task conflict differs from relationship conflict, which focuses on the interpersonal orientations of the team members. Thus, task conflict has internal (intrateam) and external (intraorganizational) sources. Teams can therefore effectively handle task conflict by focusing on these two sources.

Consequences of Conflict

The consequences of conflict center on task, personal, group, and organizational levels.[10] Indeed, they sometimes relate to national-level outcomes. There is anecdotal evidence that the Rwandan conflict started at the individual level and spread across groups and organizations to the entire nation. In addition to the negative outcomes (e.g., deaths, vandalism, destruction of property, chaos, or instability) observed at the national level, conflict can also lead to negative reactions such as anger, resentment, and anxiety at the individual level. It may also reduce communication required for coordination, shift from participative to authoritarian styles, enhance negative stereotyping, or emphasize loyalty to one's own group.

Despite these negative consequences, conflict is not always bad. Some conflicts may have positive consequences including bringing into the open problems that have been ignored previously, motivating people to understand each other's position, encouraging new ideas that facilitate innovation and change, improving decision quality by forcing people to challenge their assumptions, and enhancing organizational commitment. As we discussed above, conflicts that lead to positive outcomes are considered functional, whereas conflicts that lead to negative effects are considered dysfunctional.

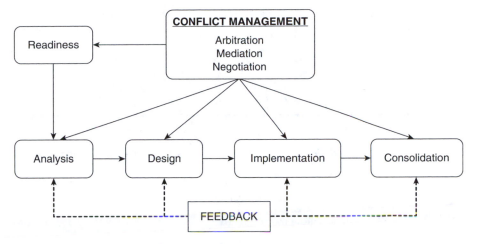

FIGURE 10.3   Conceptual Model of Conflict Management

Managing Conflict

Conflict management refers to the process of determining the cause of conflict, resolving, and evaluating resolution effects. Thus it comprises diagnosis, resolution, and evaluation processes.[11] Whether conducted by individuals, groups, or organizations, conflict management is done in stages. The stages are embedded in the processes shown in Figure 10.3.

In the first stage, actors assess their *readiness* for conflict management. Readiness includes analysis of assessment of commitment, willingness, and preparation of mechanisms for conflict management. The second stage, *analysis*, includes information gathering, minimization of resistance and biases, and solicitation of support from constituents. It refers to appraisal of conflict based on data on the emergence and escalation of conflict. In the *design* stage, actors establish conflict management systems after identifying features and parameters that make them effective. The fourth stage, *implementation*, refers to the execution of conflict management systems. It includes role allocation and backup of actors. Parties involved in conflict management have to know their roles and commencement periods. Backup actors (individuals, groups, organizations) help effectuate conflict management at this stage. The last stage is *consolidation*. Here, actors reinforce conflict management by harnessing processes and outcomes and correcting errors. It includes motivational mechanisms that help to institutionalize conflict management. These stages underlie the diagnosis, resolution, and evaluation processes.

Conflict evaluation refers to the process of appraising conflict and its resolution. It comprises impact and process evaluation. Impact evaluation refers to the examination of conflict outcomes and its impact on the parties involved. The nature of the outcomes (distributive or integrative) and post-resolution relationships are discussed at this stage. Process evaluation seeks to appraise the features and delivery of resolution to conflicting parties. The model suggests evaluation focuses on resolution and diagnosis processes. The dynamism of conflict management is shown by the feedback loop. The model also suggests that there are various systems of conflict management. The major ones include negotiation, third–party intervention, and litigation (see Figure 10.4).

Negotiation

Negotiation, sometimes termed bargaining, is a process in which opposing sides exchange offers, counter-offers, and concessions, either directly or through representatives.[12] If successful, a solution that both parties find acceptable is attained and the conflict is resolved. Negotiation explores

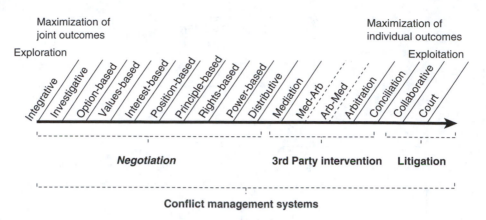

FIGURE 10.4 Conflict Management System

solutions to a conflict and seeks to maximize joint outcomes. However, if bargaining is unsuccessful, a costly deadlock may result and the conflict may even intensify. Parties involved in a negotiation may use several tactics to advance their cause. Some of these tactics include extreme offer, big lie, and misrepresenting one's position on common issues. The perspectives governing the approach to bargaining include win–lose situation (gains by one side are necessarily linked with losses for the other), win–win situation (interests of both sides are not necessarily incompatible and both sides may realize gains) and integrative agreement (offer greater joint benefits than simple compromise). Other approaches to negotiation (see Figure 10.4) include investigative, values-based, option-based, interest-based, position-based, principle-based, rights-based, and power-based. With investigative negotiation, the parties negotiate conflict by investigating, as in police investigations, the cause of the conflict. They also bargain based on values, options to leave or litigate, interests, positions, principles, rights, and power respectively.

Third Party Intervention

When the parties are unable to reach an agreement, they may seek third party intervention. The third party may play the role of a mediator or an arbitrator. A mediator is a third party who does not have the power to impose a decision on the parties involved in the conflict. However, the mediator helps facilitate communication and discussion between the parties. In arbitration, the third party has power to impose or recommend strongly the terms of an agreement. There are generally two types of arbitration, binding arbitration and voluntary arbitration. In binding arbitration, the two sides agree to accept the terms set by the arbitrator, whereas in voluntary arbitration, the two sides retain the freedom to reject the arbitrator's recommendation. Variants of third party intervention include mediation-arbitration (med-arb), and arbitration-mediation (arb-med). In med-arb, the parties mediate first before seeking arbitration. It is the opposite in arb-med. Sometimes, they may also seek conciliation where the intervener meets with the parties separately in an attempt to resolve their differences.

Conflict Resolution Styles

The parties in conflict use different styles to negotiate resolution. Five major styles include avoiding, compromising, competing, collaborating, and accommodating.[13] In using the avoiding style, the individual intends to solve the conflict by avoiding the other party. However, this style does not help to solve the conflict. Avoiding the other party helps keep the conflict dormant but not solved. In the compromising style, each party gives up something but gets something in return. In competing, one party only focuses on the gains expected from the conflict and intends to impose its will on the other party. In the accommodating style, one party tries to solve the conflict by accommodating itself to the will of the other party. It is like giving up one's request to please the other party. Finally, in the collaborating situation, both parties work together to find a common ground. This style is not a compromising style, because the parties do not give up something. Collaborative styles are associated with integrative bargaining while competing styles are associated with distributive bargaining.

Summary

In this chapter we have discussed the workplace conflict system. First, we discussed the nature and emergence of conflict. Second, we identified the various levels, sources, process, and consequences of workplace conflict. We concluded the chapter by discussing conflict management including resolution, negotiation, and third party intervention. We also discussed conflict negotiation styles.

■ Individual Learning Questions

1. What are the levels of workplace conflict?
2. How does conflict affect organizations?
3. What types of conflict are distinctly African?

■ Group Discussion Questions

- Discuss the various types of workplace conflict.
- Discuss how conflict is resolved in the workplace.
- Discuss the conflict management system.

Exercise 10.1: Case Study

Imhonopi Katongole had been a manager at Bakary Studio for 10 years. For most of those years the training program focused mostly on running the cash register, operating machinery, and proper procedures for opening and closing the studio. Katongole's management style focused on creating a comfortable environment for employees. As a result, he had only demanded punctuality and forbade employees to sit down in an area where customers are viewing products. Katongole and his subordinates took great pride in the meticulous look of the studio. A year ago, he learned from a workshop that providing a positive experience to the customer is based on the intuitive appeal of the products based on megapixel size, camera cases ordered by color and material, and film all orderly arranged by shutter speed and brand.

Oyinlola, a recent hire whom all of the customers loved for her deep knowledge of photography and willingness to educate customers on new and creative techniques, had started to come in 25 minutes late on a consistent basis. Katongole had been gently reminding her of the need for punctuality on a nearly daily basis for two weeks now. Every day she came up with a different excuse and promised to get better about it.

After Oyinlola had been there for about three months she started sitting while she took new photos from the picture finishing unit. She was neither sick nor pregnant. The first time Katongole noticed this he mentioned it immediately, telling her, "Oyi, we don't sit down while we're on the clock, especially where the customers can see you so easily." To which Oyinlola replied "I have to walk three miles just to get here because no taxi comes over here. Give me a break, OK?" Katongole walked away stunned and not sure of what to say while Oyinlola was still sitting down.

Katongoles' management and personality style are at odds with his leadership challenge. He has a good employee and dislikes the thought of going through the bother of hiring and training someone who is entirely unlikely to match Oyinlola's technical and people skills. However, he can't simply allow each employee to operate under their own set of rules. In addition, Katalongole feels as though Oyinlola's response was a direct insult to him and a threat to his authority.

Questions

1. What is the conflict between Katongole and Oyinlola?
2. How do personality attributes affect the conflict?
3. What can Katongole do to create a win–win situation?
4. What should Oyinlola do?
5. What should Katongole do?

Exericise 10.2: Self-Assessment Exercise—Conflict Management Style Orientation Scale

Purpose

The purpose of this self-assessment exercise is to help you identify your preferred conflict management style.

Instructions

Read each statement below and circle the response that you believe best reflects your position regarding that statement. Then use the scoring key to calculate your results for each conflict management style. Circle the number that best indicates how well each statement describes you.

	Rarely					Always	
1. If someone disagrees with me, I vigorously defend my side of the issue.	1	2	3	4	5	6	7
2. I go along with suggestions from co-workers even if I don't agree with them.	1	2	3	4	5	6	7
3. I give and take so that a compromise can be reached.	1	2	3	4	5	6	7
4. I keep my opinions to myself rather than openly disagreeing with people.	1	2	3	4	5	6	7
5. In disagreements or negotiations, I try to find the best possible solution for both sides by sharing information.	1	2	3	4	5	6	7
6. I try to reach a middle ground in disputes with other people.	1	2	3	4	5	6	7

7. I accommodate the wishes of people who have points of view different from my own.   1 2 3 4 5 6 7

8. I avoid openly debating issues where there is disagreement.   1 2 3 4 5 6 7

9. In negotiations, I hold on to my position rather than give in.   1 2 3 4 5 6 7

10. I try to solve conflicts by finding solutions that benefit both me and the other person.   1 2 3 4 5 6 7

11. I let co-workers have their way rather than jeopardize our relationship.   1 2 3 4 5 6 7

12. I try to win my opinion in a discussion.   1 2 3 4 5 6 7

13. I like to investigate conflicts with co-workers so that we can discover solutions that benefit both of us.   1 2 3 4 5 6 7

14. I believe that it is not worth the time and trouble discussing my differences of opinion with other people.   1 2 3 4 5 6 7

15. To reach an agreement, I give up some things in exchange for others.   1 2 3 4 5 6 7

Scoring Key

Write your circled score for each statement on the appropriate line (statement numbers are in parentheses), and add the numbers for each style category. Higher scores indicate that you are stronger in that conflict management style.

Competing   _____ + _____ + _____ = _____
                     (1)   (9)   (12)

Accommodating   _____ + _____ + _____ = _____
                     (2)   (7)   (11)

Compromising   _____ + _____ + _____ = _____
                     (3)   (6)   (15)

Avoiding   _____ + _____ + _____ = _____
                     (4)   (8)   (14)

Collaborating   _____ + _____ + _____ = _____
                     (5)   (10)   (13)

11

COMMUNICATION IN ORGANIZATIONS

Overview

By the end of this chapter you should be able to:

- Explain the importance of communication in organizations
- Describe the factors influencing interpersonal communication
- Describe the various tools for modern communication (phone, fax, e-mail, etc.)
- Describe how to improve communication effectiveness
- Discuss communication in an African context

The Communication Process

In this chapter we discuss communication as an important component of organizational life and human interactions. It facilitates coordination of work activities and motivation of employees. Communication is generally defined as the transmission and reception of thoughts, facts, beliefs, attitudes, and feedback through one or more information media that produce a response. In the following lines, we explain the communication process.

Elements of the Communication Process

The communication process includes the following elements: a) a sender, b) a receiver, c) a message, d) a channel and e) a feedback loop. Communication starts with a sender who encodes a message, which is then transmitted to a receiver. The receiver decodes the message and then provides information to the sender that the message has been received and is either understood or not (feedback) (see Figure 11.1). After encoding the message, the sender may select a given communication channel. The communication channel is the medium used to transmit the message. This medium may be face-to-face, a memo, or through electronic media. Organizational behavior scholars often contend that the richest medium of communication is face-to-face. The main argument for face-to-face communication is that both sender and receiver are able to directly observe

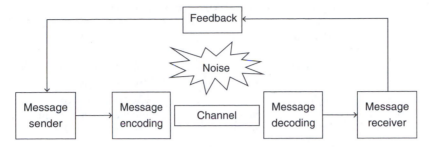

FIGURE 11.1   The Communication Process

the physical gestures and expressions of each other, which may provide valuable clues regarding individual feelings and reactions. Such observation is important in allowing each party to gauge the true reactions of the other to the message. The communication between the sender and the receiver may be disturbed by what is usually called noise. Noise is anything that prevents the sender from transmitting the message as intended. An example of noise in communication could include the language used in face-to-face communication and jargon that the receiver cannot decipher.

Communication in African Organizations

Different forms of communication occur in African organizations. They include face-to-face, electronic, non-verbal, and telecommunication. Face-to-face communication is generally more time-consuming or costly to organize due to physical distance and lack of time. Modern organizations tend to use more electronic means of communication than in the past. Such electronic means include e-mail, instant messaging, video-conferences, blogs, or social media. Organizations in Africa also use such electronic media. As an example, most organizations that we have worked with as consultants or advisors in Africa use e-mails or other forms of electronic media. The use of such electronic media helps to speed up the communication process and improve efficiency. However, it bears some limitations. E-mail messages can be misinterpreted or even poorly written. In addition, employees could use company time to engage in e-mail writing and other electronic means that are not always work-related. Table 11.1 below provides an overview of the richness of selected communication media.

Functions of Communication in Organizations

Communication serves at least four functions in organizations. These functions include control, motivation, emotional expression, and information.[2] Communication is used to ensure that employees display behaviors expected from them and follow instructions. Communication is also used to motivate employees by making clear the incentives available for displaying expected behaviors. For instance, an organization's policies related to performance-based compensation can be communicated to employees orally or in writing by managers. Employees and managers alike use communication to express their emotional state. An employee may communicate his/her frustration to a manager orally or in writing. In both cases, the employee uses communication to express his/her feelings. Finally, communication is used to provide information to facilitate decision

TABLE 11.1 Common Communication Media in Twenty-First Century Organizations

Media	Media Richness	Example	Reason to Use It
Face-to-face	Very high	Ask supervisor for a raise	Ability to adjust message according to real-time feedback
Telephone conversation Video conference	High	Meeting with virtual group members	Efficient and less costly and time consuming than traveling to central location
Memos Letters Personalized e-mail Voice-mail	Low	Communicate a customer service policy to customer	Efficient and cost-effective to communicate routine information
General e-mail Financial reports Flyers Bulletin boards Computer reports	Very low	Annual report to shareholders	Standardized information for large audience

Source: Robert H. Lengel & Richard L. Daft (1988). The selection of communication media as an executive skill. *Academy of Management Executive*, 2(3), 225–32.

making. Managers communicate important dates, such as looming deadlines, to employees. To perform effectively, organizations need to maintain some form of control over members, stimulate members to perform, allow emotional expression, and make decision choices.[3] There are several forms and types of communication in organizations. We will explore them in the following section.

Forms and Direction of Communication

There are two forms of communication in work settings: verbal and non-verbal. Verbal communication refers to communication using words. This verbal form of communication includes oral and written communication. Non-verbal forms of communication refer to the transmission of messages without the use of words. Examples of non-verbal communication are dress code and office size. Both may convey some meaning in organizations. The dress code in most banks is formal, conveying a sense of professionalism. In high-tech organizations where casual dress codes prevail, the dress codes convey a message of informality and "thinking out of the box." In most organizations, the size of the office is often related to the rank and status of the person who occupies it. High-level executives tend to have larger and fancier offices than line managers.

Communication in organizations can also be formal or informal. Formal communication refers to communication by formal means in organizations. Examples of such communication include memos, formal letters. Informal communication refers to communication that occurs beside formal communication. E-mails can also be considered a form of formal communication when they are work-related. Chatting with a co-worker in the hallway is an example of informal communication. Both formal and informal forms of communication can provide benefits to both employees and managers.

In organizations, communication has generally three directions: downward, upward, and lateral. Downward communication occurs when managers transmit information to employees.

Managers use downward communication to assign tasks to employees, give instructions, and provide guidelines. In upward communication, employees inform managers about progress made toward assigned goals, ask for clarification when needed, or express their feelings as well as expectations. Lateral communication occurs when employees at the same rank transmit information among themselves. Lateral communication may save time and ensure coordination among group members or even members of different groups.

Barriers to Effective Communication in Organizations

Several factors negatively influence interpersonal communication in organizations. For the purpose of clarity, we will divide these factors into three categories: individual factors, organizational factors, and cultural factors.

Individual Factors

Individual factors, such as personality and personal communication styles, may influence how people communicate with others. For instance, low sociability, low conscientiousness, and low intellectual openness, may serve as obstacles to effective communication. In addition, perceptual errors (perceptual defense, stereotyping, halo effect, projection, and high expectancy effect) may reduce effective communication. Individuals may filter information and provide just the piece of information they intend to provide. Filtering refers to a sender purposely manipulating information to make it favorable to the receiver. As an example, an employee receives bad news about a potential supplier. The employee may manipulate this information when reporting it to the manager. The employee's intention could be to avoid the anger of his/her manager.

Individuals can also select pieces of information they want to consider when communicating with others. Organizational scholars often acknowledge that in communicating with others, people often see and hear based on their personal motivations, needs, and expectations. Thus, communication is not always objective. In other words, we see what we want to see and hear what we want to hear. Thus, our emotions may prevent us from communicating effectively with others. We may give meaning to words pronounced by others. We may also attribute specific motives to those who communicate with us. Such tendencies and behaviors affect the way we communicate with others.

Organizational Factors

Organizational factors that impede communication include status, organizational structure, and organizational culture. People from different physical locations within a company may not often communicate between them. The same is true for the physical design of the workplace. It is common that employees and managers working on the same floor will be more likely to communicate frequently among themselves than with their peers from other floors. Therefore, organizations must be careful in designing office spaces. The use of cubicles is an attempt to facilitate interaction and communication among employees.

Cultural Factors

Cultural factors influence interpersonal communication. The same words may have different meanings. Some gestures may have different meanings across cultures. To understand the effect of cultural factors on interpersonal communication, organizational scholars identified two types of cultural contexts: *high-context culture* and *low-context culture*. In a high-context culture, the establishment of social trust before engaging in work-related discussions characterizes interpersonal communication. There is a high value placed on personal relationships and goodwill. People also value the surrounding circumstances during an interaction. In a low-context culture, individuals directly and immediately address the tasks, issues, and problems at hand. There is a high value placed on personal expertise and performance. People emphasize clear, precise, and speedy interactions.

What do Africans value when they communicate with each other? What manners are appropriate when discussing with others? We address these questions in this section. Communication is important for task coordination and understanding in every organization. However, the way people communicate and the manners that are deemed acceptable and appropriate may differ from culture to culture. In most African cultures, as in other cultures around the world, interrupting people when they talk is considered rude and disrespectful. Specifically in an African context, communication bears some formal protocol that needs to be respected when interacting with superiors or people holding high social status. It is common and expected to address people by their formal title. In Francophone Africa, a supervisor should always be addressed using the word *vous*, a sign of deference, whereas the supervisor can address a subordinate using the term *tu*, commonly used with friends or acquaintances. In Anglophone Africa, however, people tend to be a little informal. Regardless, in Africa, communication is more formal than in countries such as the United States. For example, people usually defer respect to those who are older than themselves. Thus, in communicating with a senior colleague, one must show respect due his or her age. It also happens that in some African cultures, a verbal agreement may not always be carried out. Agreeing to commit to a course of action may not necessarily indicate that the person will perform the action.

How to Improve Communication Effectiveness

At the Individual Level

One of the best ways to improve one's communication skills is to use the KISS principle (Keep It Short and Simple). When you are communicating with someone in writing or otherwise, you want to make sure that the other party understands clearly and effectively the message you are trying to convey. People are more likely to remember messages that are succinct and clear than long and wordy ones. Thus, senders should always have the audience in mind when encoding their messages. People communicate effectively when they strive to convey a message rather than impressing others.

People can also improve their communication skills by becoming effective listeners. If you were asked to measure the time you speak to others rather than listening to them on a daily basis, the answer would probably be that you listen more than you talk to others. Yet people do not tend to develop listening skills. We all think that we are good listeners. However, the evidence proves otherwise. Strategies, such as asking questions, putting the speaker's ideas into your own words, avoiding jumping to conclusions or making evaluative remarks, and making sure that you understand the speaker's ideas before responding could help you become an active listener. It happens very often that during conversations, people tend to think more about what they will say rather than listening carefully to the speaker.

At the Organizational Level

To improve communication at the organizational level, managers should allow suggestion systems; for example, develop corporate hotlines, brown bag meetings, and employee surveys. *Skip level meetings* which refer to meetings of employees from different levels of the organization, can also help improve communication. The existence of suggestion systems could help employees provide valuable insights to management related to improving processes or introducing new methods. They could also help employees vent their frustrations. Corporate hotlines allow employees to report suspicious behaviors, which could help managers make timely decisions to prevent major crises. Having brown bad meetings could help employees and managers communicate directly and share timely information. They could also provide avenues for informal interactions. Brown bag meetings held in the West could be replaced by lunch-time meetings in African organizations. Employees and managers could discuss work-related issues while eating lunch together. Frequent communication in organizations allows managers and employees to avoid gossip. When communication is lacking, employees tend to use gossip and rumors to fill the gap. The American Management Association (AMA) suggests 10 ways to improve organizational communication.[4] They are often referred to as the Ten Commandments of Good Communication. They are displayed in Table 11.2. These Ten Commandments could apply to African organizations.

TABLE 11.2 AMA's Ten Commandments of Good Communication

Commandments	*Actions*
1. Seek to clarify your ideas before communicating.	Make sure you know what you are trying to say.
2. Examine the true purpose of each communication.	How many times have we all said something that we wish we had not said? Thinking about the purpose of the communication will prevent this from happening so much.
3. Consider the total physical and human setting whenever you communicate.	For example, having a business conversation in a non-business setting may not be taken seriously or remembered by the receivers.
4. Consult with others, where appropriate, in planning communications.	It might be a good idea to ask another person if he or she understands the message before giving it to others.
5. Be mindful of the overtones as well as the basic content of your message.	People can read things into our message by the voice tone and gestures that are used in the delivery process.
6. Take the opportunity, when it arises, to convey something of help or value to the receiver.	One way to build good communications is by helping other people. If you have helped them in the past, they will probably listen favorably to you in the future.
7. Follow upon your communication.	It is a good idea to make sure that the receiver has gotten the message. You might follow up on the original message with another message, perhaps using a different medium.
8. Communicate for tomorrow as well as today.	Remember that the way you communicate with someone today sets the tone for that relationship in the future.
9. Be sure your actions support your communications.	People speak louder with their actions than they do with their words. A boss who is always late for work will have difficulty trying to tell people to be on time.
10. Seek not only to be understood but also to understand—be a good listener.	People must take the time to listen to what others have to say if they want people to take time to listen to them.

Source: The Ten Commandments of Good Communication, *Management Review*. American Management Association, October, 1955.

Applying these Ten Commandments could help improve communication in every organization, including those operating in Africa.

Summary

In this chapter, we have discussed the communication process, identified barriers to effective communication and highlighted strategies to improve communication in organizations. We have also discussed cultural influences affecting the communication process.

■ Discussion Questions

1. Describe the communication process.
2. Using your personal experience, describe the functions of communication.
3. Identify some of the advantages and disadvantages of electronic communication.
4. Using your understanding of this chapter, propose a plan to improve communication in your organization.

Exercise 11.1: Self-Assessment Questionnaire for Assertiveness

The purpose of this exercise is to provide you with feedback on the extent to which you use an assertive communication style. Go to the following website: http://cl1.psychtests.com/take_ test.php?idRegTest = 3126. Click on "Take the Test." Take the test by answering all 10 questions. Click on "Score my Test" to receive your score. Read the interpretation of your score.

NOTE: The questionnaire is for instructional purposes only and does not constitute an endorsement of any products that may or may not suit your needs.

Exercise 11.2: Self-Assessment Exercise—Active Listening Skills Inventory[5]

Check the response to the right that best indicates the extent to which each statement describes you when listening to others. This inventory helps you assess your listening skills.

Items	Not at all	A little	Somewhat	Very much
1. I keep an open mind about the speaker's point of view until he or she has finished talking.				
2. While listening, I mentally sort out the speaker's ideas in a way that makes sense to me.				
3. I stop the speaker and give my opinion when I disagree with something he or she said.				
4. People can often tell when I'm not concentrating on what they are saying.				
5. I don't evaluate what a person is saying until he or she has finished talking.				
6. When someone takes a long time to present a simple idea, I let my mind wander to other things.				
7. I jump into conversations to present my views rather than wait and risk forgetting what I wanted to say.				
8. I nod my head and make other gestures to show I'm interested in the conversation.				
9. I can usually keep focused on what people are saying to me even when they don't sound interesting.				
10. Rather than organizing the speaker's ideas, I usually expect the person to summarize them for me.				
11. I always say things like "I see" or "uh-uh" so people know that I'm really listening to them.				
12. While listening, I concentrate on what is being said and regularly organize the information.				
13. While a speaker is talking, I quickly determine whether I like or dislike his or her ideas.				
14. I pay close attention to what people are saying even when they are explaining something I already know.				
15. I don't give my opinion until I'm sure the other person has finished talking.				

Scoring Instructions

Use the following table to score the response you checked for each statement.

Write your circled score for each statement on the appropriate line (statement numbers are in parentheses) in the table below. Then calculate the overall active listening inventory score by summing all subscales.

Scoring Key

For statement items 3, 4, 6, 7, 10, 13: Not at all (3), A little (2), Somewhat (1), and Very much (0).
For statement items 1, 2, 5, 8, 9, 11, 12, 14, 15: Not at all (0), A little (1), Somewhat (2), and Very much (3).

Score interpretation

Avoiding interruption (AI) _____ + _____ + _____ = _____   High: 8 to 9;
                                  (3)   (7)   (15)   Medium: 5 to 7;
                                                            Low: Below 5.

Maintaining interest (MI) _____ + _____ + _____ = _____   High: 6 to 9;
                                 (6)   (9)   (14)   Medium: 3 to 5;
                                                              Low: Below 3.

Postponing evaluation (PE) _____ + _____ + _____ = _____   High: 7 to 9;
                                 (1)   (5)   (13)   Medium: 4 to 6;
                                                              Low: Below 4.

Organizing information (OI) _____ + _____ + _____ = _____   High: 8 to 9;
                                 (2)   (10)   (12)   Medium: 5 to 7;
                                                               Low: Below 5.

Showing interest (SI) _____ + _____ + _____ = _____   High: 7 to 9;
                                 (4)   (8)   (11)   Medium: 5 to 6;
                                                               Low: Below 5.

Active Listening Skills (total): High: above 31; Medium: 26 to 31; Low: Below 26.

Exercise 11.3: Case Study

Jeanne Mpwana has just been promoted as Marketing Manager of Compagnie Electronique, a medium size company located in Kigali, Rwanda. Jeanne was born in Kigali on May 20, 1982 from a Rwandan mother and a Congolese father. Her father was born in the Democratic Republic of Congo in 1960 and immigrated with his family to Kigali shortly after he was born. Jeanne studied at the University of Kigali where she obtained a Bachelor of Science in Economics in 2005. She interned at the Compagnie Electronique as a student before being recruited in 2005 as a market research analyst. Shortly after her promotion, Jeanne decided to improve the communication process in the marketing unit that employs 12 people.

She suggested that each employee use his or her e-mail account to directly communicate with her concerning problems or issues within the unit along with possible suggestions for improvement. She also conducts weekly meetings to ensure that everyone is on the same page. Further, she holds a type of meeting that she calls Tiger Meetings to deal with pressing issues and crises, such as reductions in marketing shares or problems related to customer complaints. Despite these efforts, some of the employees often complain about the lack of transparency in making decisions and rewarding good performance. They also complain about Jeanne because of her young age and her Congolese heritage. One employee even confided to his peers that "this girl thinks that she knows everything. I am older than she is and I know what I am doing. I was first recruited in this company when she was still a child." Another employee was also heard stating that "this Congolese girl thinks that we are in Kinshasa; but we are here in Kigali, Rwanda.'

Discussion Questions

1. Identify the potential communication barriers that Jeanne is facing.
2. What would you advise Jeanne to do to persuade some of the employees?

PART III

12

STRUCTURE AND DESIGN OF AFRICAN ORGANIZATIONS

Overview

By the end of this chapter you should be able to:

- Explain organizational structure
- Describe the six factors of organizational design
- Explain the different types of organizational structure
- Explain the impact of organizational structure on employee behavior

Types of Organizations

Before we discuss the structures of organizations, it is important to understand the nature of organizations in Africa. In doing so, we need to distinguish traditional organizations from modern ones. Organizations are "systems of coordinated action among individuals and groups."[1] In that regard, organizations in Africa may be considered traditional and modern. Traditional organizations tend to dominate the rural sectors, and basically focus on two or more individuals coordinating activities to achieve individual or collective goals. The pre-colonial organizations tended to be voluntary and subsistence-oriented. They lacked clearly defined structures and formality and tended to be primarily informal.[2]

Colonialism introduced modern organizations with formal structures in Africa. Modern organizations are based on Western models because the colonial countries that established state organizations to provide jobs, welfare, and governance adopted industrial models from the West. After independence, the state-owned enterprises maintained their structures and formality. African organizations can therefore be classified into informal and formal on the one hand, and traditional and modern, on the other. Modern organizations dominate the urban sectors of African countries and traditional organizations dominate the rural sectors. Both formal and informal organizations are present in urban areas. Both types of organizations structure themselves in a way that affects their conduct and performance. This is the structure-conduct-performance (SCP) paradigm.

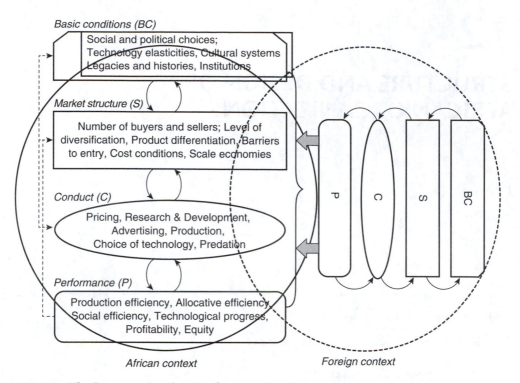

FIGURE 12.1   The Structure–Conduct–Performance Paradigm

Dominant from the 1950s in Economics and Strategy, SCP proposes that the market structure in which organizations exist affects the way they conduct themselves which in turn affects their performance. Enhancements to the paradigm suggest that basic or environmental conditions (see Chapter 1) affect the market structure. Figure 12.1 shows BC (basic conditions)-SCP as it relates to African organizations.

Within Africa, socio-political, historical, and cultural legacies affect market structures. From the colonial period till the 1990s most African economies had monopolistic structures because of the dominance of state-owned enterprises. However, structural adjustment programs eliminated those structures. The decisions (e.g., choice of technology) and behaviors (e.g., predation) stem from the market structure. The behaviors also influence performance (e.g., production efficiency, social efficiency, profitability, and equity). The model shows the dynamics (feedback and feedforward processes) in SCP. BC-SCP of African organizations is affected by African and foreign contexts. The SCP of foreign organizations (e.g., multinationals) that expand to African economies as well as environmental conditions of foreign economies affect African organizations' conduct and performance. African organizations therefore have design structures that are assumed to help them fit within the industry so that they can perform well.

Organizational Design System

Organizational design refers to the process by which work processes, jobs, and tasks are structured to facilitate achievement of organizational goals. It ranges from the macro design that involves the entire organization (see organizational forms) through functional processes to specific jobs and tasks. As a system, it comprises determinants, processes, and outcomes (see Figure 12.2).

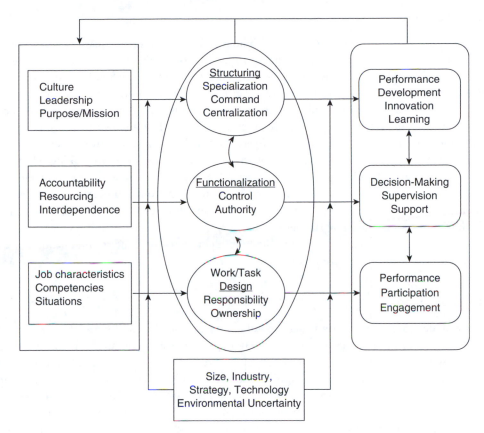

FIGURE 12.2   A Multilevel Determinants and Outcomes Model of Organizational Design

Organizational design involves tasks or jobs, departments or functions, and the system-wide form or structure. The characteristics of the tasks or job (e.g., autonomy), competencies of the job incumbents, and organizational situations (e.g., crisis) determine how jobs and tasks are designed. Through design, tasks and jobs are performed efficiently and effectively. Job design also engages the employees responsible for those jobs and increases their participation or involvement in organizations. Job design system is related to the functional or departmental system. At that level, accountability, resourcing, and delegation affect how departments are designed. Functionalization or departmentalization has a number of outcomes including support, supervision, and decision-making mechanisms. Departmentalization processes relate to organizational forms. As discussed below, organizations can be structured by departments or functions. System-wide design depends on the culture, leadership, purpose, and mission of the organization. Organizations with open values may be boundaryless. Organizations can also be structured based on leadership systems. The organization can be designed depending on the purpose or mission. System-wide design leads to such outcomes as organizational learning, innovation, performance, and development.

Design Processes

Design processes take two forms: top-down and bottom-up. The bottom-up approach is associated with new companies that tend to focus on specifying tasks and jobs for employees to execute so as to facilitate growth and development.

Task/Job Design

At the bottom is task or job design. Responsibilities and ownership (i.e., quasi–rights or control associated with the job) are specified. As the organization grows, jobs are grouped by functions or departments. The number of functions or departments tends to be small and basic (e.g., production) but increases as the organization grows. Termed unitary (U)-form, the basis of the functional units could be common expertise/experience or because the units use the same resources or focus on the same activities. U-form structures (see Figure 12.3a) tend to be common among small to medium firms that predominate in Africa. Generally U-form structures have the advantage of increased specialization, economies of scale, and centralized decision making. However, they cannot handle complexity of multiple activities well as sub-goal pursuit problems can become acute. Operational concerns can also divert attention from strategic, competitive, and entrepreneurial issues. An example of an African organization that has a U-form structure is Kenyan Airways.[3] It has seven departments which include finance, information systems, commercial, technical, human resources and administration, flight operations, and ground handling. Each is headed by an executive director reporting to the Group managing director.

Functionalization

Unlike task design that focuses on structuring of tasks performed by employees, functionalization focuses on structuring of the department or functional unit. Departments are structured according to their responsibility for management of human resources, sales and marketing, production, and finance. That process facilitates specialization and accountability. The human resources department of Kumba plc of South Africa, for example, is responsible for managing the acquisition, maintenance, utilization, and development of its 5,600 people working in the operations of the company.[4] The projects department is responsible for the production and logistics of Kumba plc.

Forms of Organizational Structure

The structure of the entire organization emerges after the various departments are established. It is the formal framework by which tasks, jobs, units are grouped and coordinated. This formal structure tells employees what to do and to whom they should report. An organizational chart usually illustrates the structure of the organization.

All organizational structures can be categorized into multidivisional, holding, matrix, team, network, and virtual. They are variously termed M-form, H-form, X-form, T-form, N-form, and V-form respectively. A multidivisional (M-form) structure (see Figure 12.3b) is designed to manage diversification while controlling bureaucratic costs and control-loss problems.

M-Form structures decentralize operating decision making to the business unit/division level where all necessary competitive and operational decisions are made. However, strategic decision-making responsibility is retained at the headquarters. Some benefits of the M-form include objective use of market/output performance measures, bureaucratic controls, and cultural controls which encourage exploitation of economies of scope across divisions; facilitation of diversity and growth. However, it introduces additional levels of hierarchy. This often magnifies the problem of information distortion. Managers of the divisions tend to develop myopia, and compete at the expense of cooperating.

Holding (H) structures (see Figure 12.3c) seek to exploit the advantages of internal capital markets. As a conglomerate, the Dangote Group is one of the "most diversified business conglomerates in Africa with a hard-earned reputation for excellent business practices and products' quality."[5] H-form organizations tend to be involved in multiple, usually discrete, products. The H-form design enables organizations to minimize economic and market risks. Matrix (X)-form structures (see Figure 12.3d)

(A) Unitary (U) Form

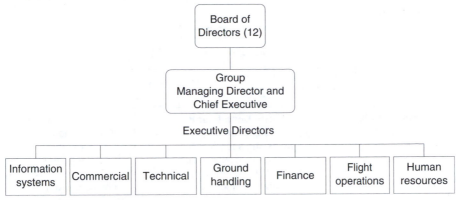

Kenyan Airways (http://www.kenyanairways.com)

(B) Multi-divisional (M) Form

Source: http://www.oandoplc.com/

(C) Holding(H) Form

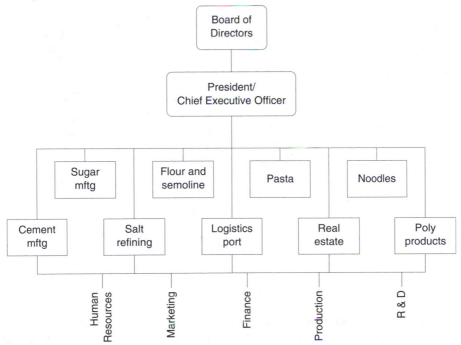

http://dangote-group.com

(D) Matrix (X) Form

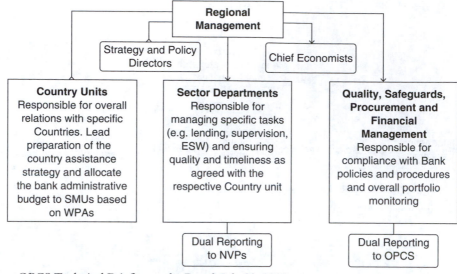

Source: OPCS Technical Briefing to the Board, July 28, 2009

http://www.worldbank.org

(E) Network (K) Form[#]

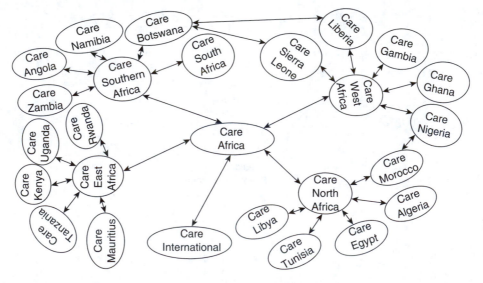

http://www.careafrica.org.au/

[#]Care is in every country of Africa. However, this constructed network is partial and purely illustrative. It does not suggest that those are the only countries which have CareAfrica (for details see www.careafrica.org.au/)

FIGURE 12.3 Forms of Organizational Structure

combine functional or unitary forms with some geographical or product dimensions. They seek to maximize the strengths while reducing the weaknesses of functional and decentralized forms.

Three modern forms – Network (K)-form, Team (T)-form and Virtual (V)-form have recently emerged. The K-form organizational structure (see Figure 12.3e) involves organizing business processes around interconnected and coordinative mechanisms. Some structures are based on out-sourcing business operations to third parties. Managers in network structures spend most of their time coordinating and controlling external relations, usually by electronic means. Most multinational corporations (MNCs) tend to outsource their production to networks of suppliers from low-cost Asian and African countries. Such organizational arrangements can help lower production costs.

The advent of new technology, particularly the Internet, has resulted in a move toward the V-form structures to address critical resource, personnel, and logistical issues, leading to the creation of virtual organizations. A virtual organization is a flexible network of independent entities linked by information technology to share skills, knowledge, and access to expertise in non-traditional ways. V-form structures are special kinds of boundaryless organizations. They are rare in Africa at the moment because of the lack of efficient information technology and telecommunication infrastructure.

The Team (T)-form structure emerged during the 1990s and was implemented by large corporations such as Toyota, Honda, Ford, Procter and Gamble, and General Motors. The T-form enables organizations to address various issues such as internal and interdepartmental communication within larger organizations. This type of structure is not widespread in Africa. Most organizations are adopting teams but avoiding organizing their processes around team structures. As we discussed in Chapter 8 (Groups and Teams), there are several advantages of T-forms that can be exploited by African organizations. T-forms facilitate creativity and innovation in organizations.[6] They can also optimize human capabilities.[7]

These different forms of organizational structure may be simple or bureaucratic. A simple structure is not an elaborate structure. It has low departmentalization, a wide span of control and authority is centralized in a single person. Further, there is little formalization. This structure is fast, flexible, and inexpensive to maintain. It is characteristic of small organizations. The bureaucratic structure is characterized by rules and regulations. It is based on order, logic, and the legitimate use of authority. A bureaucratic structure can be a functional structure or a divisional structure.

Some organizational theorists distinguish mechanistic structures from organic ones. A mechanistic structure is often a rigid structure, characterized by high specialization, rigid departmentalization, clear chain of command, narrow spans of control, a relatively centralized decision process, and high formalization. An organic structure on the other hand, is characterized by a more flexible structure, cross-functional teams, cross-hierarchical teams, free flow of information, wide spans of control, relatively decentralized decision process, and low formalization.

Usually, organizational structure involves work specialization, departmentalization, chain of command, span of control, centralization and decentralization, and formalization. *Work specialization* describes the degree to which tasks in an organization are divided into separate jobs. The essence of work specialization is that one individual does not do an entire job in an organization. Work is broken down into several activities and people perform each of these activities depending on their skills. *Departmentalization* refers to the process of grouping jobs that are similar into departments. Most companies group departments by functions such as human resources, finance, marketing, production or service, and so on.

The *chain of command* is the continuous line of authority that extends from higher levels to lower levels. It is basically the succession of authority within a company. The *span of control* refers to the number of employees a manager oversees. A manager who has a narrow span of control oversees fewer employees than a manager who has a wide span of control. Wide spans of control are more efficient in reducing costs. However, if these spans of control are too wide, managers may not be able to provide the support and leadership needed.

Centralization/decentralization refers to the levels at which decisions are made. In centralized organizations, decisions are made at top levels and imposed on employees. In decentralized organizations, however, those close to the action often make the decisions. Small organizations tend to be highly centralized. However, in some large organizations (e.g., Dangote) high decentralization in different groups is combined with low centralization. *Formalization* refers to the degree to which jobs within the organization are standardized and the extent to which employee behavior is guided by rules and procedures. Formalization and standardization of work leave little room for employees to have input in how to do their jobs or how to behave in the workplace.

Contemporary Designs and Structures

The goal of these new structures is to make organizations more flexible and efficient. In addition to the forms discussed above, boundaryless organizations and learning organizations represent modern forms that enhance organizational effectiveness.

Boundaryless organization

Jack Welch, former CEO of General Electric, first coined the term boundaryless organization. His intent was to reduce the artificial boundaries of his organization and make it more flexible and responsive to the needs of its multiple constituencies. Boundaries may be vertical, horizontal, and external. The purpose of the organization is to break down these boundaries. A boundaryless organization intends to eliminate artificial boundaries including specialization, authority, tasks, and identity boundaries. Organizations can eliminate such boundaries by using cross-functional teams and cross-hierarchical teams. Learning organizations don't involve new organizational structures per se.

However, organizations create an internal environment that facilitates continuous learning. In such organizations, employees constantly seek new knowledge and opportunities to learn and apply their knowledge. Even though the major characteristics of these organizational designs—interdependency and trust—are inherent attributes of the African culture they are not so common in Africa for two major reasons. First, the hierarchical culture of Africa which relies on authority and hierarchy counteracts the equality attribute in boundaryless organizations. Second, most organizations have foreign origins or owners who generally have stereotypical views of Africans as unreliable, corrupt, and unethical.

Informal Organizations

There are two meanings of informal organizations. The internal meaning focuses on the social processes, interactions, and relationships of employees that are not prescribed by the organization. Friendships and other networks function within this informal organization. One behavioral outcome—grapevine—typifies this structure. Communication patterns, affective orientations, and behaviors within the informal organization tend to be different from, but complementary to, the formal organization. Not only does work get done through this informal structure, but also personal and collective outcomes (e.g., promotions) are achieved through it. The second meaning is external and refers to entities that have no legal or regulated activities and structures.[8] It is associated with the informal economy, economic activities that are conducted by unregistered firms or by registered firms but hidden from taxation. Such organizations have no structures even though they engage in value-creating business activities. They also tend to be non-bureaucratic and illicit within the regulatory systems of the countries. Both have implications for employee behavior.

Determinants of Organizational Design

The determinants of organizational design vary by level. Some factors affect task and job design while others affect the departmentalization process. Still others affect the system-wide design.

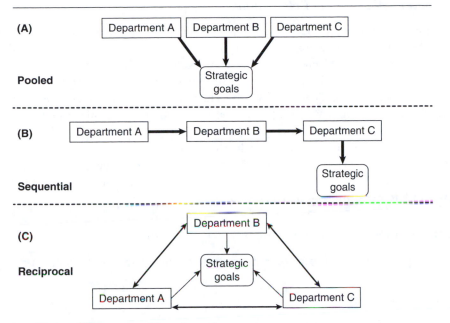

FIGURE 12.4   Types of Departmental Interdependence

Job Design Determinants

The characteristics or content of the task or job affects how it is structured. Tasks that require inputs from others have to be designed interdependently, particularly if they cross departmental boundaries. The design of decision-making tasks also differs from those of psychomotor tasks. The competencies of the person also influence how the job is designed. Jobs performed by highly competent individuals may be designed not to involve supervision while those performed by less competent individuals may include supervisory involvement. With regard to situations, tasks designed in crisis are likely to be structured differently from those designed in stable conditions.

Functional Design Determinants

At the functional level, one factor influencing departmentalization is interdependence. Three types of interdependence include pooled, sequential, and reciprocal (see Figure 12.4).[9] Departmentalization based on pooled interdependence involves each department performing its own separate functions and does not directly depend on other units, although it contributes to the success of the whole organization (Figure 12.4a). Sequential interdependence occurs when one department in the overall process produces an output necessary for the performance by the next department (Figure 12.4b). An example is a marketing department that depends on a production department. Reciprocal interdependence involves the two departments depending on each other reciprocally such that the output of the first department becomes the input of the second department and the output of the latter becomes the input of the former (Figure 12.4c).

The degree of accountability also influences departmentalization. Organizations that desire a high level of accountability have many supervisory structures embedded in departments while those that desire low accountability have fewer structures. Further, organizations that seek to preserve resources tend to have few departments. They combine functional units to increase efficiencies in using their financial, human, and social resources.

Organization-Wide Design Determinants

At the organizational level, the purpose of the organization affects the structure. The mission statement is a statement of the purpose of a company or organization. It guides the actions of the organization, and provides the framework or structure within which the company's strategies are formulated. Organizations with profit motives structure themselves to maximize value creation to meet shareholder needs. They contrast with organizations that have social welfare purposes. Second, the values, beliefs, and normative standards (i.e., culture) determine the structure of the organization. Organizations with trusting or constructive cultures tend to emphasize departmental boundaries while those with competitive cultures tend to insist on departmental structures. The leadership may also influence the structure. Executives can redesign current structures consistent with their strategic objectives or motivations. Albeit low in Africa, it is not uncommon in the West for new CEOs to restructure organizations to make them "ready" for acquisition or mergers.

Outcomes of Organizational Design

Organizational design yields outcomes related to task/job, functions, and the entire organization.

Job Design Outcomes

Jobs are performed well when they are designed properly. They also motivate and engage, so incumbents rarely move. That motivation leads to involvement or participation or elimination of alienation.

Functional Design Outcomes

Functionalization leads to effective decision making, appropriate supervision, and establishment of support structures for subordinates. Given that decision making has strategic and operational components, design also influences organizational outcomes by facilitating achievement of organizational objectives.

Organization-Wide Design Outcomes

System wide design facilitates organizational learning by enabling employees and departments to acquire, store, distribute, and utilize knowledge to improve organizational processes. Such learning contributes to innovation and development of the organization. We must point out that the outcomes of one level influence those of another level. They also vary with different types of organizations. Organizational structures can change depending on contingencies. Mechanistic and organic structures for example depend on two factors, the environment and the technology used by the organization. A mechanistic structure is more fitted when the company has standardized processes and operates in a relatively stable environment. However, an organic structure fits situations where the company has non-routine technology and operates in a dynamic environment.

Contingencies of Organizational Design

There are five major contingency factors: size, industry, strategy, technology, and environmental uncertainty of organizational design. With regard to *size*, large organizations (number of employees equal or greater than 500 employees) tend to have more specialization, departmentalization, centralization, and rules and regulations than do small or medium-size organizations. Organizational structure can also be influenced by organizational *strategy*. For instance, if an organization intends to innovate, it needs a flexible structure. However, if the organization wants to minimize costs, it should ensure tight control to cut costs down. If the company wants to follow an imitation strategy, (follow the market leaders), it needs to combine both an organic and a mechanistic structure. Organizations adapt their structures to their technology. When the organization uses a routine technology, it would have a mechanistic structure. When it uses a non-routine technology, it would have an organic structure. Finally, the external *environment* influences the structure of an organization. In a simple and stable environment, the organization would adopt a mechanistic structure. In a complex and dynamic environment, the organization would adopt an organic structure. The industry is also another dynamic factor that may influence organizational design. Organizations in competitive industries might be structured differently from those in cooperative industries.

Organizational Design and Employee Behavior

We indicated at the beginning of the chapter that one paradigm of organizational design is that the way organizations are structured influences their conduct. From an OB perspective organizational design influences the behavior of individual employees, teams, and the entire organization. Further, organizational design influences decision making, supervision, and support behaviors. Interdepartmental cooperation, coordination, and communication behaviors also result from organizational design. For instance, does work specialization have an impact on employee behavior? Work specialization contributes to higher employee productivity at the expense of reduced job satisfaction. A segment of the workforce may prefer routine and repetitive jobs. However, there is no clear relationship between span of control and employee behavior. Less centralization and greater decision-making participation are strongly related to job satisfaction.

Studies of organizational design's influence on the behavior of employees in Africa are lacking. As a result, it is not clear how much the structures of African organizations affect the behavior of employees. There are no "uniquely African" structures of organizations. However, the modern forms such as boundaryless designs seem to fit the culture of most African countries.

Summary

In this chapter, we have discussed organizational design by identifying the processes influencing task and work design, functional design, and organizational structures. In addition, we have discussed the determinants of these multilevel processes. Third, we identified some outcomes of each design. We concluded the chapter by discussing the contingencies or dynamics of the organizational design system. We also discussed the lack of, and reasons for, the unique African organizational designs.

■ **Individual Learning Questions**

1. What is organizational design?
2. What factors influence job design but do not influence departmental design?
3. List the major forms of organizational structures.

■ **Group Discussion Questions**

1. Discuss the organizational design system.
2. Discuss the outcomes of organizational design.
3. Given the African context, what design will you recommend to an entrepreneur starting her business in the next two months?

Exercise 12.1: Case Study

Tingdong has been selling local sleepers in downtown Kajetia, the center of Kumasi for over five years. Usually he buys the wears and sleepers from his village, Sheagah in the Upper East region, embroiders them in Tamale, and sells them for a meager profit of GHC1.65 after paying his five employees (he calls them "boys"). The income of the "boys" depends on how many sleepers they are able to sell in a day. His first "boy" started with him six years ago and apparently knows the business more than the others. He has added almost one "boy" every year thereafter. To illustrate his frustration in an informal organization, consider Tingdon's experience last year. He bought sleepers from the makers in the village for about GHC3.50, embroidered them for GHC1.10, and sold the finished product for GHC6.40. Throughout the years, he has not been able to formally register his business. And, throughout the years, he has constantly been driven off the market. Last year, he had to change location because of harassment by the police. It is not that he does not want to register his business; he does not see the need to do so since his current approach enables him to avoid taxes. He also knows he cannot stop the "harassment" because he cannot afford to go to court, and would likely not win if he took legal action. He has thought about the other alternative—"supporting the chief"—but that will reduce his profit since he has five "boys." Through his pidgin English (he only finished Amanguase elementary), Tingdong expresses his resignation at his fate, particularly his lack of capital and prospects. He does not like his GHC100 per month income because his personal expenses—rent, siblings' school fees, clothing, and so on, come from that income.

Questions

1. Using the systems model identify the factors influencing the structure of Tingdong's business.
2. What advice do you have for Tingdong to grow his business?
3. What design would you recommend for him to achieve his strategic objective of 5 percent growth within five years?

Exercise 12.2: Self-Assessment Exercise—Identifying Your Preferred Organizational Structure

Purpose

This self-assessment exercise is designed to help you understand how an organization's structure influences the personal needs and values of people working in that structure.

Instructions

Read each statement below and indicate the extent to which you would like to work in an organization with that characteristic. When finished, use the scoring key to calculate your results. The higher your score, the more likely you are to prefer the organization with the characteristics described.

Organizational Structure Preference Scale

I would like to work in an organization where

1	A person's career ladder has several steps toward higher status and responsibility.	0 1 2 3 _____
2	Employees perform their work with few rules to limit their discretion.	0 1 2 3 _____
3	Responsibility is pushed down to employees who perform the work.	0 1 2 3 _____
4	Supervisors have few employees, so they work closely with each person.	0 1 2 3 _____
5	Senior executives make most decisions to ensure that the company is consistent in its actions.	0 1 2 3 _____
6	Jobs are clearly defined so that there is no confusion over who is responsible for various tasks.	0 1 2 3 _____
7	Employees have their say on issues, but senior executives make most of the decisions	0 1 2 3 _____
8	Job descriptions are broadly stated or non-existent	0 1 2 3 _____
9	Everyone's work is tightly synchronized around top management operating plans.	0 1 2 3 _____
10	Most work is performed in teams without close supervision.	0 1 2 3 _____
11	Work gets done through informal discussion with co-workers rather than through formal rules.	0 1 2 3 _____
12	Supervisors have so many employees that they can't watch anyone very closely.	0 1 2 3 _____
13	Everyone has clearly understood goals, expectations, and job duties.	0 1 2 3 _____
14	Senior executives assign overall goals but leave daily decisions to frontline teams.	0 1 2 3 _____
15	Even in a large company, the CEO is only three or four levels above the lowest position.	0 1 2 3 _____

Scoring Key

Step 1

For items 2, 3, 8, 10, 11, 12, 14, and 15: Not at all: 3; A little: 2; Somewhat: 1; Very much: 0

For items 1, 4, 5, 6, 7, 9, 13: Not at all: 0; A little: 1; Somewhat: 2; Very much: 3

Step 2

Write the score for each statement on the appropriate line below (statement numbers are in parentheses) and add the scores for each scale. Then calculate the overall score by summing the scores for all scales.

Tall hierarchy   (H)   _____ + _____ + _____ + _____ + _____ = _____
                       (1)   (4)   (10)   (12)   (15)   (H)

Formalization   (F)   _____ + _____ + _____ + _____ + _____ = _____
                       (2)   (6)   (8)   (11)   (13)   (F)

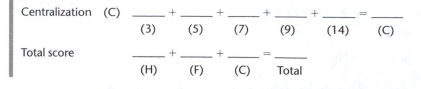

Centralization (C) _____ + _____ + _____ + _____ + _____ = _____
               (3)   (5)   (7)   (9)   (14)   (C)

Total score _____ + _____ + _____ = _____
              (H)   (F)   (C)   Total

Profile: Dangote Group President and Founder

Alhaji Aliko Dangote, founder of the Dangote Group, currently presides as President and Chief Executive. Dangote, a graduate of Business Studies from the Al-Azahar University, Cairo, Egypt, started business in 1977 trading in rice, sugar and cement, before he ventured into full-scale manufacturing. Currently, the Dangote Group has 13 subsidiaries spread all over Nigeria. The subsidiaries include cement, sugar, salt, flour, pasta, noodles, poly products, logistics, real estate, telecommunications, steel, oil and gas, and beverages. The Group also operates in 14 African countries including Senegal, Zambia, Tanzania, South Africa, Congo (Brazzaville), Ethiopia, Cameroun, Sierra Leone, Cote d'Ivoire, Liberia, and Ghana, among others. The Group, whose core business focus is to provide local, value-added products and services that meet the "basic needs" of the Nigerian population, recorded a turnover in excess of $3 billion (N450 billion) in 2010.

The Dangote Group has risen to win several awards—both locally and internationally. Last year, Dangote Cement plc, one of the four listed subsidiaries of the Group, made history when it became the largest quoted company in the country, following its historic merger with sister company Benue Cement Company plc (BCC) and the eventual listing of the emergent company on the Nigerian Stock Exchange (NSE). The Dangote Group was rated among Top 40 African Challengers in 2010 by the Boston Consulting Group (BCG) and was also adjudged the Investor of the Year 2010 by the Nigerian Investment Promotion Commission (NIPC) and the Commonwealth Business Council (CBC).

Source: http://dangote-group.com/aboutus/managementteam.aspx

13

CULTURE AND STRATEGY

Culture and Strategy are like a rope and a swing; the rope helps you swing left and right.

Overview

In this chapter we examine corporate culture and strategy. We discuss the antecedents, processes, and consequences of both. We also show the contingencies to each of them. By the end of this chapter you should be able to:

- Define organizational culture
- Discuss the organizational culture system
- Define strategy
- Discuss the strategy system

Organizational Culture

Organizational culture is determined by a number of factors and yields certain outcomes. It also involves some processes. As a result, it is sometimes referred to as a system. What then is the organizational culture system?

Defining Organizational Culture

There are several definitions of organizational culture. However, they all view organizational culture as a cognitive framework consisting of attitudes, values, behavioral norms, and expectations shared by an organization's members. Three major characteristics of this definition are 1) cognitive framework, 2) content, and 3) sharedness. Organizational culture is a *cognitive framework* because it involves observation, analysis, and interpretation of information on the psychological attributes of organizational members. The psychological attributes constitute the *content* of culture. As specified in the definition, the content relates to beliefs, values, norms, expectations, and attitudes. For example, if you had to negotiate with managers from Heglig Co. in Khartoum, Sudan, you are likely to

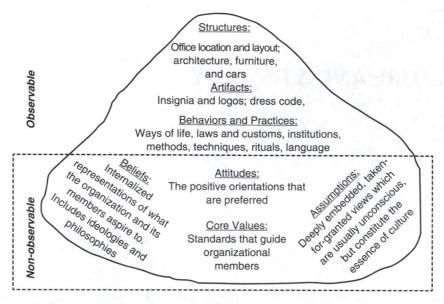

FIGURE 13.1 Iceberg Model of Organizational Culture

observe that they interact in a certain way during business transactions. What you might notice is some commonality in their communication, attitudes, and behaviors. That is the *sharedness*; they are socialized to think, respond, and act in a way that is unique to Heglig. Members of the organization must exhibit congruence in their cognitions, affect, and behaviors.

Elements of Organizational Culture

Organizational culture has often been defined to constitute observable and unobservable elements. Figure 13.1 shows the model as it relates to African organizations.

At the very bottom are assumptions, deeply held, taken-for-granted views which are usually unconscious, but constitute the essence of culture. Beliefs, values, and attitudes are also unobservable. However, attitudes are closer to the surface. Behaviors and practices are observable just as artifacts and structures.

Organizational Culture System

Though African organizations have assumed Western structures, the underlying elements of culture—artifacts and behaviors, espoused values, and assumptions—tend to combine traditional and Western content. As a system, organizational culture is characterized by distinct processes, antecedents, and outcomes (see Figure 13.2).

Antecedents

There are six major determinants of organizational culture: societal culture, purpose or mission, human resources management, leadership or founder, industry, and operating environment (see Figure 13.2).

Societal culture. With regard to *societal culture*, organizations function within societal contexts. The cultural elements of countries therefore affect the culture of organizations. South African cultural

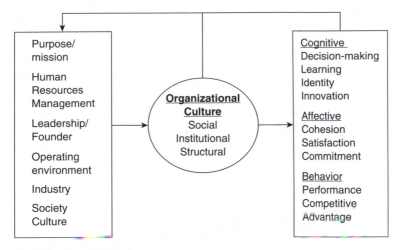

FIGURE 13.2 Organization Culture System

values, for example, impact the cultural values and behaviors of AngloGold Ashanti just as the culture of Nigeria influences values and beliefs of the Dangote Group of Nigeria. One of the values of AngloGold Ashanti is diversity, an attribute that is identical to the diversity of South Africa.

Leadership/founder. Another determinant of organizational culture is the founder or leadership. In starting his company in 1977, Alhaji Dangote of the Dangote Group, for example, espoused certain beliefs and values that he expected all his employees to share in or be guided by. Those values have contributed to transforming his company from trading in cement to a conglomerate that includes sugar, salt, flour, pasta, noodles, poly products, logistics, real estate, telecommunications, steel, oil and gas, and beverages in Senegal, Zambia, Tanzania, South Africa, Congo (Brazzaville), Ethiopia, Cameroun, Sierra Leone, Cote d'Ivoire, Liberia, and Ghana, among others. Besides the founder, successive leaders can also influence the culture. Through transformative leadership, executives can imprint values that enable the organization to achieve superior outcomes.

Purpose or mission. The third factor is the purpose or mission of the organization. Every organization has a mission which is undergirded by its values. The mission of the Poulina Group of Tunisia, for example, is "to mobilize thousands of men and women who develop common values, who create wealth and who set up a healthy corporate culture."[1] The values of the company—integrity, meritocracy, responsibility, transparency, and rigor—are intended to fulfill its mission.

Human resources management. Another determinant of organizational culture is the way in which the company manages its employees (i.e., the human resources management practices).[2] The human resources management (HRM) policies (staffing, training, compensation, performance appraisals, career management, recruiting, etc.) send messages to the employees as to what behaviors are considered desirable. HRM departments also socialize employees about acceptable and unacceptable behaviors. Through HRM, organizations reward desired behaviors and punish unacceptable ones. Zain Company emphasizes this in its culture by noting that "If the right culture is in place and the staff buy into it, are inspired by it and see its benefits, then it will impact positively on the perception of our corporation and its standards on the part of our employees and customers alike."[3] Its human resources management philosophy is also included in its culture definition, showing the central role of HRM in organizations.

Industry. As open systems organizations interact with their internal and external environments. As a result, they are affected by environmental factors. The industry is one factor that determines the culture of an organization. If the industry is competitive, the organization is likely to emphasize competitive values. However, if the industry is cooperative, the organization is likely to value cooperation.[4] Organizations in the banking sector are perceived to have competitive cultures because of the high level of competition in the financial and banking industries.

Operating environment. The operating environment generally refers to the circumstances surrounding and potentially affecting the way something operates. In business it refers to the combination of economic, social, and political factors that affect a company's activities. The environment is also important in creating organizational cultures. Some values and practices work better than others in particular industrial or market niches. Development of shared interpretation of events and actions thus helps to create an organization's culture. Some environments are munificent (supportive), as in periods of economic prosperity, while others are constraining, as in periods of economic recession. Companies in conflict-laden environments (e.g., Sudan) have cultural systems that differ from those in non-conflict environments. They espouse values and behaviors that either support or oppose the conflict.

Process

There are three major processes of organizational culture: social, institutional, and structural.

Social processes. Social processes focus on the interactions of employees. As social agents, current employees tend to interact (i.e., socialize) with new ones about the cultural elements of the organization thereby facilitating transmission of values and behaviors within the organization and across time. Socialization of new organizational members often involves not only transmission of particular patterns of behavior but also the values and beliefs underlying those behaviors. Socialization occurs through stories, symbols, ceremonies, and statements of principles, jargon, and statements of ethics.

Institutional processes. These focus on mimetic, normative, and coercive processes by which the structural and dynamic aspects of culture become nested, taken-for-granted, and transmitted. Employees, particularly new ones, often imitate other employees' behaviors and attitudes. They also are persuaded to adopt norms they observed in other places. Finally, they are controlled or coerced (e.g., through reward mechanisms) to enact values and behaviors they have observed. In sum, individual and organizational pressures induce employees to enact cultural values and behaviors. Poulina of Tunisia, for example, notes that its culture is intended to enable the organization to maximize performance like Western companies. This mimetic process is due to the pressure to perform well.

Structural processes. These are the systems and structures around culture that are established, maintained, and developed, and which instill values in employees. The artifacts that are displayed and the images associated with them transmit messages to current and new employees about cultural elements of the organization. For example, an open office layout transmits messages of transparency which is inscribed within the core values of the Dangote Group of companies.[5]

Outcomes

Culture permeates all levels of the organization: employees, departments, and the organization as a whole. It facilitates effective decision making. Managers of Zain Company, for example, are likely to make decisions on hiring women because the company emphasizes freedom or openness, "an openness in which employees can work and express their views without fear." Culture also promotes ongoing learning through the incentivization of acceptable behaviors and punishment of unacceptable behaviors. It enables vicarious learning as employees observe the consequences to other employees of specific behaviors. The sharing of values leads to a sense of collective identity. Organizational culture provides a sense of identity by helping organizational members feel part of the organization and generates commitment to the organization's mission. Organizational culture also clarifies and reinforces standards of behavior. In addition, it leads to innovation, particularly when it emphasizes creativity. In an organization that has a risk-prone culture, employees and managers may be empowered to take risks and generate novel ideas. Such a culture is likely to foster innovation as compared to a culture that is risk averse. Although organizational culture concerns the overall organization, it is possible to have subcultures within the same organization. For example, the marketing department may have a subculture that is quite different from that of the production department. However, these subcultures should not be in conflict with the dominant organizational culture. This could lead to dysfunctional behaviors.

Affective outcomes center on the enhancement of employees' affective reactions. Organizational culture prescribes norms of acceptable and unacceptable behavior, making it clear to employees what they should say or do in a given situation. Cultural norms also help employees work together (i.e., cohere) to meet customers' needs and respond to external pressures. Furthermore, culture provides structure and control without relying on an authoritative management style that can lessen motivation and creativity. In other words, it induces employee commitment and increases satisfaction. Employees who stay do so because the values of the organization fit with some or all of their interests.

Culture influences individual, departmental, and organizational performance. When organizations promote a certain set of values (e.g., respect for people and fair pay for good performance), they create social energy or motivation that influences employees' attitudes and behaviors. An organizational culture is sensitive to the needs of customers and employees alike. For example, an organizational culture may express an interest in having employees generate new ideas, take risks, and be open to communication and innovation. By maximizing employee performance, culture enables organizations to achieve market leadership or competitive advantage. Culture can also lead to cooperative advantage if it emphasizes cooperation.

Dynamics

The organizational culture system model suggests that culture is dynamic (see Figure 13.2). Organizational culture often changes to reflect adaptation. The occurrence of dramatic crisis such as facing a situation of bankruptcy can lead to changes in the organizational culture. When leadership changes hands, organizational culture also tends to change. Further, young and small organizations tend to change their cultures as they grow; the infusion of new members results in value and belief changes over time. Additional factors influencing culture change include the ethnic, gender, and age composition of the workforce. Such recomposition not only changes the overall organizational culture but it also creates subcultures within the organization. Mergers and acquisitions may also change an organization's culture. Take the example of two companies with different cultures that merge to create a new entity. One must expect some cultural clashes. It will take time for the new entity to forge a new culture that is different from that of the previous companies. Very often, the companies whose executives take over management roles in the new company impose the culture of their initial company. Finally, organizational change may lead to the creation of a new culture or the alteration of the original organizational culture. A company may change from a risk-averse to a more innovative culture if doing so helps the company better compete in its industry and environment.

It must be noted that culture is resistant to change because it is made up of relatively stable and permanent characteristics. Strong cultures are particularly resistant to change because they are deeply shared by individuals. The Dangote company culture has been affected to some extent by all the above factors as it transformed from a company focused on just one product to a conglomerate.

Organizational Strategy

As we mentioned at the beginning of this chapter, strategy enables African organizations to swing left and right. It is based on the notion that organizations cannot compete with only culture; they have to supplement it with strategy.

Defining Strategy

Organizational strategy is concerned with envisioning a future, creating value for stakeholders, and building and sustaining a strong position in the marketplace. It refers to the process of developing, implementing, and evaluating how an organization can evolve over time to meet its objectives along with a detailed assessment of what needs to be done. The strategy serves as a foundation for the behaviors of employees to achieve the goals in the strategic plan. It is the game plan for the company to compete.

Elements and Forms of Strategy

The first critical element of strategy is vision and mission. The vision of Orascom, an Algerian company, is to be "recognized as the contractor of choice for large, complex and demanding construction projects in North Africa and the Middle East." This vision is linked up with the company's strategy, which is to become "a world leader in the production of nitrogen-based fertilizers," one that is "committed to delivering quality work and products, safely and on schedule," and "driven to deliver exceptional value."[6] The vision spells out a focus and a purpose, a long-term goal the company is pursuing. The mission, on the other hand, is the reason the company exists, its *raison d'être*.

The second element of strategy is assessment of the external environment which involves gathering and analyzing essential market data (competitor profiles, studying macro and micro economic information, identifying industry opportunities and threats, and understanding what it takes to be successful in a given market). A third element, internal assessment, focuses on the internal environment of the company and includes appraisal of the company's management processes and how effectively it utilizes its internal resources (research and development, production, marketing, sales and customer service, i.e., value chain). Both external and internal evaluations focus on appraising the situation of the company. The outcome of that appraisal is used to develop objectives, initiatives, and goals. The objectives and goals articulate what the company seeks to accomplish, how to do so, and when they can be achieved. This element involves defining the direction, aligning financial and human resources, instilling accountability, and determining critical measurements.

The elements of strategy are used to develop specific strategies. There are diverse strategies and as many plans as there are organizations. However, strategies can be categorized as competitive or cooperative. *Competitive strategies* enable organizations to successfully compete against rivals within the industry. They include cost, differentiation, and focus or niche strategies. A low-cost strategy is based on producing a product or service at the lowest conceivable cost. As a consequence, employees are encouraged to maximize efficiency. The differentiation strategy focuses on unique or distinguishing attributes (quality, competence, clientele, etc.). A focus strategy targets a small segment of the marketplace that is not well served by existing businesses. The African Development Bank, for example, focuses on only development issues and avoids commercial activities.

Cooperative strategies involve firms working together to achieve a shared objective. They are intended to achieve cooperative advantage which enhances competitive advantage of organizations.

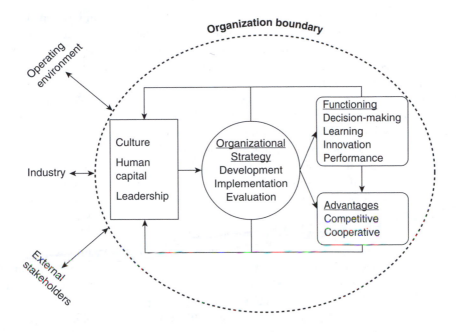

FIGURE 13.3 Organizational Strategy System

Companies can cooperate by establishing strategic alliances, joint ventures, or mergers. They all involve cooperating with other firms to create value for the customer, exceeding the cost of constructing customer value in other ways, and establishing a favorable position relative to competitors. In joint ventures, two or more firms create a legally independent company by sharing some of their resources and capabilities. Strategic alliances have two forms—equity and non-equity. In equity alliances, partners own different percentages of equity in a separate company they have formed. In non-equity alliances, two or more firms develop a contractual relationship to share some of their unique resources and capabilities.

Companies can combine both competitive and cooperative strategies. Orascom of Egypt typifies this approach. The strategy of the company involves "Targeting large, complex construction projects in emerging markets" (competitive); "expanding investments in fertilizer production and selecting downstream activities" (competitive); "working in partnership with local and global leaders" (cooperative); "investing in the best people and technologies" (competitive); "maintaining our commitment to quality and safety" (cooperative and competitive); and "providing products and services for people in developing economies" (focus and competitive).

Organizational Strategy System

The organizational strategy system functions within the internal and external boundaries of the organization. It comprises four elements: 1) inputs, 2) processes, 3) outputs, and 4) feedback (see Figure 13.3). We discuss each of these four elements next.

Inputs

There are two categories of inputs: internal and external. Internal inputs include human capital, leadership, and culture. Human capital refers to the aggregate composite skills, knowledge, attitudes of employees of the organization. As resources, they facilitate implementation of the organizational strategies, and achievement of strategic goals. They are also critical to the value chain activities and instrumental in creating and capturing value for the organization. Orascom Construction Industries emphasizes the importance of human capital by noting that it invests in the best people as part of its strategy.[7]

Through leadership executives develop the strategy of the organization. The personality, attitudes, capabilities, experiences, and behaviors of organizational leaders therefore influence initiation, execution, monitoring, and evaluation of organizational strategy. The leadership of Alhaji Dangote has been instrumental in the expansion and cooperative endeavors of the Dangote Company. As we discussed in the first part of this chapter, culture is a resource that can be leveraged to influence a company's strategy. The values and behaviors constitute a foundation for development of strategy. As a result, culture influences the types of strategy an organization pursues. Organizations with competitive cultures are likely to have competitive strategies while those with cooperative cultures are likely to develop cooperative strategies.

Industry is an external input that affects the strategy of organizations. Organizations in competitive industries are likely to adopt competitive strategies while those in cooperative industries are likely to prefer cooperative strategies. Banks in Ghana, for example, tend to have competitive strategies because of the high level of competition in the banking sector.

The economic, social, and political environment affects not only a company's activities but also its strategy. Some are beneficent in that they favor development and execution of strategies while others constrain strategy execution. Value creation tends to be higher in economic boom periods than recessionary ones. As a result, strategies that focus on growth are likely to be achieved during boom periods. Organizations have a number of external stakeholders including customers, suppliers, and governments. Customers purchase the products and services of organizations and suppliers provide raw materials. Governments regulate business activities and economic transactions. In other words, they set the rules of the game. As a result, governments influence strategy evaluation, development, and execution to some extent.

Process

Organizational strategy is a process that involves development, implementation, and evaluation subprocesses. In order for Sefalana Holding Co. of Botswana, for example, to come up with a strategy that guides its members, executives have to use the elements discussed above. Strategy development requires consideration of the leverage, constraints, problems, and vulnerabilities of the company based on situational analysis of the company.[8] Once the strategy is developed, it has to be implemented. The implementation involves execution by the actors using the required resources, time frame, and mechanisms. Strategy execution does not occur overnight. As a result, the implementation has to be monitored periodically and evaluated at the end of the stipulated period. The evaluation subprocess involves examination of the strategic objectives that were set, the resources used, and the agencies involved. Unlike the past, today's organizations engage in continuous evaluation to avoid "surprises." Reports are often generated to track progress.

Outputs

Strategy yields outcomes for organizations. An organization without a strategy is like a ship without a rudder. To avoid being buffeted by the winds of uncertainty, Air Mauritius of Mauritius developed a strategy a decade ago to be "approved as a Part 145 Maintenance Organization by the European Aviation Safety Agency (EASA)" which allows the company "to provide aircraft and aircraft components maintenance services to European aircraft operators and other airline operators that require a Part 145 Certificate of Release to Service." It is a strategy that enables the company to participate in the global air transport industry.

This example illustrates that strategy influences the functioning of Air Mauritius. It underlies decisions of its managers and top executives. It also enables the organization to learn from its failures and successes. Furthermore, strategizing facilitates innovation by harnessing creative resources to develop products and services which enhance performance. To the extent that organizations achieve their strategic goals which are often linked up to profitability, sales, and growth, they are likely to achieve increased market leadership. In addition to governing internal operations, organizational strategy facilitates achievement of competitive and cooperative advantages. In 1995 Wafa Assurance of Morocco strategically reorganized itself. This enabled it 12 years later to be a market leader with 21 percent market share and be ranked the best assurance company in Morocco and Africa.[9] An organization can use strategic alliances and joint ventures to innovate, expand, and learn, all of which contributes to organizational effectiveness.

Feedback

Organizational strategy is dynamic (see Figure 13.3). The dynamics occur due to interactions of the organization with the internal and external environments. Changes in the operating environment affect the strategy process and the outcomes. The global recession, for example, affected the strategic plan of most companies including those of Africa. Internal changes such as leadership, reorganization, labor–management conflicts, as well as external political, social, and cultural changes affect the strategy process and outcomes. The feedback loop illustrates that dynamic. The controls which are often built into strategy evaluation can also lead to changes before the a priori goals are achieved. The firm learns from its environment. For instance, if the company is implementing a strategy that allows it to extend its market share, this may be considered a signal that the strategy is working. However, if the company's market share is declining, it may signal poor strategy execution of a product quality problem.

Summary

In this chapter we have discussed the organizational culture and strategy systems. We identified the factors that influence organizational culture and strategy. We also discussed the processes and subprocesses of organizational culture and strategy. Further, we identified some outcomes of culture and strategy, and concluded with the dynamics that occur as a result of the open systems of organizational culture and strategy.

■ Individual Learning Questions

1. What is organizational culture?
2. What is organizational strategy?
3. What is the relationship between organizational culture and organizational strategy?
4. What are the various types of strategies African organizations pursue?

■ Group Discussion Questions

1. Discuss the factors that influence corporate culture.
2. What outcomes do organizations achieve from their cultures?
3. What are the major processes and forms of organizational strategy?
4. What are the dynamics of organizational culture and strategy?
5. Explain the relationship between culture and strategy.

Exercise 13.1: Case Study—Swinging the Rope

SWINGRO,[10] an energy and chemical company, was established in the mid-twentieth century to make and sell coal-to-liquids technology. Inspired by its vision—robustness, innovation, and excellence—and its cultural values of safety and integrity, the company grew rapidly to be a conglomerate by the beginning of the twenty-first century. The company's products expanded to include chemicals storefront, datasheet library, fuels and oils storefront, gas storefront, convenience center storefront, and supplier application. Today the company is in more than 30 countries and employs more than 30,000 people. In order to live by its vision which is firmly at the very core of its strategy and everything it does, employees are socialized to focus on excellence and ensure "delivery of guaranteed value" to customers and stakeholders. That strategy has enabled it to expand its international presence.

Toward the end of the first decade of the twenty-first century, Pat Dalanvies was appointed CEO of SWINGRO. He was driven to excellence to the exclusion of competitors. Consequently, a "culture of anti-competitive conduct" developed. Consistent with this counter- or subculture, Pat implicitly facilitated "price-fixing, collusion, abuse of dominance, price discrimination and cartel activities across the sectors in which it does business." In fact, the five key divisions of SWINGRO were under investigation by competition authorities in the country and abroad including the European Union's competition authorities.

Further, the company lost about $4.2 million as payment to the European Union's competition authorizes in the last quarter of 2008 for its part in a wax industry cartel. The company also agreed to pay a record domestic fine of $22.04 million for settling some of the charges leveled against its fertilizer arm, S-Nitro. There are also civil claims from companies for millions of dollars in damages. Some major customers, N-Flo and P-fert, also launched complaints about the behavior of SWINGRO which prevented the investigative body to show leniency to SWINGRO. Other behaviors included collusion with potential-but-disapproved companies. The regulatory commission is also investigating between 10 and 20 products in the oil division of SWINGRO. The chief executive of PIC, the single largest shareholder (10.73% stake) called for SWINGRO's "senior management and chairperson to be held accountable for the charges of collusion and cartel activity the company faces." It seems all is not well with SWINGRO. Other shareholders have agitated for the replacement of the CEO.

Even though Mr Dalanvies expressed remorse and acknowledged that he and management accepted full responsibility for the behavior of the company, they were replaced after three months.

Questions

1. How did SWINGRO's culture drive its strategy?
2. How did SWINGRO's strategy influence its culture?
3. What advice would you give to Mary Jones, a new CEO who replaces Pat?
4. What type of CEO would you recommend to replace the outgoing CEO?

Exercise 13.2: Self-Assessment Exercise—Corporate Culture Preference Scale

Purpose

This self-assessment exercise is designed to help you identify a corporate culture that fits most closely with your personal values and assumptions.

Instructions

Read each pair of statements in the corporate culture preference scale, and circle the statement that describes the organization you would prefer to work in. Then, use the scoring key to calculate your result for each subscale.

Scoring Key

All item numbers are listed in parentheses in the equations below. For each item, in the space provided, write 1 if you circled that item and 0 if you did not. Then, add the numbers for each subscale. The maximum score for each subscale is 6, and the minimum score is 0. The higher the score, the more likely that you would feel comfortable in that type of culture.

Control culture _____ + _____ + _____ + _____ + _____ + _____ = _____
  (2a)　(5a)　(6b)　(8b)　(11b)　(12a)

Performance culture _____ + _____ + _____ + _____ + _____ + _____ = _____
  (1b)　(3b)　(5b)　(6a)　(7a)　(9b)

Relationship culture _____ + _____ + _____ + _____ + _____ + _____ = _____
  (1a)　(3a)　(4b)　(8a)　(10b)　(12b)

Responsive culture _____ + _____ + _____ + _____ + _____ + _____ = _____
  (2b)　(4a)　(7b)　(9a)　(10a)　(11a)

Control culture. This culture values the role of senior executives to lead the organization. Its goal is to keep everyone aligned and under control.

Performance culture. This culture values individual and organizational performance and strives for effectiveness and efficiency.

Relationship culture. This culture values nurturing and well-being. It considers open communication, fairness, teamwork, and sharing vital parts of organizational life.

Responsive culture. This culture values its ability to keep in tune with the external environment, including being competitive and realizing opportunities.

Corporate Culture Preference Scale

I would prefer to work in an organization:

1a. Where employees work well together in teams OR
1b. That produces highly respected products and services.

2a. Where top management maintains a sense of order in the workplace OR
2b. Where the organization listens to customers and responds quickly to their needs.

3a. Where employes are treated fairly OR
3b. Where employees continually search for ways to work more efficiently.

4a. Where employees adapt quickly to new work requirements OR
4b. Where corporate leaders work hard to keep employees happy.

5a. Where senior executives receive special benefits not available to other employees OR
5b. Where employees are proud when the organization achieves its performance goals.

6a. Where employees who perform the best get paid the most OR
6b. Where senior executives are respected.

7a. Where everyone gets his or her job done like clockwork OR
7b. That is on top of innovations in the industry.

8a. Where employees receive assistance to overcome any personal problems OR
8b. Where employees abide by company rules.

9a. That is always experimenting with new ideas in the market place OR
9b. That expects everyone to put in 110 percent for peak performance.

10a. That quickly benefits from market opportunities OR
10b. Where employees are always kept informed of what is happening in the organization.

11a. That can respond quickly to competitive threats OR
11b. Where most decisions are made by top executives.

12a. Where management keeps everything under control OR
12b. Where employees care for each other.

14

CHANGE AND INNOVATION IN AFRICAN ORGANIZATIONS

Overview

By the end of this chapter you should be able to:

- Explain the change process
- Explain Kurt Lewin's three-stage model of change
- Describe Kotter's model of change
- Identify factors that lead to resistance to change
- Explain how to overcome resistance to change
- Explain and describe innovation in organizations

The Nature of Change

You will have heard the adage the "only thing that remains constant is change." Change permeates social and organizational life. For most managers and employees, the only constant of today's corporate life is change. Organizational change refers to any alteration in people, structure, or technology. Change is ever present in organizations and cannot be eliminated. This chapter describes the nature of change, Lewin's three-stage model, Kotter's eight-step model, the forces that influence change, the barriers to change, how to overcome resistance, and how to effectively manage change. It also discusses innovation as a specific form of change.

Defining Change

Change is often defined as the movement from one point to another point. Suppose that you are at point A and you move to point B. This could be construed as change. In organizations, change concerns any alteration in people, structure, and technology. Suppose that at stage 1, the organization operates in a certain way. At stage 2, the organization behaves in another way based on modifications previously introduced. We could say that the organization has changed. But why do organizations change? Several reasons may explain why an organization may decide to change. An organization may change because it faces a particular problem, such as profit reduction, loss of

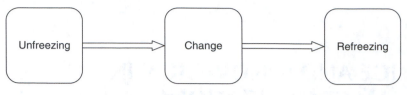

FIGURE 14.1 Lewin's Three-Stage Model of Change

market share, or competitor's actions. In this situation, the change is reactive. The organization reacts to situations in its environment. However, some changes may be proactive. For instance, an organization may anticipate some opportunities in the external environment. To exploit these opportunities, the organization may decide to introduce change.

Lewin's Three-Step Process of Change

Lewin identified three stages of change: *unfreezing, changing,* and *refreezing.*[1] Unfreezing implies the recognition that the current state of affairs is undesirable and that change is needed. It can be accomplished in one of three ways: increasing the driving forces, which direct behaviors away from the status quo, decreasing restraining forces, which hinder movement from the existing equilibrium, or combining the two approaches. Once employees and managers consider the actual state of affairs as undesirable, they may be willing to change. The change stage is a planned attempt to create a more desirable state for the organization. At this stage, the organization introduces the change process. Refreezing implies that the organization incorporates changes into employees' thinking and organizational operations (see Figure 14.1). As we discussed in the Introduction, there are three targets of change: technology, people, and structure. Organizations may try to change their employees' attitudes and behaviors. They may also change their structures by modifying existing rules and procedures, changing responsibilities, or introducing new equipment or processes.

Three conditions are necessary to create the need for change in an organization. First, organizations must consider the degree of dissatisfaction with the current state. To the extent that people are strongly dissatisfied with the current state, they may contemplate change. Second, a desirable alternative should be available. Third, a plan to achieve the desirable alternative should be available. When these three conditions are present, people will proceed to a cost-benefit analysis of the change process. If the costs are higher than the benefits, it is obvious that change will not occur. However, if the benefits are greater than the costs, change is likely to occur.

As we argued, to create a need for change, managers should create a discomfort with the current state of affairs. But how do they do this? Managers should explain the reason why the status quo is untenable and change is needed. Once they have explained the situation and created a discomfort with the current state of affairs, they should propose another alternative (a better alternative). If employees see that there is a better alternative, this may increase a discomfort with the current situation. Managers should also have a strategy to implement the new alternative. In summary, managers can create the need for change by 1) creating a discomfort with the current situation; 2) proposing a new alternative; and 3) having a way to implement the new alternative. Lewin used the force field analysis to explain how both driving forces and restraining forces could be influenced to introduce change. Figure 14.2 illustrates the force field analysis.

Kotter's Eight-Step Model of Change

Building on Lewin's work, Kotter[2] developed a model of change that identifies eight steps: 1) establish a sense of urgency, 2) form a coalition, 3) create a new vision, 4) communicate the

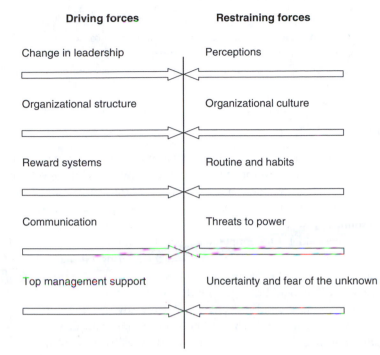

FIGURE 14.2   Force Field Analysis

TABLE 14.1 Kotter's Eight-Step Model for Implementing Change

Steps	Actions
1	Establish a sense of urgency by creating a compelling reason for why change is needed.
2	Form a coalition with enough power to lead the change.
3	Create a new vision to direct the change and strategies for achieving the vision.
4	Communicate the vision throughout the organization.
5	Empower others to act on the vision by removing barriers to change and encouraging risk taking and creative problem solving.
6	Plan for, create, and reward short-term "wins" that move the organization toward the new vision.
7	Consolidate improvements, reassess changes, and make necessary adjustments in the new programs.
8	Reinforce the changes by demonstrating the relationship between new behaviors and organizational success.

Source: Adapted from J. P. Kotter (1996). *Leading change.* Boston: Harvard Business School Press; and J. P. Kotter (1995). Leading change: Why transformational efforts fail. *Harvard Business Review,* January.

vision, 5) empower others by removing the barriers to change, 6) create and reward short-term wins, 7) consolidate, reassess, and readjust, and 8) reinforce the changes. The first four steps correspond to the unfreezing stage; the fifth, sixth, and seventh steps correspond to the change itself; and the eighth step corresponds to the refreezing phase described by Lewin. Table 14.1 summarizes Kotter's eight-step model.

Forces Influencing Change

We call forces for change, the conditions that push managers in an organization to decide to initi-ate and implement a change program. These forces can be both internal and external to the orga-nization. Internal forces for change come from within the organization, whereas external forces come from the external environment.

External Forces for Change

External forces for change concern those factors in the external environment that create a need for change. These factors include the economy, government laws and regulations, technology, labor markets, the competition, population demographics, and globalization. For instance, a slowdown in the economy can lead an organization to change its hiring practices. An organization may have planned to hire additional personnel. However, a slowdown in the economy may lead the organi-zation to freeze the hiring of new personnel. An example is the global economic crisis that started in 2008. This global crisis had a direct impact on companies and their hiring prospects. Some companies were even forced to downsize their workforce. Thus, remaining employees were compelled to do more with less. Technological changes could also have important implications for how organizations operate, communicate, and structure themselves. Advances in information and communication technologies have dramatically changed how organizations operate through-out the world. African organizations have also joined the trend of using information technology to improve their internal processes, albeit to a lesser extent than Western organizations. The use of e-mails, video-conferences and social networks is now ubiquitous in the workplace.

Changes in the labor market as well as changes in the demographics of the general population could also affect the internal workforce dynamics of an organization. A recent *Wall Street Journal* article indicates that in the United States, the birth rate has shifted from whites toward minorities. For the first time in U.S. history, whites of European ancestry account for less than half of new-born children, marking a demographic tipping point that is already changing the nation's politics, economy, and workforce. Among the roughly four million children born in the U.S. between July 2010 and July 2011, 50.4 percent belonged to a racial or ethnic group that in previous generations would have classified them as minorities.[3] This shift in demographics could affect the workforce composition in the years to come. The same could be true when there are more women entering the workforce. Although they may be professionals, women still carry the social responsibility of caring for their families, especially young children. Thus, to meet this shift in the composition of the workforce, organizations could establish flexible time work arrangements, allowing women to balance work and family responsibilities. Such demographic changes may well be happening in African organizations. In several countries, governments have raised the mandatory limit for retire-ment from 55 years to 60 or even 62 years. This could imply the existence of a multigenerational workforce in the workplace. The competition a company faces could alter its internal strategies. Companies competing in a fierce environment may feel the pressure to be more flexible and adaptable not only to the competition but also to changes in the external environment.

Internal Forces for Change

In contrast to external forces for change, internal forces for change originate primarily from within the company. They include changes in strategy, changes in the workforce, the use of new equipment, and change in employee attitudes. For instance, an organization may decide to change its strategies to compete better. Such change in strategy may lead to a change in culture or structure. It may also happen that an organization introduces new technologies, such as new software to improve its internal processes. Such internal change may lead to training employees and/or revising existing processes or assigning new tasks and responsibilities to employees. Change in management may also lead to the alteration of processes and policies. Very often, when new managers come into an organization, they tend to initiate new policies, processes, and strategies to make their mark on the organization. Employees would have to modify their attitudes and behaviors to cope with new realities introduced by new managers.

Barriers to Change

Barriers to change in organizations can come from both individual employees and the organization itself. Next, we explore the individual and organizational causes of resistance to change.

Individual Sources of Resistance to Change

As you have probably learned in your personal or professional life, making change is no easy task. People do resist change. They do so for a variety of reasons. People resist change because it brings uncertainty and ambiguity, and people experience concern over personal losses, and a feeling that change is not beneficial to them. Several reasons underline employee resistance to change. They include: *direct costs to employees, saving face, fear of the unknown, habits, threat to personal power and privileges*. Employees usually weigh the benefits of change against their personal fortune within the organization. If they believe that the change will help them improve their lot, they are likely to embrace it. However, if they believe that the change will bear detrimental consequences for them, chances are that they will resist it. Employees may also resist change as a political strategy to prove that the decision to make the changes was wrong in the first place. Change may require that employees learn new skills, which could imply that their current skills have become obsolete. Change always creates uncertainty about future events. Because of this employees will likely resist it unless they have received clear information about the reasons and benefits of change.

Organizational Causes of Resistance to Change

Organizational causes of resistance to change include structural inertia, limited focus of change, group inertia, threat to expertise, threat to established power relationships, and threats to established resource allocations. Organizations may have structures, policies, and cultures that are too rigid to be easily changed. Such factors lead to what is called structural inertia. The organization is simply too rigid to change. Thus, the resistance to change lies in the organization's internal mechanisms. Imagine someone who is too big to walk. Some changes may also be too narrow to have a real impact on the organization. Such change efforts could be resisted because not everyone in the organization sees their actual importance.

Group inertia is similar to structural inertia but differs from it to the extent that it is limited to a given group within the organization. The internal dynamics of some groups may render change impossible. Change may imply a threat to expertise and power relations within organizations. Those groups whose interests are threatened by change may oppose it. Suppose that an organization decides to reduce its layers of management and push decisions further down to employees. Who would be likely to be threatened by such a move? Of course, managers who could see their power reduced by this new policy may resist it. Change could also modify the way resources are allocated in organizations. Should the change involve a reduction in the power of those who used to allocate those resources, it is likely that they will resist it. To reduce both individual and organizational resistance, managers must develop the skills required to successfully implement change.

Managing Change

Managing change is both an art and a science. As an art, it depends on the savvy and stamina of the change champion. As a science, it requires knowledge and understanding of the processes that can facilitate the success of a change effort. To successfully manage change, organizations need to have change agents or champions. A change agent is a person who is responsible for implementing the change. Change agents may be managers, staff specialists, or outside consultants. These change agents must recognize that there will be some resistance to change. Change agents must build "the case for change" by "proving that the pain of not changing will be greater than the pain of changing."

Overcoming Resistance to Change

Reducing resistance to change is important for implementing a change program. In the following lines, we discuss several strategies that managers can use to reduce resistance to change.

Education and communication. One way to ease people's fears about a change program is to provide clear explanation concerning the benefits and costs of the change. Managers can overcome resistance to change by educating and communicating with employees, by negotiating with the parties affected by the change.

Participation. Managers may also include employees in decisions regarding the change process. When employees are involved in the decision leading to changes, they are more likely to support them.

Manipulation and cooptation. Resistance to change can also be overcome by manipulation and cooptation. Managers can explain to employees the personal benefits of embracing change. By doing so, they can offer them more responsibility as change agents. Such tactics may help secure employee support for the change.

Support and commitment. Ensuring that employees support and commit to the change is of paramount importance. Managers should do whatever it takes to align employees to their vision for change.

Select those who accept change. When initiating and implementing any change effort, there will always be those who are likely to accept the change and those who are likely to oppose it. Managers should build a coalition with those who accept the change. They can become advocates when it comes to implementing the change.

Coercion. Managers could also threaten employees who might resist change. Such measures could be successful but also backfire, especially when those who resist the change might have other types of power or political connections within the organization.

Fairness. To implement changes successfully, managers and change agents must ensure that the change is done fairly.

Conditions within the organization could also facilitate change. Such conditions include dramatic crises, leadership challenges, a weak organizational culture, and the organization's size. Organizations are likely to change when they face a situation of crisis that threatens their very existence. Organizations are also likely to change when they have new leaders or when the existing leadership is no longer able or willing to redirect the organization toward a brighter future.

Strategies for Implementing Change

Despite resistance to change, there are strategies which when well implemented could facilitate the success of the change process. To facilitate the successful implementation of change, organizations need to identify and explain the goals of change. Examples of such goals include reducing costs, improving efficiency, or increasing market share. Once the goals are clearly explained, managers should ensure that they have the "buy-in" of their employees. Managers should also designate change agents for implementing the change. The change agents should be empowered to make decisions related to implementing the change. Organizations should also reward "small wins"—progress made toward the change. Such a strategy could help improve morale and encourage those who are working toward implementing the change. Managers should identify the barriers to change and eliminate them. The section on reducing resistance to change is informative in this regard. Early in the process, managers should identify the potential sources of resistance to change and reduce or eliminate them.

Organizational Change in an African Context

Most research in organizational change has focused on Western organizations. However, research in cross-cultural management indicates that culture influences people's belief in the possibility for change. Some cultures may easily embrace change, whereas others may resist it. For instance, it is possible that time orientation will affect implementation of change. Likewise, reliance on traditions could increase resistance to change. The importance of traditions and customs in African cultures has been recognized. It is likely that this could affect the extent to which African organizations are predisposed to transform themselves and embrace the challenges of modern technologies and management practices. For instance, information and communication technologies have invaded Africa. In most countries, the use of the cell phone has become ubiquitous, so much so that land line usage has dramatically declined in most countries. Such technologies could be effectively used in the workplace to improve communication and productivity, and increase efficiency.

We have described most African cultures as being high on power distance. Power distance can modify implementation methods. For instance, change agents could act differently in different cultures. One could expect that change agents would tend to act more autocratically or not involve employees in the change process in high power distance cultures than in low or even moderate power distance cultures. It is also possible that cultures that are high on uncertainty avoidance would not easily embrace change. Change brings anxiety and uncertainty. Cultures where people prefer stability over uncertainty and risk could be reluctant to embrace change. Such cultures can be less innovative than those that are low on uncertainty avoidance.

Innovation

Innovation is a particular form of change. It has been of central interest to organizational scholars because it is vital for organizational adaptation and renewal.[4] Organizations can benefit from change if they have employees and managers who are creative and innovative. Before we discuss the concept of innovation, we explore the concept of creativity because creativity is the seed of innovation.

Creativity and the Creative Process

Creativity involves the combination of new ideas in unique ways or associating ideas in unusual ways. Theresa Amabile, a psychologist and organizational scholar who has worked extensively on creativity, defines it as the generation of novel and useful ideas.[5] The creativity process involves four stages, *preparation*, *incubation*, *insight*, and *verification*. Creative people are generally intelligent, persistent, they have subject-matter knowledge and experience and an inventive thinking style. Organizations can foster the creativity of their workforce by transforming themselves into learning organizations, by intrinsically motivating their employees, by encouraging open communication, and providing sufficient resources and support from leaders and co-workers. Creativity lies at the beginning of the innovation process within organizations.

Innovation: Challenges for African Organizations

Innovation consists of turning creative ideas into useful products, services, or methods of operation. There are three sets of variables—structural, cultural, and human capital—that stimulate innovation in organizations. The structural variables include organizational structure, high inter-unit communication, and the abundance of resources. These structural variables could impede or facilitate innovation. Cultural variables include the belief systems, values, and traditions within the organization. Such cultures could foster an environment that is conducive to innovation. Other cultures could inhibit innovation by not accepting new ideas. For instance, most African cultures have been described as high on power distance, which could imply that to be successful, initiatives to innovate must be top-down. In fact, research in management and organization behavior suggests that new ideas can come from the bottom as well. Very often, employees who know their work processes can have better ideas on how to improve processes than their managers.

There are generally four steps in the innovation process.[6] 1) *Idea creation*. Ideas are generated through spontaneous creativity, ingenuity, and information processing. 2) *Initial experimentation*. This step corresponds to the establishment of the idea's potential value and application. 3) *Feasibility determination*. This step consists of identifying anticipated costs and benefits. 4) *Final application*. This final step in the innovation process consists of producing and marketing a new product or service, or implementing a new approach to operations. Flexible organizational structures tend to spur innovation, whereas rigid ones tend to inhibit it. Research shows that organic organizations tend to be more innovative than mechanistic ones. Cultural variables concern the acceptance of ambiguity, tolerance of the impractical, tolerance for risks, and a focus on ends rather than means. The human resource variables involved in innovation concern hiring creative people, having a highly committed workforce, and providing job security. Creative people can be found everywhere. A recent book by Vijay Govindarajan and Chris Trimble on reverse innovation shows the trend toward using innovation from emerging countries to develop new products that can be marketed in developed markets.[7] African organizations can benefit from such an innovative process.

Summary

In this chapter, we have discussed organizational change and innovation. The chapter has discussed the importance of change and innovation for modern organizations. We have explained the causes leading to change as well as the potential barriers to change. We have suggested strategies to successfully manage change in organizations and particularly those operating in Africa. We have also discussed creativity and innovation. African organizations can foster change and innovation by adopting flexible structures and developing work environments that facilitate change and innovation.

■ Discussion Questions

1. Explain the reasons why people resist change.
2. Describe the different strategies change agents could use to facilitate the implementation of change.
3. What is meant by the expression "change is the only constant?"
4. Explain the difference between creativity and innovation.
5. What factors could lead African organizations to resist change and innovation?
6. What can be done to stimulate creativity and innovation in African organizations?

Exercise 14.1: Self-Assessment Exercise—Are You Tolerant of Change?

Purpose

The purpose of this exercise is to help you understand how people differ in their tolerance to change.

Instructions

Read each of the 16 statements and circle the response that best fits your personal belief. Then use the scoring key to calculate your results. To what extent does each statement describe you? Indicate your level of disagreement by marking the appropriate response. You have the choice among seven categories: Strongly agree (StA), Moderately agree (MA), Slightly agree (SlA), Neutral (NE), Slightly disagree (SlD), Moderately disagree (MD), and Strongly disagree (StD).

Statements	StA	MA	SlA	NE	SlD	MD	StD
1. An expert who does not come up with a definite answer probably does not know too much.							
2. I would like to live in a foreign country for a while.							
3. There is really no such thing as a problem that can't be solved.							
4. People who fit their lives into a schedule probably miss most of the joy of living.							
5. A good job is one where it is always clear what is to be done and how it is done.							
6. It is more fun to tackle a complicated problem than to solve a simple one.							
7. In the long run, it is possible to get more done by tackling small, simple problems rather than large, complicated ones.							
8. Often the most interesting and stimulating people are those who don't mind being different and original.							
9. What we are used to is always preferable to what is unfamiliar.							
10. People who insist on a yes or no answer just don't know how complicated things really are.							
11. A person who leads an even, regular life in which few surprises or unexpected happenings arise really has a lot to be grateful for.							
12. Many of our most important decisions are based on insufficient information.							
13. I like parties where I know most of the people more than ones where all or most of the people are complete strangers.							
14. Teachers or supervisors who hand vague assignments give people a chance to show initiative and originality.							
15. The sooner everyone acquires similar values and ideas, the better.							
16. A good teacher is one who makes you wonder about your way of looking at things.							

Adapted from S. Budner (1962).[8]

Scoring Key

For statements 2, 4, 6, 8, 10, 12, 14, 16, Strongly agree = 7, Moderately agree = 6, Slightly agree = 5, Neutral = 4, Slightly disagree = 3, Moderately disagree = 2, and Strongly disagree = 1. For statements 1, 3, 5, 7, 9, 11, 13, Strongly disagree = 1, Moderately agree = 2, Slightly agree = 3, Neutral = 4, Slightly disagree = 5, Moderately disagree = 6, and Strongly disagree = 7.

Score Interpretation

This scale is known as the tolerance for ambiguity scale. A score between 81 and 112 indicates a high tolerance for change and ambiguity; a score between 63 and 80, a moderate level for tolerance for change; and a score below 63 a low degree of tolerance for change.

CASE STUDIES FROM CAMEROON

Caisse Nationale de Prévoyance Sociale: Dealing with Politico-ethnic Issues

CNPS administers social security payments under a national social insurance scheme, as an agency of the government. Here the Directeur Général (DG) describes as problematic the low levels of skills of employees who lack basic training and sufficient education levels for the job. At the higher levels there are leaders who lack vision and are too concerned about the day-to-day business. They do not take the time to reflect on what they are doing and why. Managers do not have a clear understanding of the general mission. There is an attempt by top management to try to share the vision of social responsibilities toward the clients they serve, although there appears to be some resistance by managers lower down.

Yet without sharing the mission, the DG believes, managers cannot be involved in the decision process. He says:

> there is a tendency to rely on the DG as far as decisions are concerned, but decision-making has to be a collaborative process. I consult a lot, although in the end I make the decision when it is something for which I have responsibility. Some decisions are taken within committees, others are taken at lower levels because they are too technical or relate to operational use of resources.

One of the issues appears to be that some people are only motivated by money and see a refusal of management to respond to their money demands as a form of punishment, and this affects their engagement to their work. Those who have understood the message of what is trying to be achieved are more prepared to make the necessary sacrifices. The DG explains one of the problems of management motivation:

> I found here an insane situation. The organization was ruled on a clan basis. You were close to the DG or you were not. People were motivated by what individual benefit

(Continued)

they could obtain by this. People were not motivated by the desire to leave a mark, but only by the immediate return on their commitment to the DG. I am trying my best to be a guiding force in motivating people by the desire to succeed.

This issue, which is illustrative of misplaced motivation through adherence to politico-ethnic loyalties, has implications for the reward system in the organization. The DG explains that:

the reward system we have here is in line with public sector practices, that is reward and monetary advantage is gained through promotion. Therefore people spend a great deal of energy in fighting for promotion. I am in the process of putting an appraisal system in place. Such a system, with measurable criteria will make it easier to assess the performance of each individual. This is going to take quite a time to implement, but finally we may have a proper appraisal system.

This appears to be a drive to assert a formal system, rather than be driven by an informal system. Yet this is difficult because:

here people try to impress you by the supposed relationship they have with decision-makers. You have to be very careful. We have some problems in the management of our organization. The controls are loose. They are purely formal. Yet you also have to rely on feelings and Africa wisdom.

The process of change they are in, involving the questioning of what they are, and what they are trying to become, causes a lot of resentment because "we lack vision and the knowledge of our mission, we have to constantly put it back on the agenda. It isn't easy." This is in part because:

the influences of inter-ethnic relations in the organization are real, but you have to transcend them. The principal of ethnic equilibrium exists, but you have to refuse to encapsulate yourself in tribal logic. People who tend to use the tribal card are those who do not have the quality of their performance to fall back on. As DG you have to do your best to stay above all that.

The DG, coming from the Bulu group, asserts that he tries not to let that influence his duty. Yet he admits still, "the tribal reflex does exist."

In this case, politico-ethnic issues have moved the organization towards an informal system of favoring certain groups, and encouraging motivation toward currying favor rather than toward organizational output. Post-colonial systems of management here combine both formal and informal systems of control, although top management is attempting to move away from this towards more results-oriented organizational forms. Coercive control mechanisms may well give way to more remunerative control mechanisms. Although mentioned, indigenous approaches are looked upon warily. This situation may well be repeated in the private sector, particularly in foreign (Western) companies, which are attempting to develop productivity-focused management systems along Western lines, moving away from coercive forms of management control, yet being mindful (although still wary) of indigenous influences. Such an example is Guinness Cameroun.

■ Questions

1. What effect behaviors are present or lacking in the case?
2. What leadership challenges are posed in the case?
3. What is the effect of tribal identities on the organization's effectiveness?
4. Discuss the interaction between the informal organizational system and tribal diversity.
5. Evaluate the effectiveness of the motivational mechanisms discussed in the case.

Guinness Cameroun: Adapting Western Techniques

Guinness Cameroun has seen a continued expansion in Cameroon. From offering a range of products, including lager and "black products" (that is "Guinness" proper and a non-alcoholic drink Guinness Malta), they have focused on the latter class of products. In the *Guinness Cameroun News* circulated to all employees the Managing Director declares the year ended June 2001 as the most successful in the 30 years history of the company. Malta sales increased by 21 percent while Guinness itself saw a 19 percent growth. Although not one of the highest paying companies in Cameroon, employees appear to stay. It is also unusual in Douala, the commercial heart of Cameroon, as the company is predominantly anglophone.

However, the MD believes that more emphasis should be placed on recruiting franco-phones in order to get a better cultural balance.

Developing a Performance Culture

Guinness Cameroun is a Western company with Western principles. Yet the MD states that "although sometimes these principles, coming from London, seem a bit academic, we have to adapt them in a practical way to the situation." With a workforce of 1,300 people, "for the second year running we are putting in a performance culture, that is not Cameroon" says the HR Director.

> We have a target of 530 thousand hectolitres for our black products. If reached we pay out a bonus of two months' salary. Managers also have a bonus for, among other things, managing their costs. Managers have 15 months' salary here, and workers about 13 months' salary.

Educational Constraints

However, top management recognize that there are a number of constraints that have to be addressed. In particular they relate to the lower levels of education and the shallowness of the talent pool. For example the MD says that:

> in areas of functional expertise there is not a great depth in the country. Although people will go to university, the general standard isn't high. The engineering expertise is okay, but in marketing and sales it is lacking. So we try to find bright graduates and put them through our programmes.

This also reflects the general emphasis of higher education in training graduates for adminis-tration rather than for management. At the lower artisan and trade levels standards are good,

(Continued)

but the HR director believes that people are not taught to "think outside the box. People are trained to be subordinates." This leads on to the next constraint.

"Cultural" Constraints

People expect a boss/subordinate relationship. According to the MD "people won't address me by my first name, I am 'patron'." But they are working to change this.

> People believe that the boss is there to make the decisions. We meet on a regular basis with managers. At my second meeting with the managers a second-tier manager asked what management was doing about a particular issue. I said, you are a manager, what are *you* doing about it. The managers here are more supervisors than managers.

Yet there is a belief by this Western manager that "it comes out of African culture and respect for elders and authority," and he states that "we are more trying to change the culture of a country rather than just a company." He explains that they have people there who have authority within their community, and will not tolerate being challenged in their own community. "So, in a junior position in the company, they will not challenge authority here." They are attempting to change that, the HR Director explains. "We are trying to get people to take calculated risks, that is giving people the freedom to succeed, including making mistakes, and giving managers the opportunity to manage things the way they want."

Political and Ethical Constraints

In addition, in common with other companies in Cameroon, they have difficulties with the administrative authorities within the country:

> The economy is being dictated from the IMF and World Bank. There are pressures on the government to collect more taxes from the companies they know will pay, rather than widening the tax base. They will reassess tax liability and backdate it for 30 years. They will reinterpret the tax laws to do this. We can contest this, but it takes time, and the collection arm still tries to collect the tax in the meantime, even coming down here and putting padlocks on the door to close down the factory. There is also a lot of shady dealing. So your documentation has to be in top order. If not, officials will fix it for you if you are prepared to deal with the problem in a pragmatic way. As a company we are not prepared to do this. It is against our code of practice. We know that other companies, whose MDs belong to certain political parties have less trouble than others.

Opportunities Through Change

Internally, the MD explains that the company used to be very directive and run on an expatriate basis, "following the pattern of a colonial master, copying the French way of working." The company then introduced a program to transform the culture and business in the early 1990s. The HR Director added that "Top managers now have to lead by 'walking the talk'." But there have been problems with this. In 1994, when the CFA Franc was devalued, half the staff was laid off. This has left an element of cynicism that the company is trying hard to change.

(Continued)

Fortunately, "Cameroonian people are very open, and open to change and experimentation. We just need leaders to capitalize on this." However, this may well be a two-edged sword, as people live for today. There is little forward planning.

Employee Benefits

This is being partly addressed through the structure of employee benefits, as the HR director reports:

> This [lack of forward planning] has a positive impact as people are ready to change, but also a negative effect as people may run out of money. This puts pressure on, as they make no provision, no contingency for future problems. So as managers we have to introduce practical things like pensions and saving schemes.

The other aspect of this short-termism is that "you cannot run a business on this basis: people don't think what the long term may bring."

This company therefore appears to be adopting Western techniques of performance management, but adapting them in addressing environmental constraints, such as lack of educational opportunities, the nature of educational opportunities, uncertainty in political and ethical dealings, and a lack of performance culture including a perceived deference to authority and short-termism. Yet at the same time the top management appears to view indigenous culture in a negative light, largely ignoring any benefits to be drawn from it. This is in sharp distinction to the approach of Afriland First Bank.

■ Questions

1. What are the organizational development challenges discussed in the case?
2. Identify individual-, group-, and organizational-level behaviors discussed in the case.
3. Using your knowledge of systems, identify the antecedents, process, and consequence of performance culture.

Afriland First Bank: Developing Indigenous Approaches to People Management

Adapting Western HRM principles to the Cameroonian situation may be one way of working used by foreign multinationals. There also appears to be a new generation of indigenous firms that are now beginning to get past the "small" stage and establishing themselves as players among medium-sized firms. Such an example is Afriland First Bank.

When Afriland First Bank was set up in Cameroon in 1987 it was with a mission to promote a class of entrepreneurs in Africa. The organization began with five people, and today it has a staff of 300, including 50 trainees and around 100 managers. It now has a subsidiary company in Equatorial Guinea, and offices in Congo, Paris, and Beijing. We interviewed the senior management team as a group, and we have tried to select statements that represent the collective

(Continued)

views expressed, and which convey a picture of the approaches being used to forge what we believe to be one of the closest examples to the African "renaissance" management system (albeit, of course, in a hybrid form).

Reaching Out to the Community

When the company was first being put together:

> the question was put: how can we contribute to the development of our community? Here [in Cameroon] the community rather than individuals influences processes. We decided to create a tool to create wealth through business promotion. This would deliver new products suited to our environment and would fit in this culture.

So, for example, micro-finance is a key issue that is linked to the development process in Cameroon. "We don't go into an area to open a branch, but to help people to develop themselves, so this can be linked to the development of the country. It is a community approach." This is based in part on the fact that 70 percent of the economy is in the informal sector, so to develop this they needed to create a link to the formal sector. "When you want to promote African entrepreneurs you face the problem of lack of capital. So we have promoted venture capital for micro businesses."

"At the strategic level we are building a new country. The country we find ourselves in was not built for us." According to the management team, this artificially created country is only one of the constraints they find themselves confronting. "It is difficult to build the [work] group as the boundaries of the country are artificial." This has led to tremendous ethnic diversity within the country. "People are going back to their roots all the time, we need cross-cultural management."

Environmental and Operating Constraints

In addition, other constraints are numerous. These include the importance of the state and an ethos of the civil service in the country that operates against the spirit of entrepreneurship. There is also a spirit of consumption rather than production in the country. There is a problem of rules, where these rules are dictated by the operating and strategic constraints. "It is easy also to talk about corruption," says one senior manager. This group of managers also pointed to the judicial and legal system. "You can't do business unless this is effective, it is difficult where you have an arbitrary system." The lack of infrastructure is also seen as a problem. This includes the telecommunications industry, electricity, and the education system. The latter "does not prepare people for technical or managerial jobs; it prepares people to be civil servants. Business people are not celebrated in this country, and there is a lack of political will to develop business."

One manager suggested that after the country came out of its financial crisis during the 1990s "our internal resources were limited. You therefore need outside sources to help you." However, a fundamental problem is that "the leader in our country is the IMF and World Bank." It is they who are making the rules that fundamentally affect business in the country. So, although the immediate environment of relative social and political peace and stability and

(Continued)

the economy present opportunities, it is still difficult to utilize these opportunities. There is a need to have plans and objectives. "But these are strongly influenced by external forces." This is not only the IMF and World Bank. "We also have the strong influence of France."

Decision Making and the African Culture

Despite these difficulties, there appears to be a strong motivation to address these issues from an African perspective. This first involves decision making. This, in Afriland First Bank, is a group process, unless a quick decision has to be made as an emergency case.

> This comes from our African culture. We set up a college to take decisions. In traditional culture it isn't the chief who makes the decision. Every stone is turned, by bringing people together. With individual decision making there is a chance that you will make a mistake. So decisions are taken at the group level. We are like an African family that is trying to ensure our stability for the longer period. We don't think African is best, if we can obtain value from, for example, Japanese ways we will take it. But in our family the chief cannot always see that he is doing wrong. If he is doing wrong he is punished. You listen to your brother if he is telling you that you are making a mistake. We have noticed that working in committees is a collegiate way. This is a very strong training ground. We have been trained within those committees. Our philosophy is that we are a family and no one has an advantage. We all contribute. You have an opportunity to say what you think. If you are a member of a family you have to put controls first at your own personal level. You are the first level of control. You are then acting for the family. The family is the next level of control. In the bank we have levels of control at branch and headquarters levels. But the most important is at the personal level. Everyone in the bank is a controller. We have an evaluation process that ensures this.

Normative control systems therefore appear to be important within the bank.
   Within the bank there is a discussion forum:

> In the north of the country you have isolated big trees in savannah areas. So people gather around the tree. They solve community matters, preventing small problems becoming destructive. This is the model here. Every month people gather without consideration of rank, to discuss internal matters. There is no general manager present. We look at good news. We discuss things that are not right. We ask people what they think and decide upon the issue in respect of their individual operating unit. For the entire bank we meet informally once or twice a year, to develop a spirit of togetherness. Everyone can open the door of the Managing Director, and put an important problem to him.

Internal Climate, Motivation and Normative Control Mechanisms

So, there is:

> fraternity and respect, solidarity, communication, and a high critical feeling. You can't just do what you want. Everyone is looking at you. You may be the best in one way, but

(Continued)

equal opportunities are not an individual matter. We are going to share the bonus. The climate is that you have to be able to stay in your place, or I am going to take your place tomorrow.

However, there may be a problem of size now that the company has grown bigger from its origins. "If there is a death of a relative for example, we can't all go to the funeral as we used to, as we would be travelling to such things the whole time."

One of the managers thought that it is obtaining results that get noticed. That motivates managers. But he suggests that the question should be asked "What kind of results?" "As a family you have opportunities and you have the environment to stimulate motivation. But this is strongly linked to the individual's ambitions. Pay, for example, is just an incentive. The true motivation is the driving force of the individual." But management motivation may also be driven by higher ideas. "Most of our managers are motivated by the objective to build a country. This is an inner thing to motivate you."

We have specific human resource management processes. At the beginning of the year everyone in each function has specific evaluation criteria. If I am a cashier the first evaluation might be the number of bank notes I have counted over the year, and the number of counterfeit notes I have taken. At the end you have the commercial criteria. At the beginning of the year you have norms. After that you set your own objectives depending on your own ambitions. At the end of each month you have to fill in a form to compare the difference between the norms and objectives and achievements. You send one copy to Human Resources, and you keep one copy. This gives you an opportunity to compare your performance, as well as being a form of control.

We have a career profile for each function within the bank. According to that profile you know where you are and where you need to be. Promotion can be made in the same function but you can grow in grade. If you meet objectives three times you are promoted by rank. Also you can be promoted by function. We try as much as possible to have something quantifiable to treat everyone objectively. But qualitative actions are also taken into consideration. But there should be a relation between objectives and results.

As discussed above, this evaluation process is also considered a part of an element of control. "If you make an error this has to be explained: so there is an element of control in this."

So, although other control mechanisms are in place, mainly through remunerative incentives, emphasis is placed on normative control with the moral involvement of employees and managers who share a common vision. Hence:

the inner force is an African culture, but it is also strongly influenced by state and government controls. Also foreign countries controlling Cameroon influence the industry. As we are a francophone culture we try to take an Anglo-Saxon approach that is more specific. The French approach is less specific. Indirectly, there may be a Japanese influence, but this is only through the US influence.

Things are changing within the country and this affects the management of the bank. "The country is becoming more liberalized and democratic. It is moving slowly, but in the right

(Continued)

direction. There is a sort of African renaissance, but we have also to remove the negative things." Yet managing with African principles is not always easy:

> It is not easy in the African culture to manage more than about 300 people. The richness of the company is in its human resources. But we have to invest a lot to meet the challenges presented to us. As we are no longer a very small bank we are looking at human resource management. We have more democracy in the country, so this affects the way we talk to staff and do things.

Yet, one of the stumbling blocks to developing the business and changing people is that "to do things you have to be good in your own head. This is a colonial thing. Black people don't think they are good enough, so how can black people build and run a good bank? People didn't use to talk about these things, but now they are more in the open." However, within this African perspective there are still problems of ethnicity.

Managing Ethnic Diversity and Recruitment

For example, one manager said that:

> Since being in the bank I have never had to discuss the inter-ethnic aspect. But in meetings when people take the floor you see people are doing this from their own cultural education. In the North you have a big hierarchy and people behave according to their position in the hierarchy. It is similar for people from the West. In the Centre and the East there is not this hierarchy. People come with their culture. But this isn't very direct.

This diversity can be both negative and positive:

> There are more than 200 ethnic groups in the country, so we are representative of the whole of Africa in our diversity. This is the problem of this country, but it can also be a source of progress. We are moving in the company to cultural diversity. First we are addressing the francophone/anglophone issue by giving first preference to new recruits who are English-speaking in order to obtain an equilibrium between English and French speakers, as well as helping us to operate internationally. Secondly, we are mainly a Bamileke culture, so we are taking people from other ethnic groups to bring diversity and to bring in other mentalities. By asking a person from another ethnic group, you may get a different perspective, and therefore arrive at a good answer.

However, the company avoids using a quota system, and the quality of the recruit is paramount in a recruitment decision.

Afriland First Bank, despite problems of managing environment constraints, and the problems associated with the growing size of the organization, has made a conscious decision to develop in an African direction. This is in distinction to both Guinness, which predominantly employs Western techniques yet adapts them to the local environment, and to CNPS who are attempting to overcome politico-ethnic issues by negating the informal system, and strengthening the formal HRM systems in echoes of Western approaches.

(Continued)

Through these three cases, it is possible also to discern the type of control mechanisms being employed. CNPS is attempting to change from a predominantly coercive system of control via both formal and informal means by employing aspects of remunerative control systems. Guinness is attempting this same transformation, yet is introducing a more thoroughgoing productivity-based system by using more directly Western post-instrumental approaches. Here the issue is not to defeat an informal system, but to strengthen a results-focus in order to make the company more efficient and competitive. Afriland First Bank appears to be strengthening its normative control system through developing a moral basis for employee involvement, where people share a sense of community (whilst trying to retain this in the face of a growing organization).

Source: Jackson, T. (1994). *Management and Change in Africa: A Cross-Culture Perspective*. New York: Routledge (pp. 76–81; 84–6; 220–31). Reproduced with permission.

■ Questions

1. Discuss the challenges of indigenous management.
2. How easy will it be to develop indigenous OB in Africa? Discuss.
3. Discuss the environmental factors influencing Afriland First Bank.
4. Do Western models of decision making fit well within the African context?
5. Assuming Afriland is contemplating a new structure that is uniquely African, how does the African culture limit the structural configuration of Afriland First Bank?
6. Can Afriland leverage ethnic diversity for a competitive advantage?

NOTES

Chapter 1: Introduction to Organizational Behavior

1 Roxburgh, C., et al. (2010). Lions on the move: the progress and potential of African economies. McKinsey Global Institute (MGI). Available from: http://www.mckinsey.com/mgi/publications/progress_and_potential_of_african_economies/pdfs/MGI_african_economies_full_report.pdf. Downloaded on December 23, 2011.

2 Charmes, J. (1998). *Women working in the informal sector in Africa: New methods and new data*. New York: United Nations Statistics Division.

3 See http://www.safaricom.co.ke. Downloaded on January 3, 2012.

4 See http://www.greatplacetowork.com/what_we_do/model.php. Downloaded on January 3, 2012.

5 See http://www.haygroup.com/ww/best_companies/index.aspx?id=155. Downloaded on January 3, 2012.

6 See http://www.financialtechnologyafrica.com/admired/cwg.html. Downloaded on January 3, 2012.

7 Bertalanffy, L. von (1968). *General systems theory: Foundations, development, applications*. New York: George Braziller.

8 This is similar to the tacit–explicit knowledge dichotomy of I. Nonaka and Michael Polanyi: Nonaka, I. (1994). A dynamic theory of organizational knowledge creation. *Organization Science*, 5(1), 14–37; Polanyi, M. (1958). *Personal knowledge*. Chicago: University of Chicago Press.

9 See Mbiti, J. S. (1990). *African religions and philosophy* (2nd edn). Norfolk, UK: Heineman Educational. See also Noorderhaven, N. G., & Tidjani, B. (2001). Culture, governance, and economic performance: An exploratory study with a special focus on Africa. *International Journal of Cross-Cultural Management*, 1(1), 31–52.

10 Taylor, F. W. (1911, reprinted 2003). *The principles of scientific management*, New York: Harper.

11 Follett, M. P. (1918). *The new state: group organization, the solution of popular government*. London: Longmans.

12 Mayo, E. (1949). *Hawthorne and the Western Electric Company: The social problems of an industrial civilization*. London: Routledge.

13 Some scholars in this domain include Woodward, J. (1958). *Management and technology*. London: Her Majesty's Stationary Office; Blau, P. M., & Schoenherr, R. A. (1971). *The structure of organizations*. New York: Basic Books; Burns, T., & Stalker, G. M. (1961). *The management of innovation*. London: Tavistock; Lawrence, P. R., & Lorsch, J. (1967). *Organization and environment*. Cambridge, MA: Harvard University Press; and Child, J. (1972). Organizational structure, environments and performance: The role of strategic choice. *Sociology*, 6, 1–22.

14 The nascent Positive Organizational Behavior (POB) field is growing fast and there are several scholars from diverse disciplines. For pioneering work, see Luthans, F. (2002). The need for and meaning of positive organizational behavior. *Journal of Organizational Behavior*, 23, 695–706 (p. 59), and Luthans, F. (2002). Positive organizational behavior: Developing and managing psychological strengths. *Academy of Management Executive*, 16(1), 57–72.

15 The Chinese government established the first African school in Accra, Ghana. See http://www.ceibs.edu/africa/. Downloaded on August 1, 2012.

16 See "The hopeful continent: Africa rising," *The Economist*, December 3, 2011, and *The Africa Report* magazine which publishes detailed business, economic, social, cultural, and political information on Africa.

17 Lewin, Kurt (1943). Defining the "field at a given time." *Psychological Review*, 50, 292–310.

18 Miner, J. B. (2005). *Organizational behavior: Behavior 1: Essential theories of motivation and leadership.* Armonk, NY: M.E. Sharpe.

19 Mischel, W., & Shoda, Y. (1995). A cognitive-affective system theory of personality: Reconceptualizing situations, dispositions, dynamics, and invariance in personality structure. *Psychological Review*, 102, 246–68.

20 Borman, W., & Motowildo, S. (1997). Task performance and contextual performance: The meaning for personnel selection research. *Human Performance*, 10(2), 99–109.

21 Cameron, K. S. (2003). Organizational virtuousness and performance. In K. S. Cameron, J. E. Dutton, & R. E. Quinn (Eds.), *Positive organizational scholarship: Foundations of a new discipline*, pp. 48–65. San Francisco: Berrett-Koehler Publishers.

22 Borgatti, S. P., & Foster, P. C. (2003). The network paradigm in organizational research: A review and typology. *Journal of Management*, 29(6), 991–1013.

23 Kozlowski, S. W. J., & Klein, K. J. (2000). A multilevel approach to theory and research in organizations: Contextual, temporal, and emergent processes. In K. J. Klein, & S. W. J. Kozlowski (Eds.), *Multilevel theory, research, and methods in organizations: Foundations, extensions, and new directions*, pp. 3–90. San Francisco: Jossey-Bass.

Chapter 2: The External Environment of African Organizations

1 Hofstede, G. (1991). *Culture and organizations: Software of the mind.* London: McGraw-Hill.

2 Hofstede, G. (1993). Cultural constraints in management theories. *Academy of Management Executive*, 7(1), 81–94.

3 Hofstede, G., & Peterson, M. F. (2000). National values and organizational practices. In N. M. Ashkanasy, C. M. Wilderom, & M. F. Peterson (Eds.), *Handbook of organizational culture and climate*, pp. 401–16. Thousand Oaks, CA: Sage.

4 Hofstede & Peterson (2000).

5 Rokeach, M. (1973). *The nature of human values.* New York: The Free Press.

6 Chironga, M., Leke, A., Lund, S., & Van Wamelen, A. (2011). Cracking the next growth market: Africa. *Harvard Business Review*, May, 117–22.

7 McKinsey Global Institute (2010). *Lions on the move: The progress and potential of African economies.* Washington, DC.

8 Constructed from the Africa Development Indicators (http://data.worldbank.org/data-catalog/africa-development-indicators). Downloaded on August 1, 2012.

9 Kohlberg, L. (1981). *Essays on moral development, Vol. I: The philosophy of moral development.* San Francisco: Harper & Row.

Chapter 3: Social Perception and Diversity in African Organizations

1 Kenny, D. (1994). *Interpersonal perception.* New York: Guilford Publications.

2 Hunt, S. (2007). Different types of staffing assessments. In *Hiring success: The art and science of staffing assessment and employee selection*, pp. 39–78. San Francisco: Pfeiffer.

3 Eden, D. (1984). Self-fulfilling prophecy as a management tool: Harnessing Pygmalion. *Academy of Management Review*, 9, 64–73.

4 Babad, E. Y., Inbar, J., & Rosenthal, R. (1982). Pygmalion, Galatea, and the Golem: Investigations of biased and unbiased teachers. *Journal of Educational Psychology*, 74, 459–74.

5 Rowe, W. G., & O'Brien, J. (2002). The role of Golem, Pygmalion, and Galatea effects on opportunistic behavior in the classroom. *Journal of Management Education*, 26, 612–28.

6 Heider, F. (1958). *The psychology of interpersonal relations.* New York: Wiley.

7 Jones, E. E., Kannouse, D. E., Kelley, H. H., Nisbett, R. E., Valins, S. & Weiner, B. (eds.) (1972). *Attribution: Perceiving the causes of behavior.* Morristown, NJ: General Learning Press.

8 Nisbett, J. (1971). *The actor and the observer: Divergent perceptions of the causes of behavior.* New York: General Learning Press.

9 Weiner, B. (1974). *Achievement motivation and attribution theory.* Morristown, NJ: General Learning Press.

10 Ross, L. (1977). The intuitive psychologist and his shortcomings: Distortions in the attribution process. In L. Berkowitz (Ed.), *Advances in experimental social psychology. 10*, pp. 173–220. New York: Academic Press.

11 Heradstveit, D., & Bonham, G. M. (1996). Attribution theory and Arab images of the Gulf War. *Political Psychology*, 17(2), 271–92.

12 Gardenswartz, Lee, & Rowe, Anita (1998). *Managing diversity: A complete desk reference and planning guide.* London: McGraw-Hill.

13 Our typology is similar to but different from Cox's monolithic, plural, and multicultural organizations. We focus on all forms of diversity in contrast to cultural diversity. See Cox, T. Jr. (1991). The multicultural organization. *The Academy of Management Executive*, 5, 43–7.

14 Fine, M. J. (1996). Cultural diversity in the workplace: The state of the field. *Journal of Business Communication*, 33(4), 485–502.

15 Brownell, J. (2003). Developing receiver-centered communication in diverse organizations. *Listening Professional*, 2(1), 5–25.

Chapter 4: Personality, Affect, and Stress

1 Hogan, R., & Hogan, J. (1992). *Hogan personality inventory manual.* Tulsa, OK: Hogan Assessment Systems.

2 Brewer, M. B. (1991). The social self: On being the same and different at the same time. *Personality and Social Psychology Bulletin*, 17, 475–82.

3 See Markus, H., & Nurius, P. (1986). Possible selves. *American Psychologist*, 41(9), 954–69; Norman, C. C., & Aron A. (2003). Aspects of a possible self that predict motivation to achieve or avoid it. *Journal of Experimental Social Psychology*, 39, 500–7.

4 Mpofu, E. (1994). Exploring the self-concept in an African culture. *Journal of Genetic Psychology*, 155, 341–54.

5 Zoogah, D. B., & Abbey, A. (2010). Cross-cultural experience, strategic motivation and employer hiring preference: An exploratory study in an emerging economy. *International Journal of Cross Cultural Management*, 10(3), 321–43.

6 Holland, J. L. (2008). Award for distinguished scientific applications of psychology. *American Psychologist*, 63(8), 672–4.

7 See Csikszentmihalyi, M., & Csikszentmihalyi, I. S. (eds.) (1988). *Optimal experience: Psychological studies of flow in consciousness.* New York: Cambridge University Press.

8 Lowinger, P., Schorer, C., & Knox, R. (1963). Personality development in identical twins. *Arch Gen Psychiatry*, 8(5), 509–17.

9 Watson, D., Clark, L. A., & TeUegen, A. (1988). Development and validation of brief measures of Positive and Negative Affect: The PANAS Scales. *Journal of Personality and Social Psychology*, 54, 1063–70.

10 Tajfel, H., & Turner, J. C. (1986). The social identity theory of intergroup behaviour. In S. Worchel, & W. G. Austin (Eds.), *Psychology of intergroup relations*, pp. 7–24. Chicago, IL: Nelson-Hall.

11 Browning, V. (2006). The relationship between HRM practices and service behaviour in South African service organizations. *International Journal of Human Resource Management*, 17(7), 1321–38.

12 Meyer, M. (2004). Organizational identity, political contexts, and SMO action: Explaining the tactical choices made by peace organizations in Israel, Northern Ireland, and South Africa. *Social Movement Studies: Journal of Social, Cultural and Political Protest*, 3(2), 167–97.

13 Zoogah, D. B., & Abbey, A. (2010). Cross-cultural experience, strategic motivation and employer hiring preference: An exploratory study in an emerging economy. *International Journal of Cross Cultural Management*, 10(3) (December), 321–43.

14 Rwanda: http://www.pbs.org/wgbh/pages/frontline/shows/ghosts/today/; Liberia: http://www.pbs.org/frontlineworld/stories/liberia/facts.html (both downloaded August 1, 2012); Sierra Leone: Bellows, E., & Miguel, J. (2006).War and institutions: New evidence from Sierra Leone. *American Economic Association Papers and Proceedings*, 96(2), 394–99.

Chapter 5: Motivating the African Worker

1 Latham, G. P., & Pinder, C. C. (2005). Work motivation theory and research at the dawn of the twenty-first century. *Annual Review of Psychology*, 56, 485–516; and Pinder, C. (2008). *Work motivation in organizational behavior*, 2nd ed. London: Psychology Press.

2 Maslow, A. (1954). *Motivation and personality.* New York: Harper & Row.

3 Maslow (1954).

4 Blunt, P., & Jones, M. (1992). *Managing organizations in Africa*. Berlin: Walter de Gruyter.

5 Backer, W. (1973). *Motivating black workers*. New York: McGraw-Hill.

6 Hagerty, M. R. (1999). Testing Maslow's hierarchy of needs: National quality-of-life across time. *Social Indicators Research*, 46(3), 249–71.

7 Alderfer, C. P. (1969). An experimental test of a new theory of human needs. *Organizational Behavior and Human Performance*, 4, 142–75; and Alderfer, C. P. (1972). *Existence, relatedness and growth*. New York: Free Press.

8 McClelland, D. (1961). *The achieving society*. Princeton, NJ: Van-Nostrand; and McClelland, D. C. (1965). Toward a theory of motive acquisition. *American Psychologist*, 20, 321–33.

9 Arnolds, C. A., & Boshoff, C. (2003). The influence of McClelland's need satisfaction theory on employee job performance: A causal study. *Journal of African Business*, 4(3), 55–81.

10 Mitchell, B. C. (2001). Motivation among entrepreneurs in rural South Africa: A comparative study. Unpublished dissertation. University of South Africa.

11 Locke, E. A. (1968). Toward a theory of task motivation and incentives. *Organizational Behavior and Human Performance*, 3, 157–89.

12 Frese, M., Krauss, S. I., & Friedrich, C. (2000). Microenterprises in Zimbabwe: The function of sociodemographic factors, psychological strategies, personal initiative and goal setting for entrepreneurial success. In M. Frese (Ed.), *Success and failure of microbusiness owners in Africa: a psychological approach*, pp. 103–30. Westport, CT: Greenwood.

13 Adams, J. S. (1965). Inequity in social exchange. In L. Berkowitz (Ed.), *Advances in experimental social psychology*, Vol. 2, pp. 267–99. New York: Academic Press.

14 Vroom, V. H. (1964). *Work and motivation*. New York: Wiley.

15 Orpen, C., & Nkohande, J. (1977). Self-esteem, internal control, and expectancy beliefs of White and Black managers in South Africa. *Journal of Management Studies*, 14(20), 192–9.

16 Mueller, K. J. (1983). Expectancy theory in developing nations: Motivating Botswana public servants. *Public Administration and Development*, 3(3), 265–74.

17 Hackman, R. J., & Oldham, G. R. (1975). Development of the job diagnostic survey. *Journal of Applied Psychology*, 60, 159–70; Hackman, R. J., & Oldham, G. R. (1976). Motivation through the design of work: Test of a theory. *Organizational Behavior and Human Performance*, 16, 250–79; and Hackman, R. J., & Oldham, G. R. (1980). *Work redesign*. Reading, MA: Addison-Wesley.

18 Herzberg, F., Mausner, B., & Snyderman, B. B. (1959). *The motivation to work*. New York: Wiley; Herzberg, F. (1965). The motivation to work among Finnish supervisors. *Personnel Psychology*, 18, 393–402; and Herzberg, F. (1966). *Work and the nature of man*. Cleveland, OH: World Publishing Company.

19 Mathauer, I., & Imhoff, I. (2006). Health worker motivation in Africa: The role of non-financial incentives and human resource management tools. *Human Resources for Health*, 4, 4–24.

20 Hackman, R. J. (2002). *Leading teams: Setting the stage for great performance*. Boston: Harvard Business School Press.

Chapter 6: Power, Influence, and Politics

1 French, J. R. P., & Raven, B. (1962). The bases of social power. In D. Cartwright (Ed.), *Group dynamics: Research and theory*, pp. 607–23. Evanston, IL: Row & Peterson.

2 French & Raven (1962).

3 Pfeffer, J., & Salancik, G. (1978). *The external control of organizations: A resource dependence perspective*. New York: Harper & Row.

4 Salancik, G., & Pfeffer, J. (1974). The bases and uses of power in organizational decision-making. *Administrative Science Quarterly*, 19, 453–73.

5 Hickson, D. J., Hinings, C. R., Lee, C. A., Schneck, R. E., & Pennings, J. M. (1971). A strategic contingencies theory of intraorganizational power. *Administrative Science Quarterly*, 16, 216–29.

6 Robbins, S. P., & Judge, T. A. (2011). *Organizational behavior*, 14th ed. Upper Saddle River, NJ: Pearson/Prentice-Hall.

7 McClelland, D. C. (1975). *Power: The inner experience*. New York: Irvington.

8 Milgram, S. (1963). Behavioral study of obedience. *Journal of Abnormal and Social Psychology*, 67, 371–78; Milgram, S. (1974). *Obedience to authority: An experimental view*. New York: Harper & Row.

9 Zimbardo, P. G. (1972). *Stanford prison experiment: A simulation study of the psychology of imprisonment*. San Francisco, CA: Philip G. Zimbardo, Inc.

10 Barnard, C. (1938). *The functions of the executive*. Cambridge, MA: Harvard University Press.

11 Hinken, T. R., & Schriesheim, C. A. (1989). Development and application of new scales to measure the French and Raven (1959). Bases of social power. *Journal of Applied Psychology*, 74, 561–67; Robbins, S. P. (2009). *Self-assessment library. Version 3.4.* Upper Saddle River, NJ: Pearson/Prentice Hall.

Chapter 7: Leadership in an African Context

1 Fiedler, F. E. (1977). *A theory of leadership effectiveness.* New York: McGraw-Hill.
2 House, R. J. (1971). A path-goal theory of leadership effectiveness. *Administrative Science Quarterly*, 16, 321–38; House, R. J. (1996). Path-goal theory of leadership: Lessons, legacy, and a reformulated theory. *Leadership Quarterly*, 7, 323–52; and Wofford, J. C., & Liska, L. Z. (1993). Path-goal theories of leadership: A meta-analysis. *Journal of Management*, 19(4), 857–76.
3 Vroom, V. H., & Yetton, P. W. (1973). *Leadership and decision making.* Pittsburgh, PA: Pittsburgh University Press.
4 Hersey, P., & Blanchard, K. H. (1969). *Management of organizational behavior – Utilizing human resources.* New Jersey: Prentice Hall; and Hersey, P., & Blanchard, K. H. (1969). Life cycle theory of leadership. *Training and Development Journal*, 23(5), 26–34.
5 House, R. J. (1977). A 1976 theory of charismatic leadership. In J. G. Hunt, & L. L. Larson (Eds.), *Leadership: The cutting edge*, pp. 189–207. Carbondale: Southern Illinois University Press; and Khurana, R. (2002). *Searching for a corporate savior: The irrational quest for charismatic CEOs.* Princeton, NJ: Princeton University Press.
6 Graen, G. B., & Uhl-Bien, M. (1995). Relationship-based approach to leadership: Development of leader-member exchange (LMX) theory of leadership over 25 years – Applying a multi-domain perspective. *Leadership Quarterly*, 6, 219–47; and Zhou, X., & Schriesheim, C. A. (2009). Supervisor–subordinate convergence in descriptions of leader–member exchange (LMX) quality: Review and testable propositions. *Leadership Quarterly*, 20, 920–32.
7 Seltzer, J., & Bass, B. M. (1990). Transformational leadership: Beyond initiation and consideration. *Journal of Management*, 16, 693–703; Judge, T. A., & Piccolo, R. F. (2004). Transformational and trans-actional leadership: A meta-analytical review of their relative validity. *Journal of Applied Psychology*, 89, 755–68.
8 Van Dierendonck, D. (2011). Servant leadership: A review and synthesis. *Journal of Management*, 37, 1228–61.
9 Collins, J. (2001). Level 5 leadership: The triumph of humility and fierce resolve. *Harvard Business Review*, 83, 136–46.
10 Charam, R. (2009). *Leadership in the era of economic uncertainty.* New York: McGraw-Hill.
11 Dowden, R. (2008). Africa's leadership crisis: *Time Magazine* (June 11). Available from http://www.time.com. Downloaded on May 2, 2012.
12 IMPRODAPIM is a disguised name for a real company.

Chapter 8: Groups and Teams

1 Tuckman, B. (1965). Developmental sequence in small groups. *Psychological Bulletin*, 63(6), 384–99.
2 Gersick, C. J. G. (1988). Time and transition in work teams: Toward a new model of group develop-ment. *Academy of Management Journal*, 31, 9–41.
3 Wheelan, S. A. (1994). *Group processes: A developmental perspective.* Sydney: Allyn & Bacon.
4 Gersick, C. J. G. (1991). Revolutionary change theories. A multilevel exploration of the punctuated equilibrium paradigm. *Academy of Management Review*, 16, 10–36.
5 Belbin, R. M. (1993). *Team roles at work.* Oxford: Butterworth-Heinemann.
6 McGrath, J. E. (1984). *Groups: Interaction and performance.* Englewood Cliffs, NJ: Prentice-Hall.
7 Hackman, J. R., & Wageman, R. (2005). A theory of team coaching. *Academy of Management Review*, 30(2), 269–87.

Chapter 9: Decision Making

1 Simon, H. A. (1986). Rationality in psychology and economics. *Journal of Business*, 59(4), 209–24.
2 Sanders, R. (1999). *The executive decision making process: Identifying problems and assessing outcomes.* Westport, CT: Quorum.
3 Simon, H. A. (1960). *The new science of management decision.* New York: Harper & Row.
4 Simon (1960).

5   Saunders, R. (1999). *The executive decision making process: Identifying problems and assessing outcomes.* Westport, CT: Quorum.

6   March, J. G. (2009). *A primer on decision making.* New York: The Free Press; and Shafir, E., & LeBoeuf, R. A. (2002). Rationality. *Annual Review of Psychology,* 53, 491–517.

7   March (2009); and Shafir, & LeBoeuf (2002).

8   Simon, H. A. (1997). *Administrative behavior,* 4th ed. New York: The Free Press.

9   Osborn, A. F. (1963). *Applied imagination: Principles and procedures of creative thinking,* 3rd ed. New York: Scribner.

10 Faure, C. (1990). Beyond brainstorming: effects of different group procedures on selection of ideas and satisfaction with the process. *Journal of Creative Behavior,* 38, 13–34.

11 Delbecq, A. L., Van deVen, A. H., & Gustafson, D. H. (1975). *Group techniques for program planning: A guide to nominal and Delphi processes.* Glenview, IL: Scott Foresman.

12 Hollingshead, A. B., & McGrawth, J. E. M. (1995). Computer-assisted groups: A critical review of the empirical research. In R. A. Guzzo, & E. Salas (Eds.), *Team effectiveness and decision making in organizations,* pp. 46–78. San Francisco: Jossey-Bass.

13 Tversky, A., & Kahneman, D. (1982). Availability: A heuristic for judging frequency and probability. In D. Kahneman, P. Slovic, & A. Tversky (Eds.), *Judgment under uncertainty: Heuristics and biases,* pp. 163–78. Cambridge, UK: Cambridge University Press.

14 Tversky, & Kahneman (1982).

15 Staw, B. M. (1981). The escalation of commitment to a course of action. *Academy of Management Review,* 6, 577–87; and Staw, B. M. (1976). Knee-deep in the big muddy: A study of escalating commitment to a chosen course of action. *Organizational Behavior and Human Decision Processes,* 16, 27–44.

16 Simmons, J. P., LeBoeuf, R. A., & Nelson, L. D. (2010). The effect of accuracy motivation on anchoring and adjustment: Do people adjust from their provided anchors? *Journal of Personality and Social Psychology,* 99, 917–32.

17 Jonas, E., Schultz-Hardt, S., Frey, D., & Thelen, N. (2001). Confirmation bias in sequential information search after preliminary decisions. *Journal of Personality and Social Psychology,* 80, 557–71.

18 Christensen-Szalanski, J. J. J. (1991). The hindsight bias: A meta-analysis. *Organizational Behavior and Human Decision Processes,* 48, 147–68.

19 Plous, S. (1993). *The psychology of judgment and decision making.* New York: McGraw-Hill.

20 Hmieleski, K. M., & Baron, R. A. (2009). Entrepreneurs' optimism and new venture performance. *Academy of Management Journal,* 52, 473–88.

Chapter 10: Understanding Conflict in African Organizations

1   Pondy, L. (1967). Organizational conflict: Concepts and models. *Administrative Science Quarterly,* 17, 296–320.

2   Thomas, K. W. (1992). Conflict and negotiation processes in organizations. In M. D. Dunnette, & L. M. Hough (Eds.), *Handbook of industrial and organizational psychology,* 2nd ed., pp. 651–717. Palo Alto, CA: Consulting Psychologists Press.

3   Tjosvold, D. (2007). Conflicts in the study of conflict in organizations. In C. De Dreu, & M. Gelfand (Eds.), *The psychology of conflict and conflict management in organizations.* New York: Taylor & Francis, pp. 445–54.

4   Spector, P. E., & Bruk-Lee, V. (2007). Conflict, health and well-being. In C. De Dreu, & M. Gelfand (Eds.), *The psychology of conflict and conflict management in organizations.* New York: Taylor & Francis, pp. 267–90.

5   Tjosvold, D. (1991). *The conflict-positive organization.* Reading, MA: Addison-Wesley.

6   Walton, R. E., & McKersie, R. B. (1965). *A behavioral theory of labor negotiations: An analysis of a social interaction system.* New York: McGraw Hill.

7   O'Connor, K. M., & Arnold, J. A. (2001). Distributive spirals: Negotiation impasses and the moderating role of disputant self-efficacy. *Organizational Behavior and Human Decision Processes,* 84, 148–76.

8   De Dreu, C. K.W., Beersma, B., Steinel,W., & Van Kleef, G. A. (2007). The psychology of negotiation: Principles and basic processes. In A. W. Kruglanski, & E. T. Higgins (Eds.), *Social psychology: Handbook of basic principles,* 2nd ed., pp. 608–29. New York: Guilford.

9   Jaffee, D. (2007). Conflict at work throughout the history of organizations. In C. De Dreu, & M. Gelfand (Eds.), *The psychology of conflict and conflict management in organizations.* New York: Taylor & Francis, pp. 55–79.

10 O'Connor, K. M., Gruenfeld, D. H., & McGrath, J. E. (1993). The experience and effects of conflict in continuing work groups. *Small Group Research,* 24, 362–82.

11 Wall, J., & Callister, R. (1995). Conflict and its management. *Journal of Management*, 21, 515–58.

12 Walton, R. E., & McKersie, R. B. (1965). *A behavioral theory of labor negotiations: An analysis of a social interaction system*. New York: McGraw Hill.

13 Thomas, K. W. (1992). Conflict and negotiation processes in organizations. In M. D. Dunnette, & L. M. Hough (Eds.), *Handbook of industrial and organizational psychology*, 2nd ed., pp. 651–717. Palo Alto, CA: Consulting Psychologists Press.

Chapter 11: Communication in Organizations

1 Scott, W. G., & Mitchell, T. R. (1976). *Organizational theory: A structural and behavioral analysis*. Homewood, IL: Irwin.

2 Robbins, S. P., & Judge, T. A. (2013). *Organizational behavior*, 15th ed. New York: Pearson.

3 Lengel, R. H., & Daft, R. L. (1988). The selection of communication media as an executive skill. *Academy of Management Executive*, 2(3), 225–32.

4 American Management Association (1955). The ten commandments of good communication. *Management Review*, October, 704–05.

5 McShane, S. L., & Von Glinow, M. A. (2008). *Organizational behavior*, 4th ed. New York: McGraw-Hill.

Chapter 12: Structure and Design of African Organizations

1 March, J., & Simon, H. (1993). *Organizations*, 2nd ed. Oxford: Blackwell.

2 Leonard, D. K. (1984). *The political realities of African management*. Presented to the United States Agency for International Development for discussion at the African Agricultural Development Management Workshop in Easton, Maryland on September 5, 1984.

3 See Kenyan Airways (http://www.kenya-airways.com). Downloaded on April 13, 2012.

4 See Kumba Company (http://www.kumba.co.za/careers_main.php). Downloaded on April 20, 2012.

5 See Dangote Group (http://www.dangote-group.com). Downloaded on April 25, 2012.

6 Forrester, R. H. (2000). Capturing learning and applying knowledge: An investigation of the use of innovation teams in Japanese and American automotive firms. *Journal of Business Research*, 47(1), 35–45.

7 Daly, P., Bierly, P. III, & Miller, B. (2004). The impact of training and use of teams on dynamic capabilities of small manufacturers. *International Journal of Learning and Intellectual Capital*, 1(2), 150–76.

8 LaPorta, R., & Schleifer, A. (2008). *The unofficial economy and economic development*, Working Paper Series, pp. 1–75. Washington, DC: National Bureau of Economic Research.

9 Thompson, J. D. (1967). *Organizations in action: Social science bases of administrative theory*. New York: McGraw-Hill.

Chapter 13: Culture and Strategy

1 See Poulina Group (http://www.poulinagroupholding.com/en/vision.php). Downloaded on May 2, 2012.

2 Cabrera, E. F., & Bonache, J. (1998). An expert HR system for aligning organizational culture and strategy. *Human Resource Planning*, 22(1), 51–60.

3 See Zain.com (http://www.zain.com/Philosophy/Culture). Downloaded on May 5, 2012.

4 Gordon, G. G. (1991). Industry determinants of organizational culture. *Academy of Management Review*, 16, 396–415.

5 See Dangote Group (http://dangote-group.com/aboutus/managementteam.aspx). Downloaded on May 7, 2012.

6 See Orascom Company (http://www.orascomci.com/index.php?id=ourvision). Downloaded on May 11, 2012.

7 See Orascom Company (http://www.orascomci.com/index.php?id=ourstrategy). Downloaded on May 12, 2012.

8 See Aguinis, H. (2009). *Performance management*, 2nd ed. Upper Saddle River, NJ: Pearson Prentice Hall.

9 See Wafa Assurance Company (http://www.wafaassurance.ma/index.php/fr/la-compagnie/historique.html). Downloaded on May 13, 2012.

10 Real company name withheld. The issues are based on history, events, and activities of a real company in Africa.

Chapter 14: Change and Innovation in African Organizations

1 Lewin, K. (1951). *Field theory in social sciences*. New York: Harper & Row.
2 Kotter, P. (1996). *Leading change*. Boston: Harvard Business School Press; and Kotter, J. P. (1995). Leading change: Why transformational efforts fail. *Harvard Business Review*, January.
3 Minority births are new majority. *Wall Street Journal Online*, May 17, 2012. Available online: http://online.wsj.com/article/SB10001424052702303879604577408363003351818.html. Downloaded on May 17, 2012.
4 Nohria, N., & Gulati, R. (1996). Is slack good or bad for innovation? *Academy of Management Journal*, 39(5), 1245–64.
5 Amabile, T. (1988). A model of creativity and innovation in organizations. In B. M. Staw, & L. L. Cummings (Eds.), *Research in Organizational Behavior*, 10, 123–67.
6 Schermerhon, J. R., Hunt, J. G., Osborn, R. N., & Uhl-Bien, M. (2010). *Organizational behavior*, 11th ed. Hoboken, NJ: John Wiley.
7 Govindarajan, V., & Trimble, C. (2012). *Reverse innovation: Create far from home, win everywhere*. Boston: Harvard Business School Publishing; and Govindarajan, V. (2012). A reverse-innovation playbook. *Harvard Business Review*, April, 120–25.
8 Budner, S. (1962). Intolerance for ambiguity as a personality variable. *Journal of Personality*, 30, 29–50.

INDEX

Note: *Italic* page numbers indicate tables; **bold** indicate figures.